Sovereign Mo

.

Joseph Huber

Sovereign Money

Beyond Reserve Banking

Joseph Huber
Martin-Luther-University
Halle an der Saale, Germany

ISBN 978-3-319-42173-5   ISBN 978-3-319-42174-2   (eBook)
DOI 10.1007/978-3-319-42174-2

Library of Congress Control Number: 2016957999

Cover illustration: © Rakratchada Torsap / Alamy Stock Photo

Printed on acid-free paper

This Palgrave Macmillan imprint is published by Springer Nature
The registered company is Springer International Publishing AG
The registered company address is: Gewerbestrasse 11, 6330 Cham, Switzerland

Also by Joseph Huber
Creating New Money: A Monetary Reform for the Information Age
(with James Robertson)
Modern Money Theory and New Currency Theory: A Comparative Discussion
Monetäre modernisierung
New Technologies and Environmental Innovation

Contents

List of Tables

1

Introduction

This book aims to make people aware of the central position the monetary system occupies in today's highly monetarized and financialized economies. In coming to terms with the banking and debt crisis that started in 2008, hardly anyone has contemplated the role of the money system which, however, is the root cause of it all.

A number of scholars and commentators have identified credit and debt bubbles as the typical harbingers of financial crises, but none have asked where all the money for fueling such bubbles comes from. The financial causes of crises have a common monetary cause: overshooting money creation that does not stop until the game breaks down under its hypertrophic dynamics. Financial markets cannot work properly on the basis of a malfunctioning monetary system. To sort out banking and financial markets, one has to come to grips with the money system.

In modern economies, any major activity needs prior financing. Finance, in turn, depends on the money system, the ways of primary creation and allocation of money, and continual availability of money. Money is the very thing that makes the economy what it is. And, as with any social condition, money changes over time. The money and banking system today is different from how it was even a couple of decades ago.

The book thus deals with the functioning of the present money system (Chaps. 2–4), its dysfunctions (Chap. 5) and finally (Chap. 6) the reform perspective of making a transition from the present bankmoney regime to a central bank-led sovereign money system—which we are supposed to have, but do not. Today, there is no commonly shared state of knowledge of how

© The Author(s) 2017
J. Huber, *Sovereign Money*, DOI 10.1007/978-3-319-42174-2_1

the present money system actually works, less so a common assessment of the problems inherent in the bankmoney regime.

Instead, there is an abundance of views and convictions about money, not least among those who are supposed to be experts in the field. The reasons are plenty and one, of course, is interest—financial interests, political interests and vested interests in career and professional identity. Often enough the result is poor understanding and inadequate action.

Chapters 2–4 of this book provide an outline of the development and current functioning of the money system, and of banking in so far as it is part of the money system. This will certainly be kept as simple as possible, but the matter is complicated—and it is oversimplification which is behind much of the poor understanding.

Chapter 2 focuses on the systematics of money, embedding it into historical context to help clarify understanding of the broader picture.

Chapter 3 addresses the legal and institutional foundations of the monetary system. The topic of state versus market theory of money is revisited. Particular emphasis is placed on the historical controversy of the 1830–1840s between the Currency School, which stood for re-implementing state control over the stock of money, and the Banking School, which was in favor of unregulated private bankmoney, at the time chiefly banknotes.

Little attention was paid to the Currency School position after its heyday in the nineteenth century. What is often considered to be its successor from around 1900, the state theory of money, is ambivalent in terms of Currency-vs-Banking teachings. The state theory of money actually turned out to be the trailblazer for a hybrid public–private money system, which was set to become the state-backed rule of commercial bankmoney such as it stands today. In a way, this book can be seen as an attempt to revise chartalism or the state theory of money and to update the classical Currency-vs-Banking controversy, bringing back a renewed Currency position that keeps in pace with change, this time, however, without the gold and other fixed-rule straightjackets.

Historical retrospective is certainly not a means of creating evidence and proving something to be 'natural' or 'necessary'. But with regard to the relationships between money, finance and the economy, the systems evolution involved creates evidence indeed. Rather than finance being market-borne, markets were born by providing for extended state activities, which included funding these activities. Money then facilitated funding and finance, whereby money developed as a creature of the state rather than having been invented by merchants and markets. Markets are money-borne rather than money being market-borne.

Beyond economic functions, there is another strong reason for the state origin of money. Money is an instrument of exerting power, comparable only to legal command power backed by force. The right to be a creator and first user of money gives power and privilege over all subsequent users. In modern societies as much as in traditional ones, such power and privilege must not be private, but a sovereign prerogative, preferably under conditions of separation of powers and the liberal rule of law.

Control of the money of a realm has always been an element of sovereign rule, much as lawmaking, the judiciary, taxation and the use of force. The monetary prerogative includes the sovereign rights of determining the currency (a country's monetary unit of account), creating the money denominated in that currency (the official means of payment), and benefitting from the seigniorage thereof by spending or lending the money and thus releasing it into circulation. The constitutional dimension of money must not be disregarded, either in terms of legitimacy and state law, or in terms of economic functionality.

In the transition from traditional to modern societies the sovereign monetary prerogative has twice been challenged by private money creation. The first time was from about the late seventeenth into the beginning of the nineteenth century, when private banknotes gradually replaced sovereign coin. Private paper money issued by commercial banks enabled the funding of overseas trade, warfare and industrial production, but over time it also gave rise to major financial and economic problems, not unlike those we have today. The measure then taken was to introduce the central banks' national monopoly on banknotes while phasing out private paper money.

The second challenge was already present to a degree in the first and has become apparent in the course of the twentieth century, this time in the form of the relentless rise of private bankmoney on account replacing sovereign cash. Bankmoney made it possible, again, to finance industrial activities that could not have been financed on a limited base of gold. However, it has soon become apparent that the bankmoney regime is imposing an increasingly dysfunctional burden on the real economy, similar to private banknotes around 1800 and thereafter, but with much higher stakes for financial assets and debt, economic output and income.

Chapter 4 sets out a step-by-step outline of the functioning of the present money system. In the first instance, money today is bankmoney—that is, money on account (demand deposits), created by the banks according to their own preferences whenever they credit a nonbank customer account. The leading monetary power lies with the banking industry, not with the governments, as was the case in former times, or, as is commonly believed today, with the central banks of the nation-states in the worldsystem. Today, the monetary system is bank-led, that is, banks decide to create money at their own discretion, whereupon, if need be, they are fractionally refinanced by the central bank in cash and credits on central bank account, called reserves.

In the course of time central banks have become state authorities, or para-state bodies mainly governed by public law. However, rather than still being *bank of the state*, they are now exclusively *bank of the banks,* and instead of being cautious *lenders of last resort* they now act as *anytime refinancers of the banks.* This applies all the more in times of crisis when the central banks now habitually provide 'quantitative easing'.

The system is most often referred to as fractional reserve banking and sometimes also as credit creation 'out of nothing'. Both descriptions can basically be endorsed, despite a number of misleading assumptions about their actual meaning. It is a system of credit-borne private bankmoney accommodated by a fractional base of central bank money, and guaranteed by both central banks and governments.

In the course of this book, a number of fallacious models of banking are discussed, among these the piggy bank model, the loanable funds model and the financial intermediation model of banking, and the idea of pre-set central bank reserve positions that would enable central banks to exert control over the banks' credit creation (the multiplier model in combination with the reserve positions doctrine). What will also be discussed in this context is the low effectiveness of central bank interest rate policy as a substitute for monetary quantity policy that has become unworkable in a bank-led money system.

Chapter 5 addresses the problems and dysfunctions of the present monetary system in detail and explains why the regime of state-backed private bankmoney is no more viable than private banknotes were. The problems all start from the fact that the supply of bankmoney is in no way tied to a real value base that serves as the benchmark for money creation.

As the banking and financial industries have a strong incentive to extend their business as much as possible and as the central banks have stopped asserting control over bankmoney, the ensuing dynamics of banking and financial markets tend to cross critical lines, thus overshooting. This results in inflation (in recent years primarily in newly industrializing countries) and more markedly in asset inflation, bubble building, financial over-investment and over-indebtedness, discharging in crises that affect everyone.

There are a number of restrictions to bankmoney creation in the short term. In the long run, however, there are no limitations inherent to the monetary and financial systems, whereas real economic potential and achievable output are definitively limited at any time. Thus, the final restriction on monetary and financial expansion is set by the gravitational force of real economic productivity. Real productivity, actual output and income, determines the economy's carrying capacity for financial assets and debt. Banks and central banks create the money, but they cannot create the value of the money which derives from productivity. The harder banking and finance push to escape the gravitational force of productivity by creating bankmoney, financial assets and debt in disproportion to GDP, the greater is the accumulated gap between nominal and real values, and the harder in the end is the fall back to earth, the resulting clash between hypertrophic notional values of assets, and the actual flows of income and additional debt that can be called upon to serve the claims of those stocks.

In addition, the more the expansion of bankmoney and financial assets and debt strides ahead in disproportion to real economic output, the more they will create a distributional bias toward financial income at the expense of earned income. This is why the distribution of income and wealth today is as unequal as it was almost a hundred years ago until Black Friday in 1929.

It is in periods of minor or major crises, which in recent decades have actually grown in number and severity, that the public becomes aware of the fact that bankmoney is not only of unstable value, but is unsafe in its very existence. When a bank fails, the money perishes together with the bank since that money is nothing but a mere liability on a bank's balance sheet. The introduction of deposit insurance since the Great Depression of the 1930s has confirmed that fact. But in a systemic crisis, there will never be enough 'insurance' to avoid the ruin of insurance schemes, commercial insurance providers, and perhaps even a government as the money guarantor of last resort.

At this point one will realize that private money without state backing cannot survive severe banking and debt crises. The predominance of bankmoney today simply means that the banking industry has captured the sovereign prerogatives of money creation and seigniorage—with the governments' consent, because governments, running chronic deficits and ever higher levels of debt, have made themselves dependent on quasi unlimited lines of bank credit. As governments have stopped creating money themselves, banks are now doing this on governments' behalf beyond measure.

Finally, Chap. 6 deals with the changes necessary to implement a safe and stable money system that can serve as the basis for sound finances. The obvious core element is to recapture the prerogatives of money creation and seigniorage by making a transition from bankmoney on account to sovereign money on account—technically speaking, central bank money on account.

It should be noted from the beginning that this is not another plan for 100 % reserve banking, or narrow banking.

Any kind of reserve system includes a split circulation of different classes of money, no matter whether on a fractional or full base of central bank reserves. There is bankmoney in the public circuit, and 'high-powered' central bank money in the interbank circuit. A sovereign money system, by contrast, would constitute a single-circuit system beyond any kind of split-circuit reserve banking, easier to manage and to readjust flexibly to the economy than the present regime of bankmoney.

National central banks would then be a fourth branch of government, the monetary authority of a sovereign currency area with full control of the stock of money, acting as the guardian of a nation's monetary equity, effectively enabled to defend its purchasing power and its foreign exchange value. Central banks, as the guardians of a currency and stock of money, ought to be independent and impartial, similar to the courts, bound by a detailed legal mandate, but discretionary in pursuing policies on that basis, irrespective of the particular political and financial interests of the day. The basic benchmark for extending and perpetually readjusting the stock of money would be the growth potential of the economy at full capacity, also taking into account interest rates, inflation as well as asset inflation.

Banks would no longer hold monetary power. They would have to fund their lending activities and other proprietary business in full rather than fractionally, as does any other financial and real business as a matter of course. Notwithstanding, banks would continue to provide payment and money services, and they would again be the financial intermediaries they typically were before attaining sovereign monetary powers.

Sovereign money reform aims to achieve today with bankmoney on account what was achieved with banknotes over a hundred years ago. It is about renationalizing money, not about nationalizing banking and finance, and it thus represents a renewed approach to the classical Currency School program of separating money creation and banking. Put differently, the approach is about establishing a thorough separation of monetary and fiscal powers, and of separating both from wider financial functions that are left to the banks, financial institutions and markets.

What sort of economics stands behind the analyses in the chapters that follow? The underlying paradigm might be referred to as systemic and evolutive economics. It connects to the different areas of institutional and historical economics, and unceremoniously also associates with neoclassical and Keynesian elements of analysis (except for the equilibrium mythology) when these are coherent and supported by the facts. Modern market dynamics evolve in distinct life-cycles and learning curves, incessantly undergoing structural change in the course of economic and financial cycles. In these processes, neither supply nor demand is homogenous in the aggregate. Empirically, one never knows to what extent markets 'clear'. Market participants are usually on the long or short side, which points to the fact that markets do not operate in a power vacuum. Markets and prices are the arena of an ongoing power struggle among the parties involved, the more so under conditions of financial and industrial corporatism, collective bargaining, professions protectionism, market oligopolies, and far-reaching government interventionism.

Regarding monetary theories, most of them go back to the bank credit theory of money from around 1900 as it fed into the late Austrian School, the early Chicago School and Friedman's monetarism as well as into Keynesianism and post-Keynesianism. Monetarism, however, was unnecessarily supply-side doctrinaire and operationally inadequate under the conditions of the bank-led monetary regime in place.

Applied demand-side Keynesianism, on the other hand, degenerated into an all-seasons interventionist deficit and debt doctrine, rather than focusing the government's role in providing a coherent legal framework and regulation for the economy in general and various commodity, labor and financial markets in particular, including the legal constitution of a stable sovereign money system. A coherent approach cannot be either supply-side or demand-side. These are opposite positions in terms of vested interest-led political partisanship, but from a systemic viewpoint they represent complementary parts of the entire picture, mutually implying and confining each other.

Neoclassical economics over the last century, it must be said on this occasion, has not been particularly fertile ground for up-to-date monetary theory and for giving money and finance in economics the pivotal role they actually play. For a relatively realistic description of the money system, the post-Keynesian literature has proved to be a better source, although the post-Keynesian notion of endogenous money is overstated. It resembles the Banking School real bills doctrine of the 1830–1840s and largely ignores primary credit creation for non-GDP finance as well as money supply partly driven by the banking sector's proprietary business. Similarly, the identity of money and credit as asserted in post-Keynesianism is a pseudo-truth even in the present regime of bankmoney, and misleading from a systemic and historical perspective (Sects. 4.14 and 4.15).

Within the spectrum of theories of money, the viewpoints put forward in this book have the most common ground with circuitism as, for example, condensed in Graziani (2003), and monetary quantum theory as recently expounded anew by Cencini and Rossi (2015). Existing commonalities, however, do not include the oversimplified banks–producers–workers model of money circulation of these approaches.

The present book follows on from the author's earlier investigations into the subject, including the close collaboration with James Robertson in 1999/2000 on behalf of the New Economics Foundation, London. Of course, as occurs when something is in the air, there are contributions by like-minded contemporary scholars pursuing the same or similar ideas. Among these are Gocht (1975), Zarlenga (2002, 2014), Werner (2005), Keen (2011), Ryan-Collins, Greenham, Werner, and Jackson (2012), Benes and Kumhof (2012), Jackson and Dyson (2012), Bjerg (2014), Yamaguchi (2014), and Sigurjonsson (2015). I would finally like to thank Jamie Walton of the American Monetary Institute who has importantly contributed to improve the final version of this book.

References

Benes, Jaromir, and Michael Kumhof. 2012. The Chicago Plan Revisited. *IMF-working paper*, 12/202 August 2012. Revised draft February 2013.

Bjerg, Ole. 2014a. *Making Money. The Philosophy of Crisis Capitalism*. London: Verso Books.

Cencini, Alvaro, and Sergio Rossi. 2015. *Economic and Financial Rises. A New Macroeconomic Analysis*. London: Palgrave Macmillan.

Gocht, Rolf. 1975. *Kritische Betrachtungen zur nationalen und internationalen Geldordnung*. Berlin: Duncker & Humblot.

Graziani, Augusto. 2003. *The Monetary Theory of Production*. Cambridge: Cambridge University Press.

Jackson, Andrew, and Ben Dyson. 2012. *Modernising Money. Why Our Monetary System is Broken and How It Can Be Fixed*. London: Positive Money.

Keen, Steve. 2011. *Debunking Economics*. London: Zed Books.

Ryan-Collins, Josh, Tony Greenham, Richard Werner, and Andrew Jackson. 2012. *Where Does Money Come From? A Guide to the UK Monetary and Banking System*, 2 edn. London: New Economics Foundation.

Sigurjonsson, Frosti. 2015. *Monetary Reform. A better monetary system for Iceland, Icelandic Parliament*. Submitted to the Committee on Economic Affairs and Trade, March 2015. http://eng.forsaetisraduneyti.is/media/Skyrslur/monetary-reform.pdf.

Yamaguchi, Kaoru. 2014. *Money and Macroeconomic Dynamics. An Accounting System Dynamics Approach*. Awaji Island: Muratopia Institute, Japan Futures Research Center. http://www.muratopia.org/Yamaguchi/MacroBook.html

Werner, Richard A. 2005. *New Paradigm in Macroeconomics*. London: Palgrave Macmillan.

———. 2014. *The Need for Monetary Reform*. Presenting the American Monetary Act, American Monetary Institute, http://www.monetary.org/wp-content/uploads/2011/12/32-page-brochure-sept20111.pdf.

Zarlenga, Stephen A. 2002. *The Lost Science of Money. The Mythology of Money—The Story of Power*. Valatie, NY: American Monetary Institute.

2

Money

2.1 The Four Functions of Money: Currency, Payment, Income and Capital

The need for something like money arises with a complex division of labor and corresponding chains of provision, accompanied by administration and the documentation of supplies. Some three to five thousand years ago, what was later to become money first developed as a unit of account for the documentation and clearing of claims and duties. Such units were quantities of barley, salt, silver, work days, for example. That was not yet money, but an early form of currency, a unit of value accounting which made different things commensurable.

For archaic and early ancient economies to evolve into monetarized and financialized economies, two developments had to take place. Money as a means of payment had to be introduced, and some of the money, rather than being immediately spent on everyday living expenses, had to be put aside and used to fund undertakings that could over time create a particular benefit such as an increase in production, land, hands, riches and power, also including a financial return as we understand it today. Money put to uses in this way constitutes an investment, and potentially the formation of a stock of capital.

Money and monetarized finance began to develop in antiquity. Coins were introduced in Lydia in Asia Minor in the seventh century BC. Basic banking structures, too, played a role in classical Greece and Rome. In Christian Europe, banking and finance emerged in the high and late middle ages and became fully fledged in early modernity with deposit taking, letters of credit

© The Author(s) 2017
J. Huber, *Sovereign Money*, DOI 10.1007/978-3-319-42174-2_2

(important in long-distance trade), double-entry bookkeeping and current accounts for the clearing of claims and liabilities.

The habitually stated three functions of money have thus already been identified, traditionally referred to as the functions of serving as a unit of account, a medium of exchange and a store of value. In order to better reflect relevant realities, these functions might be restated as follows:

1. The currency function of money: the existence of a monetary unit of account which enables pricing (attributing monetary value to items) and accountancy. Today, such units of account exist primarily in the form of the official currency of a nation-state (such as the dollar, pound, yen, yuan) or a community of nation-states (such as the euro)
2. The payment function of money: the use of tokens as a means of payment, or to put it another way, using money denominated in a currency for the settlement of any kind of claims and liabilities
3. The income function: money used as a vehicle for transferring income (in the broadest sense), which in turn allows real and financial expenditure
4. The capital function: money used as a vehicle of capital formation.

The latter function has a meaning that is different from the traditional notion of money as a store of value or stock of wealth. While silver coins and gold bullion were undoubtedly real valuables, not just monetary items, the value of modern token money is conferred value, which is uncertain over time and basically no more reliable than the price of goods or the value of financial and real assets. The value of money is as certain or uncertain as is the value of income and capital generated through the uses of circulating money.

Money, as a means of payment, was never actually a functional store of value. Money is a means of circulation, in making payments, transferring income, or building capital, and in these functions a way of making the economic world go around, not something for hoarding in Uncle Scrooge's treasure bunker. Traditional hoards of coin and bullion were dysfunctional because they deprived the economy of much-needed purchasing power. In modern times, too, holding large amounts of inactive money (cash or deposits) is dysfunctional for basically the same reason and also because inflation, even if low, reduces the purchasing power of the money.

2.2   Types and Creators of Money

In the present day, three types of money are used—coins, paper money (banknotes) and money on account (bankmoney). Another type of money, tally sticks from the middle ages, fell into disuse as the historical transition from traditional to modern economies advanced. Digital cash, as a possible future type of money, is currently often seen as a modern substitute for solid coins and notes. Something like this might come about with blockchain technology in future applications. For the time being, what is called electronic cash is not yet a means of payment in its own right, but always represents an amount of money on account.

What about complementary currencies operating, for example, on 'time dollars', 'nursing hours', and local monies in parallel to official money? These are in fact used as means of payment, but cannot be seen as official money. So far, they have been of limited use, for example, as emergency money in times of crisis, or as a tool for the revitalization of depressed neighborhoods, or for the joy of social experimentation. In any case, complementary currencies represent special-community or special-purpose monies.

Something similar applies to private commercial currencies such as bitcoins. For the time being, these, too, are of limited use within a special milieu, thus not serving as a regular general means of payment.[1] Bitcoins are said to serve the underground economy and money laundering, and they are also used for the excitement of speculation.

There is the question of the institutional standing and credibility of the originators of complementary or parallel currencies, be these for-profit or non-profit. The institutional and political backing of a currency, as much as productivity and responsible monetary policy, is crucial for the continued validity and value of a means of payment.

What characterizes money is its regular and general use as a means of payment in any sort of transaction, that is, its function as a means of final settlement of any debt. This includes the general acceptance—by choice or force of law—of being paid in respective forms of money. In special settings, it is still possible to be paid in kind. The payee does not receive money, but something of equivalent monetary value. In special financial transactions, the parties involved may agree upon payment by transferring the ownership of capital items such as equity shares. This is not a transfer of money either; it is the transfer of a stock of capital, which represents a claim on money, including interest, rents, dividends, or similar. Many things can serve as a means of payment, but only a few are money, that is, tokens in regular general use as a means of final settlement of a transaction, such as coins, banknotes and money on account.

Nor are credit cards and debit cards money as such, though they have misleadingly been dubbed 'plastic money'. These cards are tools for making cashless payments through the process of transferring money on account (bankmoney). In the case of debit cards, a payer initiates a money transfer

[1] ECB (2015, pp. 14–18).

from their current bank account to the current account of the payee. In the case of a credit card, there is an interposed creditor bank which credits the bank account of a payee and collects the money once a month from the payer's bank account.

Coins and banknotes are traditional solid cash. The bankmoney in a current account is, erroneously, quite often also referred to as 'cash', even by official accountancy bodies and in the publications of central banks.[2] Cash in this sense simply refers to 'a liquid means of payment'. But calling any kind of money 'cash' blurs the difference between cash and money on account, the latter being used for cashless payment. The difference between cash and money on account is substantial in today's money and banking system and must not be blurred.

In the contemporary system, three agencies are authorized to create official money—commercial banks, national central banks and national treasuries. The treasuries have the traditional prerogative of coinage (counting for less than 1 % of the money supply today). Coins represent sovereign money, some say state money, and this continues to be the case with the national currencies of sovereign nation-states.

Central banks have generally had the monopoly on banknotes since the nineteenth century (now at about 5–20 % of the money supply, depending on the country). Central banks also create the reserves on central bank account for the banks. Banknotes and reserves are central bank money.

Most central banks across the world today are public bodies and they have assumed the status of a monetary state authority, some even by constitution, others by legal provisions, and certainly as a matter of fact. The Federal Reserve of the USA is still owned by the private banking industry, even though by law and political practice the 'Fed' has taken on the character of a para-state institution. The Fed's board of governors is a US government institution. The European Central Bank (ECB) is an intergovernmental body according to European Union (EU) law. Central bank money—reserves and banknotes, like coins—thus represents sovereign money in Europe. In the US, Treasury notes are sovereign money too, while Federal Reserve notes and non-cash reserves on Fed account have an ambivalent status.

Banks themselves were never allowed to mint coins of their own, and for well over a hundred years banks have also been prohibited from printing banknotes. Doing so would be considered counterfeiting. Equally, but for technical reasons, banks cannot create central bank reserves. What they do create and circulate are deposits, that is, money on bank account, for the most

---

[2] Schemmann (2011a, pp. 80–89, 2012a, b, p. 26).

part referred to in this book as bankmoney. In most countries today, bankmoney represents 80–95 % of the active public money supply which consists of liquid bankmoney and solid cash together. These aspects are systematically explained in Chap. 4.

How do banks, central banks and treasuries bring their monies into circulation? In this respect, the historical succession of coins, tally sticks, banknotes, bankmoney on account (deposits) and mobile e-cash is instructive.

2.3   Coin Currencies and Tally Sticks

In pre-industrial times, feudal treasuries minted coins and were at the same time the first users of new coins. They put money into circulation by paying for the expenses of the court—the army, administration, civil works, servants and the court's luxuries. The secular and ecclesiastical rulers thus enjoyed the benefit of coinage in the form of genuine seigniorage, the latter referring to the difference between the cost of production and the face value of a coin.

Coining money has always been the legal prerogative of the rulers of a realm, from ancient warlords and kings through to the governments of modern nation-states. There were interim periods, though, such as after the fall of Rome, where minting passed into the hands of private coiners (*monetarii*). However, since about AD 750, Pepin III and Charlemagne made the issuance of coin again the rulers' prerogative. One motive was to catch up with Byzantium, whose precious-metal currency was the dominant model for both Occidental and Oriental rulers.[3] There were also temporary exceptions, when over-indebted rulers had to cede coinage to private creditors, normally trading and banking houses; but then, too, private minting was carried out under licence and the control of a respective treasury. No private persons were allowed to put their stamp on coins of the realm.

Traditional coin currencies were free of debt. The coins were quasi-public money issued by the rulers. Coining came with genuine seigniorage. The coins were put into circulation to pay for quasi-public expenditure and kept in circulation if they were not hoarded or called in for re-minting.

Today, governments no longer put coins into circulation. They achieve the same kind of genuine seigniorage by selling coins to central banks on demand. In turn, central banks issue the coins to the banks by way of credit or in exchange for reserves, and the banks pass the coins on, in basically the same way, to the public, the nonbank users of cash.

---

[3] Zarlenga (2002, p. 109).

In reflecting on money in its relation to credit and debt, it is particularly interesting to consider the history of tally sticks. Tallies are known from different cultures and epochs. They were widely used in Europe from 1100 until the 1400s, in Britain until the 1600s. Thereafter, usage declined with the beginnings of industrialization.[4] A tally was made of pieces of polished wood of about 20 × 5 cm. Horizontal notches marked the quantity of money units: 1000 units were the size of a handbreadth (palm), 100 were a fingerbreadth, 1 that of a corn. The stick was then split lengthwise, with one part shortened, the other remaining longer. The short end of the stick, called the foil or stub, was kept by the issuer of a tally who had taken in a deposit, or borrowed money, or received goods. The longer part, called the stock (hence the origin of stockholder), was given to the party who had made a deposit, or lent money, or supplied goods. The notches, together with the grain of the wood, made sure that the two parts were the only ones to fit together. This was practical in times when most people were illiterate, although the issuer was noted on the reverse of the tally, often through a symbol, family emblem or initials rather than the name written in full.

Simple non-split tallies were often used as a record of debt, like running a tab, for example, for the bread bought at the bakery but not immediately paid for. In various countryside regions of Europe this was common practice even into the twentieth century.[5] In the high middle ages tally sticks were also used as a receipt of deposit, and they achieved a certain range of circulation as a means of payment.[6] Tallies were introduced as a substitute for coin because, in spite of opening new silver mines across Europe, the overall supply of silver resources remained scarce and silver mines became exhausted over time, with silver thus ever more expensive. Part of the problem was the draining away of silver and gold in the growing imports of oriental and Far Eastern luxury goods.[7] The tallies extended the coin base and relied on it.

Beyond common folk running tabs, split tally sticks were issued by both merchants and feudal lords. Merchants used them to transact business, just as in later years they used bills of exchange or cheques, especially at medieval fairs like those in Lyon, Flanders, the Champagne region and Frankfurt. The fairs were also the main places for clearing foils and stocks. Henry I of England introduced tally sticks as an official kind of money when he acceded to the throne in 1100. Purveyors and soldiers could be paid in tallies, but

---

[4] Davies (2013, pp. 148, 252) and Graeber (2012, p. 48).

[5] Ifrah (1981, p. 112).

[6] Ifrah (1981, pp. 110–116), Apostolou and Crumbley (2008), Davies (2013, pp. 148, 252), Zarlenga (2002, p. 264), and Graeber (2012, pp. 48, 268, 435).

[7] Zarlenga (2002, p. 131).

acceptance was not compulsory. Tally sticks were not legal tender in modern terms. The exchequer, though, who issued the tallies, had to accept them in payment of dues (taxes). So the bigger part of the crown's revenue consisted of tally stocks, rather than coin, flowing back to the exchequer.[8]

In this regard, tallies were a form of tax credit or private commercial credit that could be used, albeit in a limited way, as a means of payment. A tally stock was not interest-bearing, but could include a *disagio*. This was a common practice in medieval and early modern banking (as it is in Islamic banking today) when taking interest was still banned because considered sinful. When a tally stock was rejoined to the appendant foil, or vice versa, the re-completed tally was taken out of circulation, unlike coin, which re-entered circulation if not hoarded or passed to distant places.

Even if tally sticks could be used as a means of payment they were a money surrogate rather than money proper, which at the time was silver coin. But tally sticks were used like money if accepted by a payee. A tally stick thus was a credit-and-debt document, passed on in the same way as later trade bills, private banknotes, or demand deposits in a bank account today.

2.4   Banknotes and the Ascent of Modern Fractional Reserve Banking

Banknotes emerged in the course of the seventeenth century, when they were introduced by banks—hence their name. In China, paper money was in use from about AD 1100. In America, the first issuers of paper money were the governments of the later US States who issued 'colonial scrip', as the governments' bills of credit were dubbed, in the first half of the eighteenth century.[9] In Europe, however, the issuers were private banks, some of them privileged by the crown.

Private banknotes were not put into circulation like treasury coins. Instead, banknotes were issued in one operation by extending interest-bearing bank credit to a customer. If the customer agreed, the amount of credit was provided in banknotes, in lieu of coins, and the issuing bank promised to disburse the amount indicated on the note in silver or gold coin on demand of the bearer. This is why banknotes are also referred to as promissory notes. Initially, banknotes were not considered to be money proper, but a money surrogate which was used like money. In terms of accountancy, a banknote was a bank

---

[8] North (1994, Chaps. 1 and 2).
[9] Hixson (1993, Chaps. 7–13) and Zarlenga (2002, Chaps. 14 and 16).

debt, a liability of the issuing bank to pay coins to the respective bearer of that note, and an according claim of the bearer on the issuing bank.

In the early stages of banking—for example, with the Swedish Riksbank (founded 1668), the Bank of England (founded 1694) and the French Banque Royale (founded 1718)—paper money was issued in an arrangement which today would be seen as a public–private partnership. Then, like today, most governments were over-indebted and under pressure to obtain funds. They thus granted the banks the right to issue banknotes within a privileged bank–government relationship. This was no monopoly, however, and banks were not banned from issuing banknotes to private customers—which is what they increasingly did in the course of the eighteenth and the early nineteenth centuries.

Banks abused the new financial instrument from the outset, to a greater extent than coin clipping in previous centuries ever could. John Law's Banque Générale Privée in Paris did so, and even the supposedly impeccable Bank of Amsterdam eventually could not stop itself from creating many times more credit and paper money than was backed up by the coin and bullion in its vault.

This was possible because customers did not convert all their notes into coin, and if they did convert notes they did not all do so at the same time. If the coin reserve a bank needed for carrying out current payments was 30 % of outstanding banknotes, the remaining 70 % did not have to be refinanced. The bank thus created 70 % of its banknotes at almost no cost, out of thin air. The fraction of 30 % alone represented a full cost position. This is the principle of fractional reserve banking. The 70 % came with a special profit, equal to the refinancing costs avoided on the 70 %. In this sense, the special profit of fractional reserve banking represents borrowing interest avoided, thus a kind of interest-borne seigniorage, in contrast to genuine seigniorage of putting coins into circulation.

Had the banks, hypothetically, issued no more banknotes than they had reserves of coin and bullion, no problem would have arisen. The banks, however, would not have made a special profit from creating paper money. Paper money would have been of no use at all, other than for convenience. The potential benefit of banknotes, however—and this applies not only to banks, but to the broader economy as well—was to expand the money supply for financing trade and industrial growth as well as government debt for funding war, ever more public services and, in the twentieth century, the welfare state. The special profit of the banks from issuing banknotes was greater the smaller the cash reserve that they needed to cover the notes, which in turn was the case the more the public preferred to use banknotes over coins.

Fractional reserve banking had existed for a long time before banknotes. The practice is as old as are deposit-taking money lenders. In ancient Greece and Rome, however, running irregular deposits was considered fraudulent and was therefore punishable. In early modern times, fractional reserve banking was gradually reinterpreted.[10] This coincided with moves to lift the church's ban on interest-taking, culminating, in 1515, in Pope Leo X's grant to the German banker and merchant Jacob Fugger the right to pay 5 % interest a year on savings accounts that contributed to funding the investments of his trading and banking house. Although compliance with the church's anti-interest injunctions had not been previously very strict, from 1515 banking on fractional reserves was not seen as fraudulent, as taking interest was in itself no longer perceived as usury.

In addition to interest, banking profits also derive from price spreads, trading fees and capital gains. The more loans and other financial items, the more banking profit can be expected. Banks thus have a strong incentive for the endogenous expansion of their balance sheet—that is, creating as much primary credit and bankmoney, also for proprietary purposes, as they dare to risk and can fractionally refinance. This has led to recurrent overshooting of the money supply, and in connection with the new industrial cycles, also to temporary undersupply in times of crisis.

Money overshoot means that additional money cannot be quickly absorbed by the additional supply of the goods and services in effective demand. Too much money in this sense causes inflation, may lead to currency devaluation, and fuels financial bubbles and crises. This has been known since the middle of the sixteenth century when the quantity theory of money was developed in relation to Spanish colonial silver inflation. Around and after 1800, with recurrently overshooting quantities of paper money, related effects were most markedly felt in the British Empire, the leading industrializing and trading power of the time.

The ease of writing out notes may have been one reason for abusing the instrument, either by the issuers or by domestic and foreign counterfeiters (think of the Assignats of the French Revolution). More importantly, however, and to save the honor of the bankers, was an increased demand for money due to expanded trade and production in the course of industrialization. Without banknotes and bankmoney on account, the ongoing modernization processes from the late eighteenth through to the twentieth centuries could not have taken place (except for the alternative of properly-run sovereign money systems, for example, colonial Pennsylvania's system, or the US Greenbacks with the US Sub-Treasury accounts system).

---

[10] Huerta de Soto (2009, Chap. 1, pp. 1–165).

Over time, banknotes were adopted by a growing range of users and ever more banks acknowledged each other's notes, albeit always reluctantly so. A wallet is of course more practical than a coinbag attached to the belt. Moreover, from the banks' point of view, notes were, and still are, much easier and cheaper to produce than coins. People became used to paper money. From a certain point in time, notes were seen as genuine money on an equal footing with coins. This was decisively furthered by the nationalization of notes, from 1833 to the 1900s, depending on the country. From then on, banknotes represented legal tender. The power of the state stood behind the paper currency and no one really thought of converting the banknotes into coins any longer.

The Bank of England has so far continued to promise to the bearer of a note that it will redeem the note on demand in pounds sterling. Some quipsters have now and again tested the promise at the Bank's gate, but returned empty-handed. US Federal Reserve notes, by contrast, state that 'this note is legal tender for all debts, public and private'. This no-frills statement is exactly to the point. Money is just that, nothing less and nothing more. In particular it makes no reference to other monetary items and does not represent a credit-and-debt relationship, but serves the final settlement of credit or debt obligations. ECB notes display no statement, except for reprinting the respective governor's signature as if saying 'By virtue of my office I guarantee the validity of this note.'

What is more, from the second half of the nineteenth century the coins in circulation were increasingly made of alloys rather than pure copper, silver and gold. Accordingly, it became apparent to people that cash is a token of value with no or little material value in itself. However, the idea persists that the value of currency is covered in some way, be this through national land value or a national gold hoard. The myth of Fort Knox has been a source of vivid fantasy, the more so the more the gold standard was reaching its end. The only real coverage of money, however, is in real economic output, the amount and quality of goods and services for which there is a supply and demand.

2.5 Bankmoney on Account

In the decades around 1800, money on bank account, or bankmoney for short, began its ascent as a money surrogate in growing use for cashless payment. Bank-created money in a current bank account is called a demand deposit or sight deposit; money created by a central bank and kept in a central bank account is called a reserve. These are traditional terms dating way back to when a deposit was actually created by depositing coins or bullion in a bank. Today however, as will further be explained in Chap. 4, deposits are created by bank credit which creates a credit entry in a current account. A deposit and money on bank account (bankmoney) are one and the same, as are reserves and money on central bank account (central bank money).

Reserves and bankmoney are a means of cashless payment. The range of cashless payment grew with industrialization, but the monetary importance of bankmoney was not generally recognized before about 1900. At that time the share of demand deposits in advanced European countries had grown to about one-third of the public money supply. Today it has reached 80–95 %. The remaining small part is cash.

Bankmoney on account has not exactly been a new development. It is definitely older than banknotes. Ever since banking in Europe developed, around 1300–1500, merchants could maintain a current account with a bank. Credits and debits, claims and liabilities, could thus be cleared through procedures of accountancy. A credit letter from a bank, or the receipt of a money deposit with a bank were much safer and more practical than the physical transport of large amounts of coins, and also less cumbersome than having to deal with tally sticks.

The scope and functional reality of deposits, of course, have been changing over time. Seen in retrospect, one difference is the diffusion of bankmoney from only a few actors involved at the time of the Rinascimento and Reformation to close to 100 % of users in any type of household today.

Like banknotes, bankmoney is not spent into circulation, but issued by way of interest-bearing commercial bank credit, in more modern times also by way of central bank credit. There has never been a law that made private bankmoney legal tender. Numerous laws and regulations, however, refer to demand deposits and presuppose their existence and general use as a means of cashless payment. Most state bodies today, in particular the tax office and social security entities, demand to be paid in bankmoney only. Since the interwar period and certainly after World War II, bankmoney has achieved the status of official money. This is to say, even though bankmoney is not legal tender, or sovereign money, or central bank money, it is a means of payment that is officially acknowledged and used by all relevant state bodies.

Bankmoney is a promissory accountancy note to convert a deposit into cash on the customer's request, in the same way as a former private banknote was a promise to redeem that paper note in silver coin. Most of the time people were happy with the notes and some remaining coin, as we are happy today with the deposits and a remaining amount of banknotes and small change. If customers wanted to cash in all their monetary claims against the banks, the system would immediately collapse, as everybody knows. Normally we do not intend to do so, for convenience and cheapness, and banks do not want us to do so because only a fraction of the amounts of deposits is available in cash—one reason for this is the considerable cost advantage of banknotes over coins, and of bankmoney over notes.

There is an important difference between banknotes and bankmoney that contributed to smooth the general adoption of bankmoney and cashless payment practices. A coin has a sovereign stamp on it, a banknote the name of the issuing bank and the signature of the bank director—today the central bank governor. Bankmoney, by contrast, once it has entered into general circulation, is not tagged. Tracing it back to its originator is next to impossible. Bankmoney is thus anonymized and also homogenized—as if all banks and banking purposes were all the same at any point in time.

This gives bankmoney the semblance of neutrality and blamelessness, even official respectability, when in fact it creates bank immunity. An individual bank can certainly be held accountable for its liabilities, at least in theory. Liability for the entire stock of private bankmoney, however, falls back upon the public central banks (who license and now even supervise the banks) and the government, that is, the public purse and the taxpayers—even if these agencies have maneuvred themselves into a position where they are actually unable to do much about it. This state of affairs—creating as much bankmoney as desired, privatizing profits, minimizing costs by fractional refinancing to the competitive disadvantage of everybody else, socializing systemically critical losses, and blaming it on government bureaucrats and unknowing customers—is clearly the best of all possible worlds for the self-asserting 'masters of the universe'.

The more a regime of bankmoney on the basis of fractional reserves had been established, the more customers and banks came under constraint to participate in the system. If a bank wants other banks to accept the bankmoney it is creating itself it must accept any cashless payment from all other banks regardless. Otherwise the system would not work.

2.6   Electronic Money and Digital Cash

In recent years, with the emergence of the blockchain technology, a new distinction has emerged between electronic money or electronic cash (e-cash) on the one hand, and digital cash on the other. While e-cash refers to mobile varieties of bankmoney on account, digital cash refers to currency units in a blockchain and is seen as a next step in the development of modern money beyond bankmoney on account, for example, as sovereign digital cash issued by the central banks and used in public circulation as a modern replacement for traditional solid cash. For now let us consider e-cash.

E-cash takes the form of balances on a storage medium such as a magnetic strip or chip on a plastic card. E-cash cards are distinguished from prepaid cards. The latter are not subject to e-cash regulation and cannot be used as a means of payment. Instead, they are single-purpose devices issued by nonbank corporations, for example for providing mobile-phone talk time or for provisioning a predetermined amount of electric current. The issuer of a prepaid card receives the respective amount of money in advance, in cash or via a credit card or by way of direct bankmoney transfer. The respective amount is registered in an account with the corporate issuer of the card. The balances in the account are drawn down as the customer uses the card. Unused balances are not normally redeemable.

By contrast, e-cash is presented to the public as a means of payment in replacement of traditional solid cash. E-cash balances in an e-purse can be uploaded at a bank's automated teller machine (ATM). The respective amount is registered on the chip, debited to the customer's current account and credited to a special e-cash clearing account of the bank, analogous to a bank's open deposit account. Thus, the bankmoney liability is not booked out, as is the case with solid cash, but swapped for another such overnight bank liability in the e-cash clearing account. If the customer makes use of the card, for example at a ticket machine, the available amount on the chip is reduced correspondingly and the amount due transferred from the bank's e-cash clearing account to the regular current account of the payee. An e-purse is not provided with overdrafts. Unused balances on an e-cash card can be transferred back into the customer's current bank account.

The chip on a card can also be a special e-cash balance in a mobile phone app; or the mobile phone includes an app that is the equivalent of a debit card. In developing countries, where bank accounts are still not widespread, e-cash can be obtained from an e-cash agent in exchange for solid cash. The money is held in a special e-cash account and can be accessed via a mobile-phone app.

The storable amount of e-cash in its present form is limited to the equivalent of a few hundred dollars. One reason for this limitation is to prevent e-cash cards and phones being used as a store of value on a large scale. E-cash cannot circulate like solid cash from one hand to another, or rather, from one e-purse into another, without an intermediate clearing account.

It thus becomes clear that e-cash is *not* a substitute for solid cash and that an e-cash card is far from being a true e-purse analogous to a wallet for banknotes. It is still all about money on account. What is called e-cash is in fact a mobile version of money on account, a mobile bank sub-account. For the time being it is hardly imaginable that e-cash could exist without some bankmoney account behind, or some other private clearing account based on bankmoney. It is even unclear whether e-cash as a substitute for traditional solid cash has a future at all, or whether modern money is and remains non-cash money on account that can be used by way of a multitude of transfer methods, both online and offline, remote and on the spot, realtime and delayed.

Strictly speaking, e-cash and e-purse are misleading terms, just as referring to bankmoney on account as 'cash' is erroneous. Only in a possible sovereign money future beyond private bankmoney, when all means of payment is issued by the central banks, circulating in one single circuit, with the money of bank customers and banks' own money kept separate from each other, would the difference between cash and money on account cease to be highly relevant.

Confusing cash and bankmoney means pretending that cash and bankmoney are of the same nature. In a way this reflects the banking industry's factual claim to have 'sovereign' control over the entire stock of money. Bank-issued e-cash infringes on the coin monopoly of the treasury and the central bank's monopoly on banknotes, in that mobile bankmoney balances have the potential to substitute themselves for solid cash.

Traditional solid cash is bound to fall into disuse sooner or later. For both customers and firms, electronic or digital payment will soon be more convenient and less costly than handling solid cash. Tax officers and the financial police want to dispense with solid cash because it has been used as the preferred means of tax evasion and the underground economy.

Advocates of negative interest as an instrument of financial repression also want to abolish cash. If there was money on account only, that would do away with holding solid cash as a fall-back option and thus enable them to implement monetary expropriation by effectively imposing negative interest—that is, by relieving the interest burden of high public and private debt levels and making holders of bankmoney pay interest to the banks rather than the banks paying deposit interest to customers.[11]

Furthermore, bankers want to get rid of solid cash because it is labor-intensive and expensive to handle compared with the computerized management of money on account. More importantly, banks are not allowed to issue coins and notes of their own. They have to obtain the cash from the central bank at full cost. Solid cash thus maintains a degree of dependence of the banks on a respective national central bank, even if that dependence is greatly diminished.

---

[11] Buiter (2009) and Rogoff (2014). Larry Summers at IMF Economic Forum of 8 Nov. 2013, speech in full at www.youtube.com/watch?v=KYpVzBbQIX0

If, under unchanged conditions of the present system, traditional solid cash were completely phased out, the banking industry would obtain a monopoly on electronic or digital cash, whatever comes of it, extending its already established monopoly of bankmoney. This would be another step toward the total loss of the sovereign monetary prerogatives to the benefit of hegemonic banking corporations, putting central banks and governments in a subservient role. If digital cash as a means of payment independent of bankmoney on account has a future at all, it must be ensured that e-cash is sovereign money as soon as possible, rather than becoming the monetary mass medium of the future which the banking industry intends to issue and control itself. In addition, there are now promising new approaches to introducing central bank-issued sovereign digital cash for public use based on blockchain technology (Sect. 6.17).

2.7   Money as an Informational Token

Is there an overall tendency, some evolving attractor that can be identified in the successive stages in the development of the means of payment from coins to banknotes, to money on account and e-cash sub-account as well as digital cash?

A common view has it that there was an evolution from commodity money to token money. Commodity money, however, appears to be a narrative invented by classical and neoclassical economics. The quantities of salt or silver and the like that were used in archaic times for measuring the economic value of items cannot be regarded as money. Even though certain transactions were actually settled by transferring quantities of grain or a number of goats, this did not turn these items into a regular and general means of payment. These goods served as units of account.

From the first coins 2700 years ago through to present-day e-cash, all money has been token money. Englightenment philosopher John Locke spotted the difference: 'It is a very common mistake to say that money is a commodity. ... Bullion is valued by its weight ... money is valued by its stamp.'[12] Similarly, on the occasion of analysing the Indian economy in 1913, Keynes considered an Indian silver rupee to be but 'a note printed on silver', also apparent from the coin's silver content much below face value.[13] Graziani concluded that 'a true monetary economy is inconsistent with the presence of a commodity money ... and must therefore be using a token money.'[14]

---

[12] Cit. The American Monetary Institute, Monetary History Calendar, August 25–31, on the occasion of John Locke's birthday August 29th, 1632.

[13] Keynes (1913, p. 26).

[14] Graziani (1990, p. 10). In the same sense Parguez and Seccareccia (2000, p. 104).

The coins of former times, of course, were made of precious metal which represented a special commodity. The coins had a high material value, close to, at times even higher than the face value of the coins. But the mere fact that there was a difference and some oscillation between the face value and material value of the coins is evidence of the difference between the monetary token and the material from which the token was made.

In medieval and early modern societies, precious-metal coins were partially, and in the end completely, replaced with alternative additional tokens, for a couple of centuries with wooden tally sticks, then paper scrip and banknotes (in China formerly made of leather), then non-precious alloy coins, and finally money on account and e-cash. Hence Simmel's assumption in 1900 of a transsecular trend from material to immaterial money.[15] Bankmoney and e-cash in fact exist in the form of informational units. Money, however, was no different whatever the physical characteristics of the token. Any monetary token symbolizes a specified quantity of money denominated in a particular currency. What has changed is the technical carrier of the information, from cyphers stamped on metal coins, via entries in ledgers and cyphers at first written, then printed on banknotes, to electronically stored digital numbers in accounts.

Whatever the numbered materials, there were always methods of documentation and procedures for the clearing of claims and duties by bookkeeping. In archaic times these were in kind, in later and modern societies they were in terms of currencies. Precursors to money on account may thus have existed long before coins were introduced some 2700 years ago. Non-cash clearing of claims and liabilities has certainly existed since medieval banking. There were even currencies for bookkeeping only, such as the Frankish livre from the time of Charlemagne through to 1795, a time span of a thousand years. There were also French coins denominated in livres from about 1650, but for the most part the livre was a currency for the running of accounts, in a way comparable to the International Monetary Fund's drawing rights today, or the ECU (European currency unit) from 1979 to 1998, when it was replaced with the euro, on account since 1999, in coins and notes since 2002.

In a way, money on account has always existed in parallel to cash. What has changed is the proportional relationship between of the use of cash and bankmoney on account. The transsecular diffusion of bankmoney has moved it from the background to the fore, supported by wired and radio telegraphy, telephone, post offices, teleprinters and the more recent digital devices. As a result, accountancy and advanced payment systems based on digital informa-

---

[15] Simmel (1900, p. 139).

tion and communication technology have by now made it possible to do away with solid tokens and to use digital units in a current bank account or in a blockchain.

2.8 Where Does the Value of Money Come from?

According to the understanding of money as inherent in mercantile bullionism of the seventeenth to eighteenth centuries and the gold standard of the nineteenth century, the value of token money was thought to be backed up by a gold hoard or by land. Such thinking comes from misinterpreting money as just another commodity, even if seen as the commodity of commodities. In 1716 John Law claimed that the value of the new French paper money was covered by the land value of Louisiana. People actually believed in such narrative, and many still do. In 1923 the trick worked again, when the German Reichsbank declared the value of the new post-inflation currency to be covered by the value of the national territories.

More generally, it is interesting to consider whether the value of money depends on the value of assets, in particular silver, gold, real estate, or equity, or whether such assets represent a fortune of money. As explained below, the latter holds true. The sensitivity of asset prices to business and financial cycles as well as to the income situation in general is obvious. In a crisis, the value of financial assets affected spirals downwards—which even increases the value of money rather than decreasing it, because an amount of money can buy more goods and assets at a reduced price.

The erroneous idea that the value of money depends on the value of assets, or that money as a monetary asset has intrinsic value in itself, represents a half-modern understanding of money. At the same time, it conveys banking doctrine (Sect. 3.3). Yet banks create the money, not its value. When granting loans, banks in most cases require debtors to procure collateral or to have someone who stands bail. This may lead to the erroneous assumption that there can only be as much money as there are assets which can serve as collateral, while the value of the money is assumed to depend on the solvency of debtors and guarantors. However, there are large volumes of book credit not covered by assets or bail, but respectively by expectations of cash flow, or regular earned income. Furthermore, money neither disappears nor loses value when claims have to be written down. The hypothesis confounds the concept of securing loans with the concept of the value of money, thus confusingly equating credit and money (Sect. 4.15), all of which is typical of banking doctrine.

Another deceptive teaching on the value of money, based on a misinterpretation of the state theory of money (Chap. 3.1), maintains that value is given to money by the government accepting it as a means of payment for taxes. The importance of the tax element, however, does not relate to the value of money, that is, its purchasing power and the foreign-exchange rate of a currency, but to the general acceptance of token money. In this respect, the validity of a means of payment is mistaken for the value of that money.[16]

The state's main contribution is to give money validity. The value of money can be affected by a government's responsible or irresponsible dealings with money. But a state's practical use of certain means of payment only contributes to the general acceptance of these means in addition to confirming them as official money, if not necessarily declaring them to be legal tender.

Wherefrom then does modern token fiat money obtain its value? Firstly and ultimately, the value of money depends on the level of productivity, on the quantity and quality of economic output which is priced in the economic process, including price setting by pivotal corporate actors upstream and downstream in respective product chains, market dynamics and government interference (by way of taxes, tariffs, subsidies and regulation). Real economic output is the original substance of economic value ascription, and the quantity of active money in circulation is the medium for paying the finally fixed price for items on offer and in demand, so that the value of output equals the prices of all goods and services actually paid for in a period of time.

The pricing process is not confined to real economic items. It also comprises items in the monetary and financial economy. This means that the value of real and financial items is not predetermined. It is not inherent in some sort of labor-value alchemy related to the human effort that contributes to produce output, nor is the value miraculously inherent in the quantity of money as such. Economic value results from the interactive dynamics of the valuation of items in terms of currency units, on the basis of needs and necessities, utility and preferences, in the context of items on offer (supply) and the amount of active money chasing these items (demand).

Most of that value ascription is structurally entrenched in established prices and price relations, which go back to and are constantly readjusted through effective supply and demand. The purchasing power of money then depends on the market position and bargaining power of both the respective supply and demand side to impose their price expectations. This applies to goods

---

[16] Also cf. Rossi (2007, p. 5).

and services, the costs of labor, the prices of financial assets, and by analogy also taxes and tax-like social security contributions. Price formation involves a dynamic feedback process between these different factors that are interrelated but cannot entirely be derived from each other or reduced to a single factor.

In this regard, the systemic view defended here corresponds to the model of re-adaptive relative prices, without, however, assuming optimum prices or equilibrium prices, nor any sort of hermetic macro-identity between output and income, as is postulated in macroeconomic equations (such as, for example, output = income consumed + income invested), and which is also, in a different way, the starting point of the circuitist and quantum models of production.

In the judgement of an individual actor, prices can be deemed to be right or wrong, just or unjust, sufficient or insufficient. From a macroeconomic point of view, however, there are but actual prices, that is, prices definitely paid in transactions, reflecting both the actual value of the items and the value of the money.

According to Rossi, 'money and production are the two faces of the same reality which is therefore monetary as well as real'.[17] Cencini and Rossi state that 'money exists only to the extent that it is merged with current output. ... Isolated from output, money has no raison d'être. ... The payment of wages is the event enabling the structural coupling of money and output.'[18] In consequence, 'the formation of financial capital that is not backed by any production' merely involves 'empty' money rather than 'real' money.[19]

These statements can in a way be endorsed without necessarily endorsing the context of monetary theory of production from which the statements are taken. Money is not created through production, but by way of credit creation. It is the banks, not employers and employees, who create the money. It is true, however, that much money today feeds into non-gross domestic product (GDP) finance rather than GDP-related finance (Sect. 6.8). If income on the basis of non-GDP use of money is spent on real items, this changes real economic price relations. In the absence of correspondingly high real growth rates, the real value of a currency unit, thus the purchasing power of earned income, will be reduced.

Equally, the productive forces of nature, humans and technology generate output, but the economic value of that output is not determined by the amount of earned income that has to be paid in the production process, but

---

[17] Rossi (2007, pp. 40, 121). Also cf. Rossi (2001, pp. 105, 122, 152).
[18] Cencini and Rossi (2015, pp. 146–148).
[19] Cencini and Rossi (2015, pp. 173, 204, 258). Baranzini and Cencini (2001, p. viii).

rather through pricing processes that constitute a relatively independent complex of their own. For a business to be sustainable, actual prices will of course have to cover all costs of output creation, including input products and services, labor, finance, taxes, withdrawals or dividend payments. But the final prices fetched on output sold cannot be reduced to the various cost factors.

Regarding the difference between earned income and financial income, the latter can be subdivided into financial income from GDP-related investment, in contrast to non-GDP finance. The question then is whether the notion of empty money refers to both types of financial income or just to revenues from non-GDP finance. Whatever the answer, this is not about absolute 'laws of economics' or hermetic macroeconomic identities, but relates to normative questions of legitimacy and justice. Current disputes over financial income can be seen as a contemporary variant of old industrial disputes over productive and unproductive work. Labor theories of value from the nineteenth century had their point, but were not really viable in the end. Something similar might be said today about monetary theories of production in the Keynesian lineage.

Whoever has money has the power to purchase a share of economic output regardless of whether they have contributed to creating it. Those who invest money in real output generation make an indirect, financial contribution to economic output. Those who invest money in non-GDP finance do not, but can possibly contribute to maintaining (or destroying) a stock of capital and wealth. Finally, those who are in the position to create additional money 'out of nothing' and to spend that money or the financial revenue from it, have the privilege of a free lunch—free for the money creator, but forgone by everybody else.

Modern money has no intrinsic properties except its functionality as a means of payment, thereby providing income or building capital.[20] Seeing money as a 'medium of exchange' is not wrong, but incomplete and premodern. Money as a general means of payment acts as a medium of factor allocation and income distribution. Modern economies, rather than being huge barter systems, are better understood as a complex web of vertical and horizontal chains of production or provision, including cooperative relationships between suppliers and demanders, and competition among different suppliers as well as among different demanders. The markets and prices related to the chains are based on longer-term contracts and dominated by the pricing policy of the pivotal players along the chains.

In such a context, money can perhaps best be seen as a drawing right. Money represents purchasing power, an unspecified allotment of supplies on offer and demand, unspecified in category and quality, of basically unlimited

---

[20] Rossi (2003).

validity, but limited in the quantity of currency units. The value of money is conferred value, which means that the value is not in the money itself but in the price of the goods, services and assets money can buy. In this sense, money represents an unspecified, but quantitatively limited, drawing right on preferential items of the entire economic product as well as, where applicable, real and financial assets. However, money and financial assets cannot have value by themselves. Even if money and assets have a price in financial transactions, these prices are ultimately related to the actual and expected value of economic output. This is to say that prices and the value of money depend directly and indirectly on maintaining a certain level of productivity.

This in no way contradicts the converse dependence of the real economy on being financed, as finance in turn depends on the availability of money. The latter connection—from money via finance to economic output—represents a hierarchy of control, while the former—from the real economy back to finance and the monetary and banking system—represents a hierarchy of conditions to be fulfilled and restrictions to be observed.

What remains is the gravitational force of real output. The often quoted statement of that ominous Native American chieftain coursing through modernity-critical discourses—'You can't eat money'—may not be authentic, but is quite right. There are the upstream-downstream chains in real economic output generation, and linked to and dependent on this fundament, partially also detached from it, there are various chains of financial assets. The systemic hierarchy between the money system, finance, and output generation certainly works in both directions; but money and financial assets without real output would be completely pointless. The first and ultimate raison d'être of money is indeed the production of output and real assets, from which money derives its value, and, as a drawing right representing purchasing power, allows money holders to allocate economic factors and distribute income.

2.9   A Monetarized and Financialized Economy

An economic buzzword of recent years is 'financialization'. This refers to the tremendous growth of investment banking and global financial markets as they began to take off toward the 1980s. It also includes the notion of financial market capitalism, as a successor to the financial capitalism of old that was centered on direct, at times even exclusive, bank–company relations.[21]

---

[21] Cf. Hudson (2012, pp. 129, 185), Epstein (2005), Palley (2008), Hein et al. (2008), and Kay (2015). Bank-centered financial capitalism before and after WWI was reflected in the writings of Marxists Rudolf Hilferding and Rosa Luxemburg.

From a wider perspective, old industrial banking capitalism and today's financial market capitalism are just recent formations in a long lineage dating way back in history. Any post-subsistence, post-local economy needed to be 'financialized', that is, based on some method for the prior and ongoing funding of bigger enterprises. Large-scale buildings and public works, armies and warfare—such as cathedrals and crusades—are unimaginable without organized funding, including dues and taxes, and more or less sophisticated forms of credit. The pivotal players were the rulers of a territory rather than merchants and bankers, and the three of them—government, trade and production companies, and financers—developed the sort of symbiosis that has become typical of nation-states in the modern world system for around 500 years.

With the introduction of money, finance became easier and more efficient. Conversely, finance became dependent on the availability of money. And as modern money became uncoupled from precious metal, the financial economy became directly conditioned and shaped by the monetary system, as the latter was increasingly entangled with the banking system. Money, in particular bankmoney, has been the basic foundation of the entire economy ever since.

Against this background there is reason to assume that the development of markets was the result of the development of financing methods, rather than the reverse, and that the post-archaic development of finance was a result of money and banking over 2700 years. We thus arrive at a systemic pattern that is the opposite of the classical and neoclassical narrative. In modern societies, the economy is based on its financial system, which in turn is built upon its monetary system. According to this functional hierarchy, money governs finance, as finance governs the entire economy. Or, to put in pertinent language, the economy is finance-led, and finance is not just money-based, but conditioned on the monetary system, which today is bank-led. This is certainly no linear causation: it entails feedback interdependencies. These, however, unfold around the systemic hierarchy of the monetary, financial and real economy.[22] Whoever controls the issuance and first use of money, as well as the main pathways of its allocation, is in possession of the most powerful instrument of societal control other than command power based on the legal authority to issue directives backed by force.

---

[22] Huber (2014a, p. 195).

Such a view is widely shared in the social sciences with the exception of economics.[23] Within the spectrum of economic schools it appears to be circuitism and quantum theory that have developed the most explicit understanding of what it means to have a monetarized and financialized economy. According to Graziani, the money that funds real economic expenditure and financial investment alters the structure and inner workings of the economy.

> 'Money is never neutral [and] is, at the economic level, a source of profits and, at the social level, a source of power.'
>
>   'Since access to money and credit is a key factor in a wage economy, producers of money and credit ... enjoy a privileged position and are admitted as such to a share of total product.'[24]

According to circuitist and quantum theory teaching, modern economies depend on the way credit and money is managed. Similarly, levels of employment and income are thought not to be determined by relative prices, but by the conditions of credit-based funding, jointly decided upon by banks and firms, with the banks holding the whip hand. The model underlying that proposition can be questioned (Sect. 6.8), but it clearly stresses the power of banks and the overriding position of the banking and financial industry as the pivotal actor in the economy.[25]

By contrast, in most neoclassical economics the money system is given little attention. In typical textbook models, money is just a medium of exchange, an ephemeral veil over the economy. Even in Friedman's monetarism, in which, as he stated, 'money matters', too much money alters nominal price levels, but nothing 'real'. This assumption is unreal and misses the point.[26] Before money can be used as a *medium of exchange*, it is used as a *medium of finance*, thus a medium of economic and social control comparable to legal command power. Moreover, it makes a significant difference whether money is used for financing real economic expenditure or for non-GPD financial investment. Far from being just a veil over the economy, money is the constitutive component of financialized modern market economies. If the money system does not work properly, the financial system and the real economy will not work properly either.

---

[23] Cf. Häring and Douglas (2012, pp. 47, 76).

[24] Graziani (1990, p. 29, 2003, p. 26).

[25] Graziani (2003, pp. 58–62, 1990, pp. 8, 11–29).

[26] For a critical discussion of the neutrality theorem of neoclassical economics cf. Rossi (2001, p. 80).

References

Apostolou, Nicholas, and D. Larry Crumbley. 2008. The Tally Stick, the First Internal Control? *The Forensic Examiner* 70(1):60–62. Spring 2008. http://www.bus.lsu.edu/accountting/faculty/lcrumbley/tally%20stick%20article.pdf

Baranzini, Mauro, and Alvaro Cencini. 2001. The Quantum Theory of Money and Production. Foreword to Sergio Rossi. 2001. *Money and Inflation*. Cheltenham, UK: Edward Elgar, viii-xli.

Buiter, Willem H. 2009. Negative Nominal Interest Rates. Three ways to overcome the zero lower bound. *NBER Working Papers*, June 2009.

Cencini, Alvaro, and Sergio Rossi.2015. *Economic and Financial Crises. A New Macroeconomic Analysis*. London: Palgrave Macmillan.

Davies, Glyn. 2013 [1994]. *A History of Money*. Cardiff: University of Wales Press.

ECB. 2015. *Virtual Currency Schemes—A Further Analysis*. Frankfurt: European Central Bank.

Epstein, Gerald A., ed.2005. *Financialisation and the World Economy*. Cheltenham, UK: Edward Elgar.

Graeber, David. 2012. *Debt. The First 5,000 Years*. New York: Melville House Publishing.

Graziani, Augusto. 1990. The Theory of the Monetary Circuit. *Économies et Sociétés* 7: 7–36.

———. 2003. *The Monetary Theory of Production*. Cambridge: Cambridge University Press.

Häring, Norbert, and Niall Douglas. 2012. *Economists and the Powerful. Convenient Theories, Distorted Facts, Ample Rewards*. London: Anthem Press.

Hein, Eckhard, Torsten Niechoj, Peter Spahn, and Achim Truger, eds.2008. *Finance-led Capitalism?* Marburg: Metropolis.

Hixson, William F. 1993. *Triumph of the Bankers. Money and Banking in the Eighteenth and Nineteenth Centuries*. Westport, CO: Praeger.

Huber, Joseph. 2014b. Modern Money Theory and New Currency Theory. *A Comparative Discussion. Real-world economics review* 66: 38–57.

Hudson, Michael. 2012. *The Bubble and Beyond*. Dresden: Islet Verlag.

Huerta de Soto, Jesús. 2009. *Money, Bank Credit, and Economic Cycles*, 2nd edn. Auburn, AL: Ludwig von Mises Institute (1st edn. 2006).

Ifrah, Georges. 1981. *Histoire Universelle des Chiffres*. Paris: Ed. Seghers.

Kay, John. 2015. *Other People's Money*. London: Profile Books.

Keynes, John Maynard. 1971 [1913]. *Indian Currency and Finance*. London: Palgrave Macmillan.

North, Michael. 1994. *Das Geld und seine Geschichte vom Mittelalter bis zur Gegenwart*. München: C.H.Beck.

Palley, Thomas I. 2008. Financialisation. What it is and why it matters. In *Finance-Led Capitalism?* eds. E. Hein et al., 29–60. Marburg: Metropolis-Verlag.

Parguez, Alain, and Mario Seccareccia. 2000. The Credit Theory of Money—The Monetary Circuit Approach. In *What is Money?* ed. J. Smithin, 101–123. London: Routledge.

Rogoff, Kenneth. 2014. Costs and Benefits to Phasing Out Paper Currency. *NBER Working Papers,* May 2014.

Rossi, Sergio.2001. *Money and Inflation A New Macroeconomic Analysis.* Cheltenham: Edward Elgar.

———. 2003. *Money and Banking in a Monetary Theory of Production.* In *Modern Theories of Money,* eds. Louis-Philippe Rochon, and Sergio Rossi, 339–359. Cheltenham: Edward Elgar.

———. 2007. *Money and Payments in Theory and Practice.* London: Routledge.

Schemmann, Michael. 2011a. *The ABC of Sovereign Debt Redemption.* IICPA Publications.

———. 2012a. *Accounting Perversion in Bank Financial Statements. The Root Cause of Financial Crises.* IICPA Publications.

———. 2012b. *Liquid Money—the Final Thing. Federal Reserve and Central Bank Accounts for Everyone.* IICPA Publications.

Simmel, Georg. 1900. *Philosophie des Geldes.* Berlin: Duncker & Humblot. Recent English version 2004. *Philosophy of Money,* ed. David Frisby. London: Routledge.

Zarlenga, Stephen A.2002. *The Lost Science of Money. The Mythology of Money—The Story of Power.* Valatie, NY: American Monetary Institute.

3

Chartalism

3.1 State Theory Versus Market Theory of Money

Most people still relate the origin and nature of money to a narrative of classical economics, as for example in Adam Smith, and the neoclassical extension of that narrative by Carl Menger in 1871 (neoclassical Austrian School). According to this view, money is imagined to have emerged as a spontaneous creation in archaic barter and market processes for facilitating the exchange of goods. Money is seen in this context as a commodity like any other, and thus a private affair. This point of view is most often called the commodity theory of money.[1]

If a legal aspect is involved, it is private or civil law. From this angle, the classical narrative is a private-compact theory of money. It may be preferable here to speak of the market theory of money. The reason is that the classical narrative entwines at least three aspects that ought to be kept apart analytically: in addition to the question of whether money is state- or market-borne, there is the question of whether money is a commodity or a symbolic token (answered above in support of the token), and the question of whether money *is* credit and debt in a credit-and-debt relationship, or whether money is a debt-free token for the settlement of debts.

---

[1] Some useful discussion is to be found in Goodhart (1998) (private market-borne vs chartal theories of money), Hudson (2004) (barter vs debt theories of money), Rossi (2007, pp. 10–16), and Ryan-Collins et al. (2012, pp. 30–37) (commodity vs credit theory of money), even if these juxtapositions mix up different aspects, as explained.

© The Author(s) 2017
J. Huber, *Sovereign Money*, DOI 10.1007/978-3-319-42174-2_3

At this point, the focus is on whether money is state- or market-borne. In face of the empirical evidence which economic historians were able to produce—notably, and of relevance to the Occidental world, from early antiquity, Greece, Rome, Byzantium, the Arabo-Islamic world, the Christian middle ages and early modernity—the Smith–Menger narrative appears to be largely fictitious.[2] The findings back up the concept of money as a public affair and a prerogative of rulers, in short, the state theory of money, to adopt this term here.

The evolutionary pattern starts in ancient Mesopotamia and Egypt with the extended households of temple and palace complexes and their entourage, in the beginnings within local city-states some of which developed into ever larger kingdoms. The related economies were centrally managed by a specialized administration, including the labor-divisionary organization of chains of provision and public works such as irrigation systems or town walls, the redistribution of harvests and of other means of providing for craftspeople and workmen, the administration itself, later on standing armies. All this required the development of contracting, legal structures, scripture and documentation.[3]

Money is described as having emerged within those early state structures from tribal traditions of making gifts and contributions, such as dowry or bride price, paying wergeld in compensation for physical injury or sacrificial oblations, and later also including regular duties and tributes, the latter mostly imposed on conquered tribes, if they were not bound to forced labor or outright slavery. Equally, there is evidence from Mesopotamia of the practice of lending goods, the amount of which had to be returned with interest—that is, the amount of goods to be returned was higher than the amount lent.

In an extended household of hundreds and thousands of people, gifts and duties as well as current provisions of goods have to be measured and registered. All transactions were made in kind, and it is thought that some staple goods of the time, or highly valued goods, developed into general units of account, such as a weight unit of grain or silver, serving as a common denominator which made different goods comparable in relative quantity or value. Those units of account were fixed by a ruler's administration.

---

[2] Hudson (2004) and Graeber (2012, pp. 22–71). For a detailed history of money in archaic and medieval societies cf. Del Mar (1867, 1880, 1895), Ridgeway (1892), Le Goff (1956, 1986, 2010), and Davies (2013). On the European and American history of money since early modernity cf. Friedman and Schwartz (1963), Galbraith (1975), Vilar (1976), Kindleberger and Laffargue (1982), Kindleberger (1993), Hixson (1993), North (1994), Zarlenga (2002), Davies (2013), and Aliber and Kindleberger (2015).

[3] Henry (2004). Much of this has comprehensively been developed in K. Wittfogel's *Oriental Despotism*, published in 1957. Since then, research has basically confirmed that approach, even though in more specified and detailed ways.

This does not exclude the eventual development of trade and finally markets where the quasi-monetary units of account could be used for transacting goods. Apparently, local and long-distance trade developed in ancient economies early on. The important thing is that the emergence of trade and markets was tied to the 'state' households of kings, high priests or warlords, and largely tied to the centrally managed operations and supply chains they maintained. This also applies to the sovereign coins that rulers finally began to issue from around the seventh century BC.

If there are messages to be drawn from this historical survey, the most fundamental is that markets do not emerge and develop in a constitutional vacuum free of state powers. Markets build and rest upon a state's institutional and legal structure, of which the money system is an integral part. There is no evidence that trade, markets, prices and means of payment would have developed 'spontaneously' from primitive barter.[4] As Graeber put it:

> States created markets. Markets require states. Neither could continue without the other. ... We are told that they are opposites ... But it's a false dichotomy.[5]

Closer to our own times, this can again be studied in the evolution of nation-states and markets within the modern world system that began to emerge about 500 years ago. In building up this system, adventurers, colonizers, soldiers, missionaries, merchants and bankers did not create legal structures and monies of their own, but they always were, and needed to be, envoys of the states from which they originated, or contractual partners of the states across which they expanded their business and trade networks.

Rather than postulating money as a market-borne commodity, markets are more easily understood as being money-borne, or at least money-based and money-facilitated, or money-catalyzed, as is correctly stated in the neoclassical narrative in a functional sense, whereby, however, the money was not market-borne, but state- and law-borne as an instrument of sovereign rule.[6] With monetarization came a money-based financialization of the economy. Money has served the purposes of the real economy and the financial economy ever since.

Even though the commodity theory of money may historically be wrong and does not hold as a founding tenet in classical economics, there is no problem acknowledging that the Smith–Menger narrative grasps the basic functions of money in contributing to the development of markets. Money is a marvelous market catalyzer, catalyzing transactions, an intertemporal device

---

[4] Cf. Swedberg (2003, pp. 131–146).
[5] Graeber (2012, p. 71).
[6] Also see Aglietta and Cartelier in Aglietta et al. (eds.) (1998, p. 131).

for facilitating transactions that would otherwise be unimaginable, thereby enabling a match of supply and demand without necessitating a coincidence of wants (a coincidence of supply and demand at a given time in a given place). Payment in money helps avoid immemorial creditor–debtor relationships, rather than being a result of the latter. Equally, money facilitates the funding of investment, which otherwise would be quite complicated. Money itself is thus traded as a financial commodity. But trading money presupposes money to exist, and in this respect it has to be acknowledged that money was not market-borne 'bottom up', but was introduced 'top down' by a respective state authority.

To summarize what is relevant regarding the question of commodity theory versus state theory of money: in ancient times, money was developed as an official unit of account for documenting and clearing claims and obligations (debt, tributes). This took place in the extended household economies of the secular and religious rulers of the time and their related supply chains. When coins were introduced much later, 2700 years ago, coining remained under the control of rulers.[7]

The economy, including long-distance trade, developed around the extended households of the courts and temples of the rulers of a realm, under their control, including control of the monetary and financing practices at subsequent stages of development. To put it succinctly, the market economy is a creature of money rather than the reverse; and money is a creature of the state as much as the markets are framed by state powers and law rather than existing in an extraterritorial private nowhereland.

The classical and neoclassical approaches to economics tend to model the economy as a Robinson Crusoe island beyond the state, based on private law with no role for public or state law. The appearance of the commodity theory of money in the eighteenth century, as a component of that extraterritorial approach to economics, can be seen in the context of growing rebelliousness of the then middle classes against the repressive state of the ruling aristocracy.

However, amid all the justified criticism of absolutism and statist mercantilism of the seventeenth to the nineteenth centuries, the fundamental and indispensable role of the state in modern society, including the monetary system and creating a legal framework for the economy and finance, was improperly dismissed. The baby was thrown out with the bathwater. Even Marx and Engels in their earlier years took an anti-statist attitude when they imagined the dwindling of the state in communism. In hindsight this was a gross misunderstanding, but in the first half of the nineteenth century it was

---

[7] Cf. the contributions of Henry, Hudson, Gardiner and Ingham in Wray (ed.) (2004). Graeber (2012).

an element of social romanticism which fed into both anarchism and social-ism. Classical liberalism, by contrast, was rationalistic rather than romanti-cist. But all the then 'enlightened' political philosophies were united in their resentment against the state.

3.2   The Sovereign Monetary Prerogative and Its Two Historical Challenges

Money tokens, as they have been created and issued under state control from antiq-uity to the present day, are a legal instrument by state fiat, that is, money acknowl-edged by administrative fiat or law. Today, there are two basic kinds of fiat money, the first representing sovereign money issued by a respective authority, including coins issued by the treasuries and notes issued by a state's central bank; the second representing bankmoney, on account and as e-cash in mobile sub-accounts.

As money by sovereign fiat, coins and notes are legal tender. This means money which, by force of law, has to be accepted in settlement of debts. Bankmoney, by contrast, is not legal tender, although it represents official money because it is recognized by administrative fiat as a general means of payment. There is no law that puts bankmoney on an equal footing with trea-sury coins and central bank notes, yet bankmoney is regularly accepted and used by everybody, including public bodies (except the central bank). Various regulations presuppose the existence of bankmoney. As a common practice, the money surrogates of the banking sector have become so deeply entrenched that they might even claim to be a legitimate matter of customary law.[8]

Sovereign money gives a nation-state, or community of nation-states, mon-etary sovereignty. This includes three monetary prerogatives:

1. Determining the *currency* of the realm, the monetary unit of account;
2. Creating and issuing *money*, the means of payment denominated in that currency;
3. Benefitting from the *seigniorage*, the gain that accrues from the creation of money.

---

[8] In the USA, due to its special monetary history, there is a peculiar distinction between legal tender and lawful money. Definitions have changed over time, however, and court rulings on the matter have not been unanimous. Basically, lawful money is Treasury- or Congress-issued coins or notes, while legal ten-der refers to Federal Reserve-issued money (notes and reserves). Neither includes bankmoney (demand deposits and e-cash) which, however, is considered to be fiat money. So, despite that distinction between lawful money and legal tender, irritating as it is outside the USA, there is a basic international congruence of definitions.

Today only the currency prerogative is still intact. What the state has almost entirely lost are the sovereign prerogatives of money creation and seigniorage as these have devolved to the banking industry for the most part (Chap. 4). Prior to industrial capitalism, money was sovereign money as a matter of course. It was understood that the monetary prerogatives of a state were of the utmost importance, in fact of constitutional importance, as was formally recognized in the Constitution of the United States from 1789. The founding fathers of the USA understood that the monetary prerogatives were essential for the new nation's sovereignty.

The monetary prerogatives of the state became questioned in the course of the eighteenth and nineteenth centuries, first by private paper money, then with the advent of demand deposits, bankmoney on account, as a general means of payment. The private issuance of banknotes required a licence issued by parliament or the treasury. The issuance of bankmoney today still requires a banking licence from the central bank. Such licensing, however, in no way controls the monetary dynamics of privately issued money. Private banknotes, even if state-licensed, thus became the first historical challenge to the sovereign prerogatives of money and seigniorage. This was eventually reflected in the controversy between the Currency and Banking Schools, resulting in the state's recapturing of the prerogatives of paper money and related seigniorage through the British Bank Charter Acts of 1833 and 1844.

The second big challenge was already present in the first, but was not yet given due consideration. That challenge was, and still is, bankmoney on account through private primary credit creation. In the decades before Black Friday in 1929, demand deposits had started their take-off towards becoming the major means of payment. This led to the bank credit theory of money.[9] At the same time, theories of the monetarized and financialized nature of modern economies and banking capitalism arose, as did proposals to reform the money and banking system.

Among the latter there were new business models of banking as developed in the mutualist and co-operative movements of the time. In regard to monetary reform, two approaches gained particular attention, one by Silvio Gesell (the stamp scrip movement), the other by C.H. Douglas (the social credit movement).[10] Both Gesell and Douglas aimed for the full nationalization of money. They were followed by a number of approaches to 100 % reserve banking; these are detailed in Sect. 6.14.

---

[9] Cf. Macleod (1896), Withers (1909), Hawtrey (1919), and Hahn (1920).

[10] For stamp scrips cf. Gesell (1919), Fisher and Cohrssen (1934); for social credit Douglas (1920, 1924), Mairet (1934), Munson (1945), and Hutchinson and Burkitt (1997).

All these approaches had their shortcomings. In Gesell and Douglas there were a number of problematic theorems, such as the supposed structural advantage of money holders over commodity suppliers in Gesell, and the corresponding proposal of a demurrage rate on money holdings. Both Gesell and Douglas stood for a reductionist criticism of the role of interest in the vein of anarcho-syndicalism, and both lacked a detailed understanding of money in the fractional reserve system. The shortcomings of the approaches to a 100 % reserve on deposits are rooted in keeping the reserve system as such.

Politicians did not care too much about monetary reform, even though a number of renowned economists were in favor of 100 % banking and two members of Congress, Senator Cutting and Representative Patman, introduced legislative bills in the Senate and the House of Representatives in 1934.[11] Close to monetary reform, the most successful measure of monetary policy was the Canadian experience of a benign period of sovereign central bank credit to the government, de facto non interest-bearing, from 1936 to 1973.[12]

At the time, the practice provided impressive results against the background of very low levels of public debt as well as underused capacities and the country's huge untapped resources and growth potentials. Thanks to monetary financing under such conditions, Canada appears to be the only country that emerged from World War II without burdensome levels of sovereign debt. W.L. Mackenzie King, Canadian prime minister from 1935 to 1948, is reported to have said in 1935 that

> once a nation parts with control of its currency and credit, it matters not who makes that nation's laws. … Until the control of the issue of currency and credit is restored to government and recognized as its most conspicuous and sacred responsibility, all talk of the sovereignty of Parliament and of democracy is idle and futile.[13]

The reform finally implemented by the US government, as an alternative to monetary reform and as the lesser of two evils viewed from a banking point of view, was separate banking in the form of the Glass-Steagall Act of 1932–1933. This was watered down in the following decades, and then repealed by President Bill Clinton in 1999. The act set investment banking

---

[11] Cf. Zarlenga (2002, pp. 664–673) and Striner (2015, p. 54).

[12] The period of direct central bank financing of government expenditure in Canada is poorly documented. Only recently Ryan-Collins (2015) undertook to shed new light on the Canadian experience with monetary financing. Prior to this article there existed a rather informal, though highly informative paper by Will Abram, *The Canadian Experience, Bank of Canada Act 1934*, made publicly available, for example, at http://occupyourbank.ca/Money-The_Canadian_Experience.php

[13] http://www.michaeljournal.org/plenty24.htm

apart from commercial banking. This was somewhat mistaken, because separate banking cannot have a meaningful effect as long as, first, commercial banks are allowed to lend limitlessly to investment banks, governments, real-estate investors and so forth, and second, as long as the management of money on account and cashless payments is not set apart from both commercial and investment banking.

Whether due to conceptual shortcomings or banking-conservative politics, a lasting answer to the second challenge of the monetary prerogative was postponed to the contemporary wave of crises which set in with global financialization as it took off around 1980. That take-off resulted in a credit-and-debt binge unequaled by former such maldevelopments. The second challenge to the prerogatives of money and seigniorage is still waiting for a meaningful response. Following the logic of monetary modernization, that response is a transition from bankmoney to sovereign money on account and sovereign digital cash.[14]

3.3   The Currency Versus Banking Controversy

The first challenge to the monetary prerogative—the growing use of private banknotes in the eighteenth and beginning of the nineteenth centuries—came with the experience of inflation and deflation, re- and devaluation of currencies, and cyclical crises. The recurrent experience sparked the monetary controversy between the British Currency and Banking Schools in the 1820–1840s.[14]

Today, remarkably little attention is given to that controversy, even though it conveys a frame of reference for monetary policies of lasting relevance to modern money systems. The central question was whether money creation should be left to the banks (Banking School), or whether the state ought to re-establish its control over the money through an adequate institutional arrangement (Currency School).

The Currency School emanated from earlier doctrines of mercantile bullionism, namely the idea that a nation's wealth depends on its stock of money, which in fact meant the national stock of silver and gold that should be prevented from draining away abroad. At the time, the Currency School supported the implementation of a national gold standard. Now that the metal age of money is over, the Currency School is generally considered to be irrel-

[14] This outline of the Currency-vs-Banking controversy is based on O'Brien (1994, 2007, pp. 79–156), Galbraith (1995 [1975], pp. 36–44), Poitras (1998), Huerta de Soto (2009, pp. 601–605, 622–630, 631, 639–49), and Viner (1937).

evant. This is an error, because gold was not the crucial element in Currency School doctrine that it appeared to be. Two hundred years ago everybody was a 'metallist' in the sense of considering precious metals to be the base of banknotes and bankmoney. The Currency School, however, as represented by Ricardo, Torrens and Thornton, had no interest in gold as such. Torrens considered himself to be an anti-bullionist. Currency scholars wanted a modern paper currency and credit system, albeit a sound and stable one, avoiding monetary scarcity as well as oversupply.

Currency scholars and leading politicians of the time saw out-of-control issuance of private banknotes as the main cause of recurrent banking and economic crises. The analogy to banks' out-of-control credit and deposit creation today is obvious. In the absence of proper regulation, the free creation of banknotes and bankmoney tends to procyclically overshoot, temporarily shrink, and in consequence to be without restraint. It thus results in an unstable and ultimately inflationary and asset-inflationary money supply which prompts bank failures and bank runs, as well as wider financial and economic crises. The Currency School assumed causality to run from the quantity of money to the level of prices and interest. The Banking School, conversely, assumed the money supply to result from interest rates and prices.[15]

As a consequence, from a Currency School point of view, it needs to be determined by law what shall be money in the sense of currency in general circulation, and under whose control and responsibility fiat money shall be created. The Currency School wanted to establish a mechanism that would ensure control over the quantity of banknotes.

The opposing Banking School, with Tooke and Fullarton as its main representatives, contradicted the Currency Schol by invoking the law of large numbers, the law of money reflux, and what was known then as the real bills doctrine (real bills meant debt bills from creditworthy originators).[16]

The doctrine says that as long as bankers write out credit and banknotes against real bills at short notice, the money will surely be put to good use. Upon maturity of credits, the money will be taken out of circulation (reflux), making sure there is no more money than there is 'real' demand for it. The *quality* of available real bills will regulate the *quantity* of credit and banknotes created thereupon. They considered bankers to be honorable merchants of impeccable judgement.

As to the fractional reserve of coin and bullion in relation to banknotes issued, the Banking scholars maintained that, on the grounds of the law of

---

[15] O'Brien (2007, pp. 5, 117, 152).
[16] Poitras (1998).

large numbers, fractional reserve banking involves no more risk than lending on a full reserve base. Bankers know from experience how large a reserve they actually need. As long as banks observe the real bills principle, the banknotes will be trusted, not normally converted into coin, and no problem will arise.

The Banking scholars questioned inflation and deflation, and re- and devaluation of the currency as general phenomena. Official statistics were not yet available. Should these phenomena exist, there must be broader economic reasons beyond bank credit and banknotes. According to Fullarton's law of reflux, it can be excluded that inflation and boom-and-bust cycles would occur for monetary reasons. If something like an overhang of banknotes were looming, the holders would notice early on, and immediately exchange notes for coin, so that any overhang would be choked off. Sure enough, given the fractional coverage of banknotes, such a reflux of notes is not documented ever to have happened—although it has often been attempted in bank runs, when long queues of people wait in vain in front of closed banks to take their money out.

Even if the term 'real bills' is not used anymore, the real bills doctrine is a mainstay of any Banking theory from the early nineteenth century to the present day. It is also a core principle of central banking (prime quality assets eligible for monetary policy operations). The Banking doctrine today is hardly different from what it was 200 years ago. It says, let banks freely create money, then banknotes, and today digital money on account. The money supply takes care of itself. Money and capital markets continually readjust and thus establish equilibrium, so that under conditions of symmetric endowments, information and competition, banks cannot fail to create the optimum amount of credit (money) and financial markets cannot derail. No one ever asked how something like a self-limiting market equilibrium would ensue as long as the banking industry has a strong self-interest in expanding the money supply, as well as the power to create the money on which it operates, which cyclically results in a self-propelling growth of the money supply and financial assets, of credit and debt, *disproportionate* to economic output, as if defying the gravity of an economy's productive potential.

A prominent figure in Banking School teachings of the recent past was Friedrich von Hayek, who called for the radical denationalization of money.[17] The community of Neo-Austrian economists, many of them Americans, continues to spread the word. Fama's efficient market hypothesis can also be seen as a typical Banking School approach of the recent past.[18] The neoclassical Washington Consensus from the 1980s to the beginning of the 2000s held a

---

[17] Hayek (1976) and White (1989).
[18] Fama et al. (1969) and Fama (1970). For a criticism cf. Turner (2015, pp. 36–44).

generalized belief in the efficient self-regulation of markets, including banking and finance as well as politically deregulated global markets. Financial markets were seen as near-perfect information processing machines which relentlessly absorb and price in any relevant information. This is similar to the all-superior swarm intelligence which Hayek ascribed to markets, contrasting this to unknowing central planners, while ignoring the swarm madness in which markets can also become caught.

The Banking School rationale is based on the axiomatic classical belief in the 'invisible hand' of markets, which is a modernized variant of the medieval Scholastic theology of God's wise *manus gubernatoris* unfailingly creating a *harmonia mundi* unless distorted by devilish machinations.[19] In neoclassical economics, the latter are normally identified with government interference.

The Currency School's response to the real bills doctrine was the thesis of the real bills fallacy. It argues that the belief in 'good bills', 'good uses', 'good bankers', 'perfect markets' and other features of ideal worlds does not apply to real-world banking. Torrens, as leader of the Currency School, had himself been a supporter of the real bills doctrine. He became disappointed, however, with the realities of 'real' bills and with bankers' actual practices. According to Thornton, a respected banker of the time, it is impossible to reliably know in advance which bills will be 'real' and which will turn out to be fictitious. Equally, banks discounted long-term bills almost as willingly as short-term bills. Unforeseen events can throw over any calculation. The banking business itself, Thornton observed, including the Bank of England, had a tendency towards over-issuing credit and banknotes for pure self-interest, thereby becoming over-exposed to various risks, eventually bringing banks and financial markets into trouble, the more so because banknotes, to be accepted, had to be redeemable in silver coin.[20]

For the Currency School, the quantity theory of money was an essential foundation. Equally, they were aware of the pivotal role of bank credit for the entire economy. They did not expressly criticize 'the power of banks', but as far as the issue of banknotes was involved they in fact wanted to see that power tamed.

By contrast, the Banking School type of thinking tends to deny or belittle the power and importance of money. To bankers, the power of banks has always been a non-issue. This is in line with the neoclassical view of money as an ephemeral veil over the economy, simply mediating business and trade, but not being constitutive of them, also known as the doctrine of neutrality

---

[19] Cf. Vogl (2011, p. 39).
[20] Poitras (1998, p. 481).

of money, according to which changes in the money supply may change price levels but do not generally result in structural changes of investment, employment, production and consumption.

The Banking School did not reject quantity theory, and bankers up to the present day routinely speak out in favor of stable prices, stable currencies and so forth. In practice, bankers tend to be hypocritical in this respect and contribute to the volatility of currencies by unrestrained foreign exchange trading, as they contribute to fueling inflation and asset inflation by creating as much credit leverage as possible. It is in the interest of banks to expand their business and thus their balance sheets. This increases the nominal value of various bank assets, it decreases bank liabilities just like those of any other debtor, and it may temporarily even include a higher interest margin. If inflation and asset inflation are not extremely runaway, banks are happy to live with inflation and asset inflation; in fact they live on it to a degree in that they are the first users of the money.

By comparison, Currency scholars were classical market economists. They recognized, however, that money is not simply a commodity like any other. What is more, the creation and first use of money has a legal and political side. Modern money tokens can be created at discretion. Without anchorage in a value base—formerly gold, today the potential and actual output of an economy—money and capital markets will not reach a stage of equilibrium and self-limitation.

In consequence, there must be some mechanism to keep the money supply in a commensurate relation to real economic growth. The key to achieving this was, as Whale put it, the Currency School principle 'that banking ought to be separated from the control of the currency'.[21] The proposal of creating an institutional arrangement that would separate the control over the stock of money from the banking business of extending credit and funding investment was put forth in Ricardo's *Plan for the Establishment of a National Bank* from 1824. This plan provided for the national money supply to be re-established as the sovereign prerogative it used to be until the spread of private banknotes. Similar ideas were widespread in the USA. Among the American founding fathers, Jefferson was ascribed a number of statements on money and banking, some verified, others unverified. One such statement puts in a nutshell the politics based on Currency teaching: 'Bank-paper must be suppressed, and the circulating medium must be restored to the nation to whom it belongs.'[22]

---

[21] Whale (1944, p. 109).

[22] http://www.monticello.org/site/jefferson/private-banks-quotation

Separating money and credit appears to threaten the position of the bankers, in that it denies them as creators of money, and confines them to be money changers and money lenders and investors, as they have always been. To Banking scholars, moreover, as to most neoclassical, Keynesian and post-Keynesian economists today, the Currency School principle of keeping money and credit apart appears to be an impossibility, for they firmly believe in money and credit as being one and the same (Sect. 4.15).

The Currency vs Banking controversy was settled with the Bank Charter Acts of 1833 and 1844. The first Act made banknotes issued by the Bank of England legal tender, while, however, still permitting the issuance of banknotes by the country banks of the time. The Act of 1844 nevertheless triggered the process of phasing out private banknotes and establishing the central-bank monopoly of banknotes that exists to the present day.[23] The Act of 1844 also introduced a renewed gold standard. The permissible number of banknotes was tied to a specific money-to-gold ratio, the gold existing as a national hoard, backing up the central bank notes. Both Acts served as a model for similar measures in the nineteenth century across the then industrializing world.

With the control over banknotes, the national central banks—some of them only set up on this occasion—also took over the benefit of interest-borne seigniorage from the issuance of notes. Central banks do not need to refinance the notes they are loaning to the banks. Monetarily, they create the notes 'out of nothing'. The related interest-borne seigniorage is thus almost identical to a central bank's lending interest—almost, because there are the costs, comparatively low, of producing and managing the notes.

The Bank Charter Acts are most often seen as a victory for the Currency School. In practice it increasingly looked as if the banks were victorious. The gold standard was repeatedly suspended on the request of the Bank of England, under pressure from the banks to print additional money in order to further fuel the railway boom of the time—which promptly resulted in the banking panics and financial crises of 1847 and 1857. Moreover, neither Act took into account the role of credit and deposit creation by the banks, in spite of discussion from Currency and Banking scholars on the subject.[24] Periods of overshooting boom and devastating bust thus continued to occur.

To conclude, the decisive difference between Currency and Banking teachings is not about a gold standard. It is about the question of how to control the overall quantity of money, and the question of who ought to be entitled to the prerogative of issuing and controlling the money, and benefitting

---

[23] Ryan-Collins et al. (2012, pp. 42–45).
[24] O'Brien (2007, p. 102).

from the seigniorage: either the banking industry on the basis of private contracts (Banking position) or a state authority or state-controlled institutional arrangement based upon public law (Currency position).

The historical Currency School created awareness of the necessity of tying modern fiat money, since it can freely be created at any amount, to an anchor of value, or relative scarcity respectively. On the basis of the quantity theory of money this was the right response to the problem of inflation, asset inflation, bubble building and recurrent crises. However, they supported the introduction of the gold standard, which they saw as the natural anchor of scarcity. They did not recognize the problem of stagnant or sub-optimal growth due to the restrictive effects of a fixed amount of gold-related money, or even deflation and destabilizing degrees of unemployment in times of crisis. In retrospect, the gold standard appears as a flawed concept right from the beginning. It was backward-looking and half-hearted, in fact a halfway house between traditional and modern money. It came to a stepwise end with World War I, the Great Depression of the 1930s and the Bretton Woods system from 1944 until 1971 when US President Richard Nixon had to take the unrestrained dollar expansion off the gold standard once and for all.

The gold standard related only to banknotes and failed to include bankmoney on account. The relation between banknotes and the required amount of gold coverage was loosened or even suspended time and again, which also contributed to defeating the intended purpose of the gold standard. Where the standard was maintained, it induced deflation, stagnation and misery for the many poor, rather than achieving growing productivity and transmitting the wealth thereof by way of stable earned incomes and lower prices. In real-world economies, voluntary smooth downward elasticity does not exist; instead we have price and wage 'stickiness' from unemployment and stagnant productivity and purchasing power.

The major reason why the Bank Charter Acts failed to exert a lasting effect was growing adoption of bankmoney on account as the preferred means of payment. The Bank Charter Acts had left the banking sector's credit and deposit creation unregulated, the 'check system', as it was later called. In the course of the nineteenth century—in parallel with and in a sense in the shadow of banknotes—demand deposits came to be used as a regular means of cashless payment in the bank-managed clearing procedures among companies, government bodies, rich families and banks themselves.

The Currency School found its way into various subsequent theories, among them chartalism as well as neoclassical, Keynesian, and monetarist approaches to inflation and exchange-rate theory. Of course, any present-day Currency theory needs updating to contemporary conditions.[25] A number

---

[25] See website for New Currency Theory at http://www.sovereignmoney.eu

of differences would have to be worked out in detail. For example, rather than upholding an obsolete gold standard, a modernized Currency perspective aims for a pure system of sovereign fiat money, closely tied to economic productivity, capacity utilization and potential output.

3.4   Full Chartalism Versus State-Backed Commercial Bankmoney

The terms *chartalism* and *state theory of money* were coined by G.F. Knapp in 1905.[26] Both terms refer to the same subject. Knapp was a representative of the historical and institutional school of national economics from around 1870 to the 1920s. 'Charta' is derived from the Greek and Latin for paper, document or legal code. According to Knapp, 'money is a creature of the legal order'.[27] The teaching dates back via late medieval Thomism to Aristotle: 'Money exists not by nature but by law.'[28]

According to Knapp, the most important legal and political premise for establishing a currency is public law, in combination with the credible power to enforce it. A state's authentication of a token as legal tender in payment of all debts stands a much better chance of serving as the currency of the realm than do private monies not officially recognized. According to Knapp, the strength of a national currency ultimately depends on the political and economic stability and strength of the respective nation-state.[29] Keynes approved of Knapp's chartalism, and Lerner, a fervent promoter of Keynesianism in the 1940–1950s, took a stand for money as a 'creature of the state'.[30] Thereafter, chartalism has been present in much of post-Keynesianism.[31]

In one passage, Keynes's opinion of chartalism sounds rather absolute: 'all civilized money is, beyond the possibility of dispute, chartalist'.[32] This may be true, were it not for a specific ambiguity which actually blurs the difference between chartal money and privately issued money. That ambiguity was already present in Knapp. Most people will associate a 'state theory of money' with a stock of money consisting of state money (sovereign money) issued by

---

[26] Knapp (1905, pp. 27, 33–39, 394).

[27] Knapp (1905, pp. 32–33, 145, Engl. 1924, reprint 1973, pp. 92–95).

[28] Aristotle, Ethics 1133 a 30.

[29] Knapp (1905, pp. 101, 265).

[30] Lerner (1943, 1947).

[31] Lietaer et al. (2012, p. 136) quote as Post-Keynesian 'neo-chartalists' P. Davidson, N. Kaldor, H. Minsky, St. Rousseas, W. Godley, moreover Ch. Goodhart as well as Modern Money Theorists, among them W. Mosler and R. Wray.

[32] Keynes (1930, p. 4).

an authority such as the national central bank. This, however, is not the only meaning in Knapp and not necessarily what economists—neoclassical and Keynesian alike—have come to understand by the currency and money of a nation-state.

In Knapp's view it is not that important whether a nation's money is *issued* by the state. This can be the case, but is not a necessity. In Knapp, the state's basic role is to define the national currency unit. The decisive factor for the establishment of a specific token as a general means of payment then is what a state's treasury accepts in payment of taxes, or the courts in payment of penalty charges:[33]

> All means by which a payment can be made to the state form part of the monetary system. On this basis, it is not the issue, but the acceptation ... which is decisive.[34]—A state's money will not be identified by compulsory acceptance, but by acceptance at public cash desks.[35]

This teaching was carried forward by Abba Lerner:

> The modern state can make anything it chooses generally acceptable as money and thus establish its value quite apart from any connection ... with gold or with backing of any kind. It is true that a simple declaration that such and such is money will not do. ... But if the state is willing to accept the proposed money in payment of taxes and other obligations to itself the trick is done. ... Money is a creature of the state. Its general acceptability, which is its all-important attribute, stands or falls by its acceptability by the state.[36]

Scholars had long been aware of the role of taxes in establishing a currency. One recalls tally sticks as a kind of tax credit; or the adventurous life of John Law, who after the death of Louis XIV was engaged in 1719 to introduce paper money to France in order to reduce the crown's debt. Part of the plan was to have the new paper money generally acknowledged by accepting it at the treasury in payment of taxes, and then to use part of the increased tax revenue to redeem sovereign debt, in a context of economic growth which was expected to result from the increased money supply.

The tax issue is certainly crucial for establishing a means of payment, but it is not the only important element. In addition, Lerner referred to a state's bor-

---

[33] Knapp (1905, pp. 86, 99, 101).
[34] Knapp (1905, p. 86). Engl. Knapp (1973 [1924], p. 95).
[35] Knapp (1905, Intro, p. VI).
[36] Lerner (1947, p. 313).

rowing of money. Either way, the money a government takes in by way of taxes or borrowing is the means used for government expenditure. Furthermore, there were times when sovereign currency existed but taxes did not. Ancient forms of oblation, tribute, toll or similar cannot be identified with taxation in a modern sense, any more than can the decrying of coin (recall for reprocessing) in the high middle ages.[37] Moreover, taxes are absent today in a number of oil-rich states with a currency of their own.

According to the now predominant understanding of chartalism—implicit for the most part—the monetary prerogatives have been reduced to defining the currency, the national unit of account, while the creation of money denominated in that currency and the related monetary benefit (seigniorage) have increasingly been left to the private banking sector. Bankmoney now counts for almost everything, sovereign money for little. No wonder this reduced notion of chartalism creates misunderstanding. It represents an incomplete, only partial notion of chartalism, if it can still be referred to as chartalism at all. The monetary prerogatives as introduced above in Sect. 3.2 are comprehensive and unimpaired sovereign rights, in no way to be shared with banks and other financial institutions. The present-day state theory of money, by contrast, has mutated into a theory of state-backed commercial bankmoney. It thus now represents Banking teaching rather than Currency theory.[38]

The background to and reason for the mutation of comprehensive chartalism into a state-backed regime of private bankmoney was the rise of bankmoney as the preferred general means of cashless payment, in a first surge in the decades leading to Black Friday 1929, followed by a slight decline during the ensuing Great Depression and World War II and post-war periods, and a second surge from around the 1960–1970s which resumed the path toward a money supply exclusively consisting of bankmoney.

Cashless payment goes hand in hand with the development of the related two-tier banking system based on bankmoney and central bank reserves. The situation of having nationalized banknotes since the first half of the nineteenth century, while continuing with commercial bankmoney on account, developed into a new kind of parallel money system in the following decades; that is, sovereign money (coins, banknotes, central bank reserves) and private bankmoney in parallel. Toward and after 1900 this resulted in a split money circuit,

---

[37] Reprocessing meant smelting the coins down and re-minting them into more coins of the old face value, with each coin thus containing less silver. This can be interpreted as a kind of 'taxation' in times when taxes in the modern sense did not yet exist in the occidental world—except the tithe to ecclesial landlords, which normally, however, was delivered in kind rather than paid in coin.

[38] Also cf. Bjerg (2014, p. 251).

consisting of interbank circulation on the basis of reserves (non-cash central bank money) and public circulation on the basis of bankmoney (demand deposits). The remaining notes and coins have become a merely technical sub-amount that is no longer of constitutive relevance to either of the two circuits.

What is more, bankmoney on account (deposits) as well as central bank reserves have been credit-issued money from the outset, just like former banknotes. Today, banknotes are issued in exchange for reserves, or bankmoney on account respectively, and the reserves and the bankmoney are not spent, but loaned into circulation. After all, we should remember that central banks began their existence as privileged commercial banks.

The monetary importance of the take-off of cashless payment practices by transfer of demand deposits was fully recognized only between 1890 and 1920, when the bank-credit theory of money was developed. Important contributions were made by Macleod, Withers, Hawtrey and Hahn, also by Schumpeter and von Mises.[39]

Hahn, a Frankfurt banker, stressed the growing independence of credit expansion from previous savings. He knew from experience that with the rise of bankmoney and the corresponding decrease in the share of central bank notes, the deposit business was no longer a prerequisite for extending credit. On the contrary, the deposit business had become a mere reflex of the crediting business on the asset side.[40] In present-day post-Keynesianism this is wrapped in the formula 'credit creates deposits'. In the same vein, Macleod had concluded that a bank, rather than lending deposited cash, is an institute for creating bankmoney by crediting current accounts.[41]

With the advent of private banknotes and bankmoney on a large scale, banks increasingly became *monetary* institutions, capturing the sovereign monetary prerogatives to a growing extent. That seizure was recaptured by the state through the central bank monopoly on banknotes as introduced in the course of the nineteenth century. However, with the rise of cashless payment by transfer of demand deposits, the banking industry has recaptured the prerogatives of money and seigniorage to a larger extent than ever before.

The chartal concept of national currencies and state control of the money, be this in the form of state-issued money or at least state-controlled issuance of money, has never really been called into question by classical, Marxist or neoclassical economics, or even by historical and institutional economics, and certainly not by Keynesianism.

---

[39] The relevant passages in Schumpeter (1911) are on p. 110, in von Mises (1928, p. 81).
[40] Hahn (1930, pp. 41, 25).
[41] Macleod (1889, p. 594).

Most often, however, scholars of neoclassical standard economics are not sensitive to the subject; Neo-Austrians are, but tend to misinterpret the situation as misguided state and central-bank entanglement rather than perceiving the actual development of state-backed bankmoney as a path possibly leading to their goal of 'free banking' beyond the state and central banks. Supporters of private crypto currencies may presently also contribute to a belief in 'free money creation', but may end up providing proof that 'free money' beyond state power is doomed to fail.

Unfortunately, most of those who consider themselves chartalists have not objected to the development of the regime of state-backed private bankmoney. Rather than perceiving it as a serious challenge to the monetary sovereignty of a state, they tend to affirm and defend the state-backed regime of bankmoney, from Keynes up to present-day post-Keynesianism, circuitism and 'modern money' theorists.

This is partly due to an erroneous but still prevailing belief in central banks exerting control over the banks by way of reserve positions or interest-rate policy, or a partially misconceived understanding of 'endogenous' bankmoney which insinuates that the creation of bankmoney according to demand and the banks' proprietary intentions will result in an optimum money supply, thereby in fact reproducing the Banking School's real bills doctrine.

References

Aglietta, Michel, André Orléan, et al., eds. 1998. *La monnaie souveraine*. Paris: Odile Jacob.

Aliber, Robert Z., and Charles P. Kindleberger. 2015 [1978]. *Manias, Panics, and Crashes. A History of Financial Crises*, 7th edn. New York: Basic Books.

Davies, Glyn . 2013 [1994]. *A History of Money*. Cardiff: University of Wales Press.

Del Mar, Alexander. 1880. *The History of Money in Ancient Countries from the Earliest Times to the Present*. London: George Bell and Sons.

———. 1895. *The History of Monetary Systems*. New York: Cambridge Encyclopedia. Reprinted by A.M. Kelley, New York, 1978.

———. 1969 [1867]. *History of Money and Civilization*. New York: Burt Franklin.

Douglas, Clifford Hugh. 1974a [1920]. *Economic Democracy*. Sudbury, Suffolk: Bloomfield Books. Reprint of the 1920 edition.

———. 1974b [1924]. *Social Credit*. Bloomfield Books. Reprint of the revised version of 1934. First edition in 1924.

Fama, Eugene. 1970. Efficient Capital Markets. A Review of Theory and Empirical Work. *Journal of Finance* 25: 383–417.

Fama, Eugene, Lawrence Fisher, Michael C. Jensen, and Richard Roll. 1969. The Adjustment of Stock Prices to New Information. *International Economic Review* 10(1): 1–21.

Fisher, Irving, and Hans R.L. Cohrssen. 1934. *Stable Money. A History of the Movement*. New York: Adelphi Company.

Friedman, Milton, and Anna J. Schwartz. 1963. *A Monetary History of the United States and the United Kingdom*. Chicago: University of Chicago Press.

Galbraith, John Kenneth. 1995. *Money. Whence It Came, Where It Went*. New York: Houghton Mifflin (1st edn. 1975).

Gesell, Silvio. 1919. *Die natürliche Wirtschaftsordnung durch Freiland und Freigeld*. Arnstadt: Verlag Roman Gesell.

Gocht, Rolf. 1975. *Kritische Betrachtungen zur nationalen und internationalen Geldordnung*. Berlin: Duncker & Humblot.

Goodhart, Charles A.E. 1998. The Two Concepts of Money—Implications for the Analysis of Optimal Currency Areas. *European Journal of Political Economy* 14:407–432.

Graeber, David. 2012. *Debt. The First 5,000 Years*. New York: Melville House Publishing.

Hahn, Albert. 1930[1920]. *Volkswirtschaftliche Theorie des Bankkredits*, 3 Aufl. Tübingen: Mohr Siebeck. zuerst 1920.

Hawtrey, Ralph G. 1919. *Currency and Credit*. London: Longmans, Green & Co.

Hayek, Friedrich A. von. 1976. *Denationalisation of Money*. London: Institute of Economic Affairs.

Henry, John F. 2004. The Social Origins of Money: The Case of Egypt. In *Credit and State Theories of Money*, ed. L.R. Wray, 79–98. Northampton: Edward Elgar.

Hixson, William F. 1993. *Triumph of the Bankers. Money and Banking in the Eighteenth and Nineteenth Centuries*. Westport, CO: Praeger.

Hudson, Michael. 2004. The Archeology of Money. Debt versus Barter—Theories of Money's Origins. In *Credit and State Theories of Money*, ed. L.R. Wray, 99–127. Cheltenham: Edward Elgar.

Huerta de Soto, Jesús. 2009. *Money, Bank Credit, and Economic Cycles*, 2nd edn. Auburn, AL: Ludwig von Mises Institute (1st edn. 2006).

Hutchinson, Frances, and Brian Burkitt. 1997. *The Political Economy of Social Credit and Guild Socialism*. London: Routledge.

Keynes, John Maynard. 1930. *A Treatise on Money*. London: Macmillan. Dt. 1931. *Vom Gelde*. Berlin: Duncker & Humblot.

Kindleberger, Charles P. 1993. *A Financial History of Western Europe*. New York: Oxford University Press.

Kindleberger, Charles P., and J.-P. Laffargue, eds. 1982. *Financial Crises. Theory, History, and Policy*. Cambridge: Cambridge University Press.

Knapp, Georg Friedrich. 1905. *Staatliche Theorie des Geldes*. Leipzig: Duncker & Humblot.—Engl. 1924. *The State Theory of Money*. London: Macmillan & Co. Republ. 1973. New York: Augustus Kelley.

Le Goff, Jacques. 1956. *Marchands et banquiers au Moyen Âge*. Paris: Le Seuil.

———. 1986. *La bourse et la vie*. Paris: Hachette.

———. 2010. *Le Moyen Âge et l'argent*. Paris: Perrin.

Lerner, Abba P. 1943. Functional Finance and the Federal Debt. In *Selected Economic Writings of Abba P. Lerner*, eds. David C. Colander, 297–310. New York: New York University Press 1983. First publ. in *Social Research* 10:38–51. Available at: http://k.web.umkc.edu/kelton/Papers/501/functional% 20finance.pdf

———. 1947. Money as a Creature of the State. *American Economic Review* 37(2):312–317.

Lietaer, Bernard A., Christian Arnsperger, Sally Goerner, and Stefan Brunnhuber. 2012. *Money and Sustainability. The Missing Link*. Axminster, UK: Triarchy Press.

Macleod, Henry D. 1889. *The Theory of Credit*. London: Longmans, Green & Co.

Mairet, Philip. 1934. *The Douglas Manual*. London: Stanley Nott.

Menger, Carl. 1871. *Grundsätze der Volkswirtschaftslehre*. Wien: Verlag Wilhelm Braumüller.

Munson, Gorham. 1945. *Aladdin's Lamp. The Wealth of the American People*. New York: Creative Age Press.

North, Michael. 1994. *Das Geld und seine Geschichte vom Mittelalter bis zur Gegenwart*. München: C.H.Beck.

O'Brien, Denis Patrick. 1994. *Foundations of Monetary Economics, Vol. IV—The Currency School, Vol. V—The Banking School*. London: William Pickering.

———. 2007. *The Development of Monetary Economics*. Cheltenham: Edward Elgar.

Poitras, Geoffrey. 1998. R. Torrens and the Evolution of the Real Bills Doctrine. *Journal of the History of Economic Thought* 20(4): 479–498.

Ricardo, David. 1951 [1824]. Plan for the Establishment of a National Bank. In *The Works and Correspondence of Ricardo, Vol. IV, Pamphlets and Papers 1815–1823*, ed. Sraffa, Piero, and M.H. Dobb, 276–300. Cambridge: Cambridge University Press.

Ridgeway, William. 1892. *The Origin of Metallic Currency and Weight Standards*. Cambridge, UK: University Press.

Rossi, Sergio. 2007. *Money and Payments in Theory and Practice*. London: Routledge.

Ryan-Collins, Josh. 2015. Is Monetary Financing Inflationary? A Case Study of the Canadian Economy, 1935–75. *Working Paper*, No. 848, Levy Economics Institute of Bard College. October 2015.

Ryan-Collins, Josh, Tony Greenham, Richard Werner, and Andrew Jackson. 2012. *Where Does Money Come From? A Guide to the UK Monetary and Banking System*, 2 edn. London: New Economics Foundation.

Schumpeter, Joseph. 1911. *Theorie der wirtschaftlichen Entwicklung*. Berlin: Duncker & Humblot.

Shaw, William Arthur. 1896. *The History of Currency 1252–1896*. New York: Putnams. Reprinted by A.M. Kelley, 1967.

Striner, Richard. 2015. *How America Can Spend Its Way Back to Greatness A Guide to Monetary Reform*. Santa Barbara, CA: Praeger.

Swedberg, Richard. 2003. *Principles of Economic Sociology.* Princeton: Princeton University Press.

Turner, Adair. 2015. *Between Debt and the Devil. Money, Credit and Fixing Global Finance.* Princeton: Princeton University Press.

Vilar, Pierre. 1976. *History of Gold and Money 1450–1920.* London: NLB Publishers.

Viner, Jacob. 1937. *Studies in the Theory of International Trade.* New York: Harpers.

Vogl, Joseph. 2011. *Das Gespenst des Kapitals*, 5 Aufl. Zürich: Diaphanes.

von Mises, Ludwig. 1928. *Geldwertstabilisierung und Konjunkturpolitik.* Jena: G. Fischer.

Whale, P. Barrett. 1944. A Retrospective View of the Bank Charter Act of 1844. *Economica*, New Series, 11(43):109–111.

White, Lawrence H. 1989. *Competition and Currency. Essays on Free Banking and Money.* New York: New York University Press.

Withers, Hartley. 1909. *The Meaning of Money.* London: Smith, Elder & Co.

Wray, L. Randall, ed. 2004. *Credit and State Theories of Money. The Contributions of A. Mitchell-Innes.* Cheltenham: Edward Elgar Publishing.

Zarlenga, Stephen A. 2002. *The Lost Science of Money. The Mythology of Money—The Story of Power.* Valatie, NY: American Monetary Institute.

4

Money and Banking Today

This chapter deals with the functioning of the present money and banking system: the mechanisms of how money is created and enters into circulation, how it circulates, how it may temporarily be deactivated, and how it is finally deleted. There are popular as well as scholarly misconceptions about these questions—for example, the piggy bank model; the loanable funds model or the idea of banks as financial intermediaries; the multiplier model and the reserve position doctrine; and the concept of maturity transformation.

These misleading conceptions carry with them the historical sediment from earlier stages in the development of money and banking. In contrast, the previous chapters have already elucidated to a degree the real nature of the present system, that is, a system determined and dominated by bankmoney created by primary bank credit. This is the basic default to which all other components of the system are subordinate or secondary, and which they accommodate.

4.1 The Two-Tier Split-Circuit Structure

In institutional terms, the present system is described as resting on a two-tier banking structure, the two tiers being the *central bank* with the monopolies on banknotes and reserves (i.e. non-cash money on central bank account), and the *banking sector* with its monopoly on bankmoney. The national *treasuries* have the residual monopoly on coins, but they are not considered another tier of the institutional structure of money creation.

© The Author(s) 2017
J. Huber, *Sovereign Money*, DOI 10.1007/978-3-319-42174-2_4

In addition, there are the *nonbanks*, the money using public. The latter includes *public households* in the sense of government and public entities funded through taxes or tax-like contributions, *private households* and *firms*, including other private or publicly owned organizations of any type.

Another important nonbank actor group is composed of the *non-monetary financial institutions*, such as investment trusts, mutual funds or insurance companies. Banks and nonbank financial institutions must not be confused. A number of financial institutions have for some time now been referred to as shadow banks, for example, conduits (securitization vehicles), hedge funds or private equity investors. Although these often belong to a banking corporation, they are separately operating nonbank entities. Calling non-monetary financial institutions shadow banks is misleading with regard to what a bank actually is: a *monetary* institution that creates and deletes bankmoney, and temporarily de- and reactivates bankmoney. Shadow banks, contrary to what is often suggested, do not create bankmoney, but they accelerate the circulation of bankmoney and banks' refinancing. In addition, money market funds (MMF) have become creators of a new money surrogate, in that MMF shares are now being used as another means of payment.

The conventional two-tier description depicts the central bank as having the lead in the monetary process. In fact the initiative is with the banks. Today, the sequence of money creation starts with the creation of bankmoney, while the central bank refinances in central bank money (cash and reserves) the facts the banks have created beforehand. This is not the entire story yet, but this is how it starts and where the money comes from in the first instance.

The two-tier description leaves implicit the truly relevant core structure of the system, which is the circulation of money in two separate circuits. The two-tier banking structure comprises a double-circuit or split-circuit system. One of the two circuits is public circulation among nonbanks on the basis of bankmoney, operated by the banks. The other circuit is interbank circulation on the basis of central bank reserves among the banks, also including foreign central banks, operated by the central bank of a currency area. Without being aware of the split-circuit structure, the entire money and banking system cannot be properly understood.

The two circuits correspond to each other in a specific way, but they never mingle. Central bank money in the form of reserves never leaves the accounts and accountancy system of central banks, as bankmoney never leaves the accounts and accountancy system of the banking sector. Reserves are for bank use and interbank circulation only and cannot be converted into bankmoney in public circulation; conversely, a bank deposit cannot be turned into a reserve in interbank circulation. Accountancy and balance sheets certainly distinguish between reserve and bankmoney positions. It remains implicit, however, that this is about two different classes of money that cannot be substituted for each other. Even quite a few bankers do not always grasp the difference and mistake either reserves or deposits as loanable funds to the respective other hemisphere of circulation.

In the split-circuit system of reserve banking, the banks run the accounts for nonbank customers, while a central bank runs the operational accounts of banks, including other central banks. In contrast to transactions settled in *cash* among two parties, *cashless* transactions via accounts involve monetary intermediation, more precisely, transfer and documentation by a trusted third party. The third party among nonbanks is a bank; among banks it is the central bank. It should be noted in this respect that monetary intermediation is different from financial intermediation (Sect. 4.3).

Distinct from the past, central banks today deal with banks and foreign central banks only. Nonbanks are no longer admitted to maintain an account with the central bank. The only exception is government accounts with the central bank. In practice, most government transactions are processed via current accounts with commercial banks.[1]

4.2   The Unreal Loanable Funds Model of Bankmoney and Reserves: Credit and Deposit Creation in One Act

Among the usual misconceptions of money and banking is the piggy bank model, often in combination with the even more widespread fallacies of the loanable funds model and the theory of banks as financial intermediaries. The latter misconceptions come in two variants. One is considering customer bank deposits as loanable funds that are used by banks as financial intermediaries to make loans and purchases by using such funds. The other variant is the idea of banks passing on central bank reserves to customers, that is, into current bank accounts. Either variant is excluded for reasons of accountancy alone. In the split-circuit reserve system both classes of non-cash money—bankmoney and reserves—cannot be transformed into each other nor be substituted for each other.

According to the naive piggy bank model, when money is put in a bank, the money is in there, and you can take it out from there. Or, in the meantime, as the loanable funds model and intermediation model suggest, the bank is making use of the money for doing business, but can credibly promise to pay out a customer's money at any time on demand. Many people actu-

---

[1] ECB, *Monthly Bulletins*, Table 2.1.2.

ally believe that 'banks put our money to work', as if the banks were using the bankmoney in the customers' savings accounts or even current accounts, while in fact it is the customers who are using bankmoney. Things like banks borrowing deposits from nonbanks and lending them on to whomsoever, or banks borrowing from other banks and lending to customers, do not apply to banks.[2] They apply to secondary credit, in other words on-lending of already existing bankmoney among nonbanks.

'Banks put our money to work', however, is true when customers deposit cash. The bank will make use of the cash when paying out other customers in cash. For the rest, however, the modern economy is cashless, based on credit-borne money on account rather than cash, and it works in a different way.

Even if people think in terms of credit and cashless payment with money on account, they are often taken in by the second ill-conceived variant of the loanable funds model and bank intermediation. The money on account is assumed to come as a credit from the national central bank to the banks, and the banks pass it on by crediting their customers. This is wrong in two respects. Firstly, central bank money on account (reserves) can only be passed on within the frame of interbank circulation among banks, not to customers in public circulation. Secondly, the initiative for creating money lies with the individual banks. They have the proactive lead, while the central bank reactively accommodates the facts the banks have created in the first instance.[3]

In the present system, extending bank credit and creating a deposit of the same amount (bankmoney) is done in one and the same act. It all starts with a bank crediting the current account of a customer. This involves a simple booking entry. Just a booking entry. This may seem unbelievable, prompting J.K. Galbraith's observation that 'the process by which banks create money is so simple that the mind is repelled. Where something so important is involved, a deeper mystery seems only decent.'[4] According to a bon mot ascribed to McLuhan, money is among the secrets which are kept by disbelief.

---

[2] Also cf. Kumhof and Jacab (2015), Keen (2014), Lavoie (2014), and Werner (2014b).

[3] That banks have the proactive lead in money creation, while central banks afterwards accommodate the resulting bank demand for fractional reserves, was developed by Moore (1988a, pp. 162–63, 1988b) as the horizontal or accomodationist approach of post-Keynesianism, and became later on revised as the structuralist approach (Palley 2013). The position contrasts with the verticalist view which has it that central bank credit comes first and can thus control the banks' credit creation according to a multiplier mechanism. Also cf. Rochon (1999a, pp. 155–201, 1999b), Keen (2011, p. 309), Constâncio (Vice-President of the ECB) (2011), also referring to Alan Holmes in 1969 who then was vice president of the Federal Reserve of New York.

[4] Galbraith (1975, p. 18).

The case most often referred to is a bank making a loan to a customer of that bank. In this case, a bank enters a credit claim of a respective amount on the asset side of its balance sheet, and an according liability to the customer on the other side. That liability includes, on demand of the customer, having to pay out in cash the amount credited, or to transfer the amount to somewhere else. For the customer, the process includes obtaining bankmoney as a liquid asset, and the liability of having to pay back the principal plus interest.

Thus far, the process represents a balance sheet expansion. Claims and liabilities have been created that did not exist before. The credit and deposit creation was taken 'out of nothing'. This may be disconcerting for people who still think that money is 'covered' by something. In fact, however, it is the 'natural' procedure for modern token fiat money that can freely be created, particularly by banks and central banks—even though there are quite a number of preconditions and rules tied to a functional money creation 'out of nothing'. In view of the respective booking practice in the commercial banking sector, critical experts have raised doubts about the correctness of the practice. No nonbank can expand its balance sheet in this way.[5]

However, the picture thus far does not exactly make sense. It only becomes meaningful in that the credit (the bankmoney) *is being used* by the customer, and as soon as the customer is doing so, the bank can only fulfil its obligation to pay if it has available a corresponding amount of cash or reserves, depending on how the customer wants to make use of the credit.

For as long as newly created bankmoney would be circulating only among customers of the crediting bank, the circulation would consist of mere rebookings of the bank's overnight liabilities to the respective customers. No need for cash and reserves would come in. But customers will have to withdraw cash and transfer their bankmoney to customers at other banks. As a result, credit creation does not really occur 'out of nothing', and it is not about an individual balance sheet expansion, because when a bank meets its liability and pays out the credit, its balance sheet is reduced again for that moment as the corresponding amount of cash or reserves together with the related liability are deleted on the balance sheet. What remains, however, is the asset of an additional credit claim of bank A and the additional bankmoney liability of the recipient bank B, wherefrom the bankmoney flows to banks C, D, and so on. The process of balance sheet expansion is actually a cooperative process of mutual acceptance across the entire banking sector.

At this point, at the latest, it begins to emerge that the matter is not that simple. The banks, in sectoral cooperation, indeed create the bankmoney 'out

---

[5] Schemmann (2011b, pp. 16–25).

of nothing'. But they could not do so if the central bank would not be prepared to accommodate the ensuing demand of banks for cash and reserves, by way of central bank credit.

It is true, however, that by proactively extending credits into current accounts, thus creating bankmoney by primary credit, the banking sector determines the entire stock of money in public and interbank circulation. This is so because the creation of bankmoney also initiates the reactive creation of coins and notes as well as of reserves. Reserves in interbank circulation, too, thus represent a sub-amount of bankmoney, even if this is about a different class of money, that is, central bank money (reserves) in contrast to bankmoney, the base of fractional reserves for carrying out interbank payments as they result from transactions in the public circuit.

'Banks create money out of nothing' is too condensed, quasi metaphorical and misleading if taken literally. Banks create bankmoney (demand deposits) on a base of cash and reserves which is only a fraction of the bankmoney; and since central banks always accommodate banks' demand to be refinanced, banks create as much bankmoney as they deem decent.

Some scholars love to discuss whether credit and deposit creation is driven by demand or by supply. Clearly it is both. Banks create bankmoney upon demand from customers, more generally speaking, upon market demand. Banks do so, however, selectively, depending on how they assess the customer's creditworthiness, existing collateral, and more general business expectations. Furthermore, however, banks have business intentions of their own, and they are subject to cyclical business sentiment. Banks also create an additional supply of bankmoney irrespective of customer demand by self-initiated transactions, for example in various segments of investment banking.

There is no doubt that 'credit creates deposits', which applies both to bank credit creating bank deposits (bankmoney) for customers, and to central bank credit creating central bank deposits (reserves) for banks. The reverse, 'customer deposits funding bank credit', does not apply. As monetary intermediaries, banks transfer customer deposits as a payment service, but banks cannot borrow their customers' deposits and lend them out. Once credits have been entered into a current account, and thus have become a demand deposit, or are transferred into a savings account, these deposits are out of reach of any bank. Why? For the simple reason that there are two separate circuits. Bankmoney in the public circuit can never be exchanged for reserves in the interbank circuit, as reserves cannot be exchanged for bankmoney. As a result, neither demand deposits nor savings deposits are loanable funds available to banks, that is, they do not contribute to financing the loans and purchases of banks. Customer deposits are bank liabilities, a debt of a bank to its customers, not liquid assets such as central bank reserves and cash, which is what a bank needs, albeit only to a small fraction, for carrying out all the payments related to any aspect of their business.

The loanable funds model holds true, however, for the on-lending and investing of already existing bankmoney on secondary capital markets. This involves nonbank financial institutions such as investment funds or savings and loan associations, or special bank departments acting as brokers and market makers, as well as private households, firms and also public households as far as the latter use bank accounts rather than a central bank account. All these nonbank actors operate on bankmoney without having the capacity to create or delete bankmoney.

'Customer deposits funding bank credit' was true in pre-modern and early modern economies when depositing solid coins and bullion was the regular method of creating a deposit. Today, with cash in a long-term downward trend and presently accounting for 20–5 % of the money supply, the loanable funds model has become irrelevant with regard to the banking sector. At source the money is now non-cash, credit-borne money on account. Traditional solid cash, by contrast, is no longer constitutive of the monetary system. We may continue to speak of deposits, bearing in mind that in the first instance nothing is 'deposited' here and that at its primary source all money in public circulation is credit-borne bankmoney on current account. In the first instance, a deposit is the result of crediting an account. A bank can pay customers (nonbanks) with deposits which that bank creates itself in the process, and these deposits are subsequently being used by the recipient customers; a bank, however, cannot pay for its proprietary dealings with a customer deposit.

Cash has become a mere technical sub-amount of the stock of money by means of exchanging bankmoney out of and back into a current account. Cash presupposes bankmoney to exist, because cash enters circulation by being withdrawn from a current bank account, thereby booking out the demand deposit (bank liability) as well as the cash in the bank's vault or ATM (bank asset). Thereafter, cash can at any time be exchanged back into bankmoney on account. Banks obtain the cash from the central bank. Banknotes are printed on behalf of the central bank itself, while coins are minted by the treasury, on demand from the central bank, and sold to the central bank in exchange for a credit entry into a government account with the central bank.

On outward appearances, cash still seems to play an important role, in that in many countries the majority of small transactions are cash based, especially in retail, gastronomy and similar businesses where payments are comparatively small. Bigger payments, however, which represent the lion's share of the entire volume of transactions, are normally all carried out with bankmoney.

Monetary statistics can be puzzling in this regard. In the USA, for example, cash represents the larger part, bankmoney less than half of the stock of money M1. Americans, however, together with Britons and Scandinavians, pay more cashless than do actors in other advanced countries. The reason behind the many dollar notes is their use as a parallel currency across the globe, including their use in the submerged economy. In the euro area, to offer another example, the ratio of cash to bankmoney is about 20:80. However, only 10–20 % of the cash is in active domestic use. Another 10–20 % is hoarded for lack of confidence in bankmoney, and 70 % is outside the domestically registered economy, that is, in the underground or abroad. This is to say that in fact about 95 % of the active domestic money supply is bankmoney.[6]

A number of central banks have officially recognized some basic elements of bankmoney creation in the split-circuit reserve system, for example the Bank of England.[7] It is all the more astonishing that for the time being little of this, if any, has found its way into contemporary macroeconomics and textbooks.

4.3 Interplay Between the Circulation of Bankmoney and Reserves: Monetary and Financial Intermediation

Understanding modern money includes a basic understanding of today's cashless payment systems, in particular the interplay between the interbank circuit on reserves and the public circuit on bankmoney. Let us for now concentrate on the case of transferring bankmoney from a customer account A at bank X to a customer B at another bank Y. The bankmoney cannot be directly transferred from the sender's current account A to the recipient's current account B. Instead, the amount involved has to be transferred from the sender's bank X to the recipient's bank Y. The operational accounts of the banks are maintained with the central bank, and thus involve interbank transfers carried out in reserves.

---

[6] Krueger and Seitz (2015, p. 7).

[7] McLeay et al. (2014). There is a workbook published by the Federal Reserve of Chicago from 1961 to 1994. In this document, the functioning of credit creation is explained reasonably well (Nichols and Gonczy 1961–1994). At the same time, however, that document maintains the misleading story of loanable funds.

The procedure then includes the following steps: deletion of the bank-money in the current account of the sender, transfer of the respective amount in reserves from the sender's bank to the recipient's bank, and re-crediting there the amount as bankmoney into the recipient's current account. Put differently, this is about two parallel transfers, one in the public circuit (deleting the deposit here and re-crediting it there), and another transfer in the interbank circuit (transfer of reserves).[8] The technical term for the reserves involved is excess reserves, or say, liquid reserves, or still more to the point, payment reserves.

The indirect way of transferring deposits from one bank's customer to another bank's customer is often referred to as 'intermediation'. More precisely, this is about *monetary* intermediation, referring to the payment services of a bank, the conveyance of bankmoney in cashless payment processes of customers. *Financial* intermediation, by contrast, is about lending/borrowing or investing of already existing bankmoney among nonbanks. Cashless payment in the split-circuit system must not be confused with financial inter-mediation.[9] Being unaware of the difference between monetary and financial intermediation is another important source of misunderstanding.

Economists who mistake customer deposits for loanable funds consider banks as both monetary and financial intermediaries. This is incorrect. Financial intermediaries are nonbanks such as funds. They intermediate in that they take bankmoney from customers so as to lend or invest that money on the secondary capital markets. To the extent to which commercial banks also engage in investment banking, acting as brokers and market makers, they too are involved in financial intermediation. But this is not what makes a bank a bank and gives them a privileged status in competition with *nonbank financial* institutions. Banks are *monetary* institutions, acting as primary credit creators, and as *monetary, not financial* intermediaries. The banking business today is about *creating* the bankmoney on which they operate by using a base of central bank reserves and cash, temporarily *de- and reactivating* bank-money, and ultimately *deleting* bankmoney.

The astounding thing in bank-related payment processes now is that for creating, maintaining and perpetually transferring all the bankmoney, the banks need only a fraction of the entire amounts involved in reserves and cash. In fact it is a small fraction, something between 2.5–10 %, depending on the country and the size of a bank.

---

[8] On the payment finality in bank and interbank payment processes also cf. Rossi (2005, p. 142).
[9] Regarding these and related aspects also see Rossi (2003, pp. 339, 348).

How can it be like that? The practice of clearing may serve as a first proxy to understanding how large amounts of bankmoney are transferred on a small base of payment reserves. In the course of a day, a bank initiates x transfers to many other banks. During the same day, these many other banks initiate y transfers to that one bank. The payments are not immediately carried out, but documented and computationally set against each other (cleared). At the end of the day, the amounts of x outgoing transfers and y incoming transfers will result in the one bank having a positive balance with some part of the other banks (net long position), and a negative balance with the other part of the banks (net short position). On the bottom line, in final settlement of all the transfers and according to experience, the final amount of reserves which is actually due to or due from a bank is rather small. For example, in the Continuous Linked Settlement System which covers half of all international payments, the amount effectively paid in final settlement is 2 % or even much less of the total amount of the transfers carried out.[10]

Nowadays, the banks in advanced countries are connected to computerized payment systems run by the central banks or as a joint venture of the big players in the banking industry of a respective country. In 75 countries these payment systems are now based on real time gross settlement (RTGS).[11] This may mean that outgoing and incoming transfers of a bank are continuously cleared (offset against each other) over the day, so that there is a real time positive or negative bottom line at any time, while the final settlement in reserves is made only once at the end of the day; or else it may mean that actual final settlement is continuously being made, in that all transfers are immediately settled by payment in reserves. In this case there is no interim clearing, but an amount due is immediately debited in full from the central bank account of the sender's bank and credited to the central bank account of the recipient's bank.

If a bank happens to be short of reserves at some point in time, the execution of transfers will not stop. Instead, RTGS payment systems include an automated intraday liquidity overdraft, a marginal lending facility (against securities as collateral provided in advance). A central bank may also offer repo deals once a day (fresh reserves against collateral). In order to economize, different banks may agree to pool their reserves. As another alternative, and if

---

[10] The Continuous Linked Settlement (CLS) Foreign Exchange Payment System, Swiss National Bank, Nov. 2009, 5. Ryan-Collins et al. (2012, p. 166).

[11] Examples for such RTGS systems include Fedwire and CHIPS in the US, CHAPS in Britain, CNAPS in China, Target2 in the euro area, or BoJ-Net in Japan. CHIPS = Clearinghouse Interbank Payments System. CHAPS = Clearinghouse Automated Payment System. CNAPS = China National Advanced Payment System. Target2 = Trans-European Automated Real-Time Gross Settlement Express Transfer System, second generation. BoJ-Net = Bank of Japan Funds Transfer Network System.

applicable, banks may be allowed to violate temporarily the minimum reserve requirement, if the amount required is fulfilled on average for a given period. A bank may thus start the day with zero liquid reserves available, and may in the end come out with a surplus.

If a bank has a need for additional reserves reaching beyond the day, the bank will take up the reserves on the interbank money market. Normally this poses no problem since all outgoing payments in the system are at the same time incoming payments in the system, be it analyzed at the national or the international level. The payment surplus of one part of the banks thus largely equals the deficit of the other part of the banks. If, however, the entire banking sector is expanding the balance sheets, that is issuing additional bankmoney by primary credit and deposit creation, an overall deficit of reserves will occur. In this case the banks will have to take up additional reserves from the central bank in the course of main refinancing operations, for example, weekly central bank lending to banks with a maturity of one week.

Payment through RTGS systems prompts quite a few people, including bank directors and CEOs of large banking corporations, to think there is no such thing as bankmoney creation, thus rejecting the notion of fractional reserve banking. A brief look at how banks manage cash may help us understand better. Each pay-out in cash is immediately carried out in full. In the course of a day or several days, a bank has to make many cash payments totalling a considerable amount. Yet the bank does not need to have that total amount available in cash. A much smaller cash base will do. The reason is that while customers are withdrawing cash from the bank, other customers are depositing cash in the bank. The incoming amounts of cash are perpetually reused to refill the ATMs to serve outgoing cash payments. As a result, the cash base circulating in and out is much smaller than the total of all pay-outs and pay-ins.

When carrying out large transfers of bankmoney on a small base of payment reserves, the situation is basically no different, except for the fact that when customers withdraw cash they are in actual possession of that cash, whereas when they obtain a credit entry in their current account, the bank, not the customer, is in possession of the money (the reserves) while the customers get a mere promise to be paid on demand, but in cash only, because being paid in 'high-powered' reserves is the privilege of interbank circulation among banks. If there is not enough cash and interbank reserve lending available, as tends to be the case in a banking crisis, the customers are left with empty promises. It thus becomes apparent that bankmoney is not the property of the customers who, as most people will assume, are entitled to it. As far as central bank money is involved—coins and notes in vault, and reserves—it is all in the possession of the bank. Bankmoney remains the liability of a bank to a customer.

4.4   The Operating Principles Behind Modern Fractional Reserve Banking

Fractional reserve banking is a subject torn between contradictory views. One controversy is on whether the system is led (a) by the central bank or (b) the banking sector. Another divergence relates to the question of whether (a') the banks' credit and bankmoney creation multiplies an amount of pre-set reserve positions, or whether (b') banks proactively create the monetary facts and are reactively accommodated by the central bank in that it provides the residual cash and reserves as these are needed to a fractional extent. The foregoing explanations clearly support (b) and (b').

There are four operating principles for the smooth functioning of bank-led fractional reserve banking: (1) mutuality of interbank payments, (2) the condition of distributed transactions, (3) the non-segregation of customer money and (4) the principle of cooperative bankmoney creation.

Mutuality of payments refers to the fact already mentioned above that an outflow of reserves in the system is an inflow in the system. The reserve payments by banks A, B, C are reserve receipts by other banks, and the reserve payments by those other banks are receipts by the banks A, B, C. If a bank is fairly established and not too small, outgoing and incoming reserves will largely be netting out within a short time span.

The second condition, distributed transactions, means that payments are spread over actors, time, and volume. The use of bankmoney does not occur all at the same time. At any one time, only some part of the bankmoney is being used. All acts of creation and transfer of bankmoney thus include only a fraction of the entire stock of bankmoney, and the payments happen successively at different times, down to different minutes, seconds and smaller units of time. This ensures to a large extent the necessary netting out of outgoing and incoming payments. Prior to final settlement, customer payments can be carried out to a certain extent by internal rebooking and external interbank clearing. The more this is the case, the lower is the need for final settlement in reserves; and as far as final settlement in reserves takes places, the velocity of reserve circulation in the interbank circuit is much higher than bankmoney circulation in the public circuit. More precisely, the use frequency of the stock of reserves is many times higher than the use frequency of the stock of bankmoney.

The more intrabank rebooking and interbank clearing, and the higher the frequency of multilateral transfers of reserves among the banks, the smaller the reserve base needed. The bigger the banks, the more customers, and the more transactions, the greater the likelihood of very small reserve balances at any point in time. Severe operational account imbalances will not normally occur. There are dates when payment transactions are more frequent, for example, around the end and beginning of the month. This does not make a difference, for this is a general situation, a collective rhythm, affecting almost all customers and banks across the board, thus not distorting the normal distribution of interbank payments.

The examples of intraday, short- and long-term refinancing of banks show how central banks accommodate the banks' demand for a fractional base of reserves. If a central bank refused to do so, the flow of payments would come to a standstill.[12] This in turn, if too extended in time and volumes, could induce a standstill in the financial and real economy. No one will voluntarily want to pull that card.

The situation is another expression of the fact that it is the banks that have the lead in money creation, not the central banks as presumed. Teaching the two-tier story as a two-step sequence that starts with monetary provisions by the central bank, represents another layer of those outdated historical sediments, in this case regarding bank credit allegedly depending on pre-existing exogenous reserve positions. Instead, banks are fractionally refinanced upon or soon after the fact, rather than before. There are certainly reserve constraints, but the banks, supported by the central banks, obtain what they need.

A third principle underlying fractional reserve banking is the non-segregation of customer money. In contrast to companies and nonbank financial intermediaries, banks are not subject to a client money rule that requires to keep own money and customer money in separate accounts.[13] In the case of banks this would mean keeping the money in separate central bank accounts. Instead, all outgoing and incoming payments of a bank are processed via one and the same operational central bank account of that bank, regardless of whether it is about payments to and from customers, or payments to and from the bank itself. The latter, as regards outgoing payments, include the proprietary financial transactions of a bank, or payment of bank purchases, or, as regards incoming payments from external nonbanks, sales proceeds, loan redemptions, interest payments, dividends, fees and commissions. The principle of running a shared account for both a bank and its customers further enhances the condition of distributed transactions. It considerably benefits the proprietary transactions of a bank, because these would otherwise require a higher, thus costlier reserve base.

The fourth condition, finally, can be called the principle of cooperative bankmoney creation.[14] One aspect of this has been known for a long time. For

[12] Also see Keen (2014, p. 280).
[13] Also see Werner (2014b, p. 75).
[14] Seiffert (2012, p. 44).

fractional reserve banking to work, the pace and rate of the banks' primary credit and deposit creation must take place roughly in step.[15] If a single bank dares to create too much bankmoney at once, unilaterally, that bank runs straight into a costly liquidity shortage, because the bank would necessitate correspondingly more reserves for outgoing payments without these being offset by an increased inflow of reserves from other banks.

A related element of cooperative money creation seems to be so 'natural' that it is most often overlooked, namely, mutual acceptance of deposits. Balance sheet expansion does not only consist of an individual act of adding in pairs a credit claim and an overnight deposit liability on a bank's own balance sheet. Rather, it involves the cooperative act of adding the credit claim to the balance sheet, while the overnight deposit is in actual fact added to the recipient bank's balance sheet; and vice versa. The bank that creates a certain primary credit and thus bankmoney is not the same as the bank that will receive that money and thus incurs the costs of deposit management, may have to pay deposit interest, will have to fulfill related minimum reserve requirements, and may have to cash out that deposit. In spite of such liabilities, the banks have little choice. If they want their outgoing bankmoney to be accepted, they must in turn accept incoming bankmoney. Otherwise, the banking sector's credit and deposit creation could not work.[16]

---

[15] For example Keynes (1930, p. 26) and Gocht (1975, p. 29).

[16] Werner (2014a, 2015) distinguishes three banking models: (1) the financial intermediation theory of banking, which is linked to the loanable funds model, (2) the theory of fractional reserve banking or reserve circulation, and (3) bank credit creation out of nothing.

Werner rejects (1) the loanable funds and financial intermediation models as well as (2) the theory of fractional reserve banking, while (3) credit creation out of nothing is considered the only correct one. This is not quite right. Even though the typology overlaps in important aspects with the explanations given in this book, the three models of the typology are partly inaccurate or incomplete, can be misread and thus be misleading.

Rejecting the loanable funds model can basically be endorsed, but a number of related aspects should not be left out. Not only can banks not make use of customer deposits for funding bank loans or making other payments; equally, banks cannot on-lend reserves to customers. (It is different, however, with cash. Banks can on-lend cash they have received from customers, as banks can pass on cash from the central bank to customers). Beyond the banks' primary credit creation there are secondary credit markets where customer deposits (bankmoney) are on-lent to, or invested in, nonbanks. On secondary credit or capital markets, the loanable funds model fully applies. It also applies to the interbank money market on the basis of reserves. Finally, although commercial banks are definitely not financial intermediaries, they are monetary intermediaries, mediating the cashless payments among nonbanks by way of interbank clearing and/or final settlement in reserves.

Model (2) on fractional reserve circulation does not reflect the entire truth about fractional reserve banking. The model combines fractional reserve banking with the loanable funds model and equates that combination with the multiplier model and the reserve position doctrine. Even if inconsistent assumptions in this vein may have been present in authors such as Keynes, Samuelson, Tobin, Minsky and others more, this does not justify reducing fractional reserve circulation to that mishmash and then presenting fractional reserve banking and bank credit creation as 'mutually exclusive views', while in fact both elements—bank credit creation and fractional reserve circulation—go hand in hand.

That which ultimately enables the fractionality of the reserve base is the fact that the velocity of reserve circulation is much higher than that of deposit circulation. The reserves involved in the process flow back and forth between the banks much more frequently ('faster') than the customers make use of the credits (bankmoney) in bank accounts. In a way that is the whole 'secret' behind cashless fractional reserve banking. In final result, and on statistical average, the total reserves the banks need for carrying out all current payments amount to only about 1.25 % of the stock of bankmoney in the UK,[17] about the same in the USA, and 1.5 % or slightly more in the euro area. In the euro area, the 1.5 %, or slightly above, include 0.02–0.04 % payment reserves (excess reserves) and 1.44–1.65 % cash in vault.

In addition there is at present a rate of 1 % obligatory minimum reserves on all deposits subject to that requirement in the eurozone. This includes demand deposits, savings and time deposits. In the USA, the minimum reserve requirement is 10 % of deposits minus cash in vault, in Japan this is 0.81 %, in Switzerland 2 %.[18] In a number of countries there is—for good

---

Fractional reserve theory is certainly misguided, and rightly rejected, when combined with the loanable funds model and identified with the multiplier model and the reserve position doctrine. Such a mish-mash, however, does not represent the entire spectrum of fractional reserve theory, as in fact the existence of fractional reserve circulation in connection with bankmoney circulation cannot be denied.

Similarly, type (3)—credit creation out of nothing—is unspecific and incomplete. It is unspecific in that modern token fiat money, as it has no intrinsic value, is generally taken 'out of thin air', no matter whether it is about treasury coin, central bank notes and reserves or bankmoney. The value of modern money, its purchasing power, is conferred value relating to the prices of things money can buy, and ulti-mately covered by, or anchored in, real economic output. Money creation 'out of nothing' is a catchy metaphor regarding the nature of modern money. But this should not obscure the fact that creating money denominated in a specific currency, and ensuring the validity and value of that money, has many prerequisites that cannot be met 'out of nothing'. One of these, as a technical and political requirement, is the availability of a fractional amount of reserves and cash on which the banks' credit and deposit cre-ation is still dependent. Bankmoney creation and fractional reserve circulation go hand in hand indeed.

Serving as empirical evidence of credit creation out of nothing, Werner refers to the example case of crediting an internal customer account. For doing this, a bank does of course not yet need reserves or cash. If the bank in the example were to be very huge and represent, say, half of all customers within a currency area, then about half of all cashless payments would be carried out by simple internal rebooking of overnight liabilities among the internal customers. To that extent the Werner example would be right.

In the real world, however, such gigabanks do not exist. The vast majority of cashless payments include interbank transfers. And when transferring a customer deposit into an external account with another bank, the sending bank will need to have or obtain reserves, the more so in today's real time gross-settle-ment payment systems (Fedwire, CHIPS, CHAPS, Target2) all of which are reserves based. Extending credit without the credit being used does not make sense, and in this regard credit creation 'out of noth-ing', if taken literally rather than metaphorically, is misleading because using bankmoney in the split-circuit reserve system still involves a fractional base of cash and reserves.

[17] Ryan-Collins et al. (2012, p. 75).

[18] *Sources*: European Central Bank, *Monthly Bulletins*, Table 2.3.2. Schweizerische Nationalbank, *Statistische Monatshefte*, Tab. A1.17–19, B2.2–3 D1. Deutsche Bundesbank, *Monatsberichte*, Tab. IV.1–2.

reasons—no minimum reserve requirement at all, as in Canada, the UK and Denmark.

The present money system is most often considered a two-tier sovereign currency system led by the central bank and central bank money, with an embedded private banking system and bankmoney. In practice, however, on the basis of mutuality of interbank payments, distributed transactions, non-segregation of customer money and cooperative bankmoney creation, the system has effectively mutated into a state-backed regime of private bankmoney, where the banks proactively determine the creation of money, reactively and residually backed by the central banks, and warranted by the governments if need be.

4.5   Minimum Reserve Positions and the Unreal Multiplier Model

Minimum reserve requirements, in contrast to payment reserves exceeding minimum reserves, are set by a central bank for the next month as a percentage of the average stock of deposits from a recent period of months. The procedures differ in detail, but such is the basic approach.

Minimum reserves are often thought to be a liquidity safety net. The reserves of a bank, as mentioned, may temporarily fall below the set requirement, on the understanding that the bank will manage to fulfill the requirement on average over the entire period. Beyond that, minimum reserves are non-available. From the central banks' point of view they are not a fall-back position. Initially, owing to the multiplier model, they were thought to be an instrument of monetary policy aimed at limiting the banks' credit and deposit creation.

The approach was endorsed, among others, by Keynes in the 1920s and ultimately proved not to work in the era of monetarist policies in the 1970–1980s. The reasons for the failure are rooted in the proactive lead of the banks and the factual accommodation constraint of the central banks. Since the mid-1980s central banks could no longer pretend to control the quantity of money. The base-rate policy pursued nowadays claims to influence the rate of consumer inflation, while no longer considering the money supply, and not considering asset inflation at all.[19] Many central banks nevertheless continue

---

[19] Cf. Monetary Puzzlement. Why central banks perform worse than they could, and why sovereign-money reform would help to perform much better, http://www.sovereignmoney.eu/monetary-puzzlement.

to impose minimum reserve requirements. Old habits die hard, including economic paradigms rendered obsolete by ongoing change. In this case, the overridden paradigm is the money multiplier or credit multiplier model as developed by Philipps in 1920.

There is no uniform definition of the multiplier model. In most textbooks, the model starts with the banks having available a given amount of money (M), and a required minimum reserve rate (MinRes) of x % of extended credits (Cred). The available money (M) is normally assumed to come from savings and similar deposits of customers loaned to the bank, or of central bank credit, if scholars express any thought at all as to where the money may have come from.

The banks now use the money for making loans, whereby they have to set aside x % of M as required by the rate of minimum reserves (MinRes). The amount of extendable credit thus is Cred = M (1 − MinRes). The new loans will translate into new savings and deposits which in turn will again be used for making new loans, and iteratively so on. Step by step the credit multiplier will be reduced due to the amount of minimum reserves which have to be set aside, until the multiplier has shrunk to zero, and the total amount of credit equals the money divided by the minimum reserve rate Cred = M/MinRes. For example, if M = 100 million currency units and the MinRes is 10 % (0.1) of extended credit, then Cred = 100 million/0.1 = 1000 million units. If the MinRes is 2 % (0.02), the limit of the total of extendable Cred is 5000 million units. If MinRes = 0, the multiplier is basically limitless.

This is nicely put together, but is not of this world. The model does not describe a process of real world banking. Rather, it is another expression of economic model Platonism. The model, implicitly and wrongly, builds on some sort of pure cash economy. Customer deposits are wrongly considered to be loanable funds and the banks to be financial intermediaries rather than including the split circulation of bankmoney and reserves. There are neither additions to the money supply nor reductions from it. The model presupposes the money base as an exogenously pre-existing and basically invariable quantity rather than building on an endogenous and variable money supply.[20] The model puts the money base first, the banks' credit creation second, rather than the reverse which actually is what applies in the bank-led system of money creation.

In its most widespread forms, the textbook multiplier describes an all too reductionist, actually imaginary model of *circulation* of a given stock of money, but is in no way about credit and deposit *creation*. A frequently cir-

[20] For a criticism of the multiplier model also see Goodhart (1984), Keen (2011, pp. 306–312), Ryan-Collins et al. (2012, pp. 16–25), Jackson and Dyson (2012, pp. 75–80).

culating stock of money, of course, may have the same effect as an increase in the stock of money, but is not the same thing.

It is possible to build the multiplier mechanism on a basically correct representation of the split circulation of reserves and bankmoney. In this case, however, the multiplier model is still linked to the equally fallacious reserve position doctrine.[21] The doctrine assumes the existence of a pre-set amount of reserves, no matter whether these function as minimum or excess reserves. The pre-set reserve base is supposed to determine the maximum multiple of bankmoney that the banks are able to create. In fact, however, the reserve base is not pre-set, but promptly created upon the banks' primary credit and deposit creation. The banks have the proactive lead and central banks feel compelled to accommodate. In consequence, for exerting control over banks' primary credit and deposit creation, minimum reserves are utterly pointless.

The stock of existing bankmoney can of course be numbered as a multiple of the reserves. Roughly speaking, the multiplier is about 40 times the entire cash and reserve base (also including the minimum reserve requirement), more specifically, about 60–70 times the cash in vault, while amounting to over 4000 times available excess reserves (reserves for cashless payments). This, however, is just an arithmetic exercise, certainly illustrative, but not an algorithm that represents a real process. The real process is the reverse, in other words the proactive creation of bankmoney and its fractional refinancing upon or after the fact. Looked at without bias, minimum reserves are of no policy use at all. Their dual use as a marginal liquidity reserve in the eurozone could easily be replaced with other ways of providing intraday liquidity. The only point the practice has is in the amount of interest-borne seigniorage, that is that part of central bank profits that accrues from lending reserves and cash to banks.

4.6   Savings as Deactivated Deposits

In the existing split-circuit reserve system a deposit cannot be transformed into a reserve, as a reserve in a bank's central bank account cannot end up in a customer's bank account. This means that banks cannot make use of customer deposits. Banks need cash and reserves for carrying out payments. As a result, when customers put some of their bankmoney on current account into a savings or time account, this does not provide liquid assets for the bank, for

---

[21] For a critical discussion of the reserve position doctrine, also including a comparison with the short-term interest doctrine, see Bindseil (2004) and Häring (2013).

it is a mere swap of overnight liabilities into liabilities at notice or with specified maturity. The swap does not involve reserves or cash, simply a reposting record in the books.

If, in contrast, customers from other banks transfer some of their bankmoney to another bank, this may, on balance of all occurring payments in and out, result in a net inflow of reserves, or not; and if it does, that inflow of reserves will represent just a fraction of the deposits taken in, on all of which the bank will be obliged to pay deposit interest and the minimum reserve requirement if applicable.

In the banking and debt crisis beginning in 2007/2008 it must have dawned on many a banker that, seen from a technical point of view, they do not necessarily need the cost factor of savings or time deposits on their balance sheet. (Banks have recently paid higher deposit interest on small deposits, and less interest on large deposits.) However, banks need customers, and customers of course come with deposits. The customers want their banks to provide the service of managing current accounts, payments and money exchange. For some banks this is a loss-making service which they subsidize internally. Other banks charge cost-covering fees and pay zero deposit interest on current accounts. The reason why banks truly need their customers, and why they compete for the favour of customers, is related to the banks' lending, transaction, asset management and investment lines of business.

What is more, savings and time deposits are deactivated bankmoney, in contrast to overnight deposits which can be transferred or withdrawn any time, whereupon they draw on the bank's payment reserves and cash. As long as customer funds are placed in savings and time accounts, that bankmoney cannot be transferred somewhere else. Taking in savings and time deposits supports customer loyalty and prevents bankmoney from draining off in larger volumes. The latter situation would cause a liquidity problem for a bank, because outgoing reserves would no longer be sufficiently balanced by incoming ones. Savings and time deposits and similar positions cost a bank deposit interest. At the same time they enable the bank to extend additional primary credit at much higher lending rates, or for other lucrative business, while not incurring an additional liquidity risk.

For the customers, inactive deposit savings represent a particular type of short-term capital. Old industrial economies are in an advanced stage of their transsecular transition from traditional to modern society. Average real growth rates are declining over time. Consumer mass markets are more or less saturated, resulting in increased shares of income being devoted to lifestyle distinction and upmarket goods, and commodities that increasingly represent financial assets such as property, jewellery or artworks. Economic maturation also converges with a higher mean age in the population. All of this contributes to increases of deposit savings as well as financial investment, in total often higher than additional spending on real investment and consumption.

Such increases in deposit savings may basically be seen as positive. And yet the respective amounts of bankmoney are deactivated, in other words taken out circulation, representing a loss of active money in the real economy as discussed by circuitist economists. This overlaps to a degree with the Keynesian paradox of thrift, in that such inactive savings neither contribute to real economic demand nor to capital supply on secondary financial markets.

In consequence, deposit savings will induce additional, GDP-disproportionate credit and debt; otherwise, there would be a lack of capital expenditure and consumer demand. Not that there is a problem of credit and deposit creation to compensate for the deactivated money. That is the easy part; banks stand ready, most of the time at least. Hitherto, inactive deposits were compensated for to a certain extent by public deficit spending. The problem thus is additional debt burdens, in particular on governments with subpar tax revenues as well as on firms and households with subpar earnings.

Apparently, only a few economists across all schools of thought have recognized that savings and time deposits represent inactive bankmoney to which the loanable funds model does not apply, as it does not apply to demand deposits either. Even fewer economists have drawn conclusions from the finding. Deposit savings represent non-circulating bankmoney, thus a loss in circulation or, put differently, a reduced potential of aggregate demand.[22] This does not necessarily reduce the active money supply, or active purchasing power respectively, because banks can fill any supposed gap by extending additional credit. Given, however, that this then represents a compensatory debt constraint, deposit savings represent a loss of active money nonetheless.

4.7   The Golden Bank Rule and the Question of Maturity Transformation

The above findings render obsolete another model of banking economics, that is, maturity transformation. According to this concept, banks are thought to borrow from customers in the short term, and lend or invest that money in the long term. This, however, does not apply in the split-circuit reserve sys-

[22] Cf. Graziani (1990, p. 26). Quantum macroeconomics, by contrast, continues to treat M2/M3-deposits as loanable funds, and banks as both monetary *and* financial intermediaries. Cf. Cencini and Rossi (2015, pp. 53, 143, 165–169, 226).

tem. The truly relevant aspect of the maturity question is about the *timelines* of claims and liabilities as enshrined in the golden bank rule. The rule demands timelines as well as the liquidability of various classes of assets and liabilities to be congruent with each other. Maturity mismatches, that is, incongruent maturities or incongruent liquidability of claims and liabilities run contrary to the golden bank rule.

Following the rule helps avoid liquidity shortages, maybe even insolvency, which might result from having to fulfill a large number of short-term liabilities at once, while long-term claims cannot be liquidated at the same time, or would have to be liquidated at a loss. The risk must nonetheless be taken to a degree, because, corresponding to liquidity preference, most actors prefer to lend or invest short term or in easily liquidated positions rather than making long-term or hard-to-liquidate commitments.

The concept of maturity 'transformation' by borrowing short term and lending long term is in fact obsolete, as is the loanable funds model of banking. Banks do not borrow deposits from customers, they borrow reserves from other banks and the central bank, and part of the reserves in cash. Own excess reserves may be lent to other banks, but such deals are short term for the most part anyway. The reserves, however, cannot be lent to nonbank customers; and the cash which is handled by the banks on behalf of the customers is not really relevant with regard to the maturities in a bank's balance sheet.

If a recommendation can be drawn from this, it is the thorough reconsideration of the golden bank rule, certainly one of the oldest and most proven financial concepts. Simply, it does not currently refer to the banks' lending to customers through borrowing from customers. Instead, it involves the overall maturity structure of assets and liabilities. The volumes of overnight-, short-, mid- and long-term positions, or of hard-to-liquidate positions versus easily liquidated positions, on both sides of the balance sheet ought to be as congruent as possible. The more maturity mismatches there are, the higher the overall risk involved.

4.8   Restrictions to Credit and Deposit Creation

Hypothetically, the capacity of banks to create bankmoney is limitless. In practice, there are near-term restrictions, some inherent in the system of fractional reserve banking, some dependent on the market, some of a regulatory nature.[23]

---

[23] After Seiffert (2012, pp. 44, 78–97).

Since most bankmoney is created on market demand, the banking business depends on nonbanks being prepared to go into debt, that is households, firms and public bodies taking up loans; companies and government bodies emitting new bonds; listed companies issuing new shares; or nonbank financial institutions and other financial investors asking for leverage, thus raising the stakes in an attempt to profit still further in a current financial bonanza. If, by contrast, financial and business cycles are in a downswing or even a depressed state, perspectives for the banking business will also be down.

Another restriction is inherent in the principle of cooperative bankmoney creation, including the mutual acceptance of each other's deposits when these are transferred. A single bank cannot expand its balance sheet too much at once without incurring an expensive lack of liquidity, thus losing ground in cost competition. For the system to work smoothly, all banks need to proceed roughly in step so that a near balance of outgoing and incoming payments will ensue. The momentum and rhythm of the cooperative creation of additional bankmoney is in turn dependent on the respective outlook in the course of business and financial cycles.

Independently, the ability of a single bank to create bankmoney also depends on its size. Large banks have a greater potential for creating primary credit than do small banks. Large, in this respect, may mean being a universal bank rather than specializing in some segment of investment banking, mortgage banking, retail commercial banking, money exchange and the like. Being large also involves having many customers in each segment, or in many branches, scattered across the country, or online customers, even internationally in many currency areas across the globe. In small banks, there can be relatively large payment imbalances; not so in large banks. Large banks, furthermore, more easily form a consortium for doing very large business, for example in the initial public offering of sovereign and corporate bonds, or corporate equity. Smaller banks are thus placed at a major competitive disadvantage. They can compensate for this to a degree by joining a banking union with central handling of payments.

Among the regulatory restrictions relevant to balance sheet expansion are legal provisions concerning the liquidity and solvency of banks, most famously the Basel rules in subsequent generations I and II, with III being currently implemented and IV already in the making. These rules are set by an international committee of central banks at the Bank for International Settlements in Basel. Some of this now includes rules on capital adequacy in the form of an assets-to-equity ratio, or a loans-to-equity ratio. The rules tend to be complicated and partially questionable in detail. For example, sovereign bonds with a high rating at the time of issuance can still be carried at a risk coefficient of zero, regardless of numerous sovereign debt troubles and even sovereign defaults of initially highly rated bonds in recent decades.

As regards liquidity prescriptions, these often include some rule that liquid and near-liquid assets must be equal to or bigger than overnight liabilities. This is difficult by its very nature. Securities may be easily liquidated even in a crisis, but the securities' value may have heavily shrunk at that point in time. This may result in a balance sheet crisis rather than the rule reliably functioning as a liquidity buffer.

Seen from a bank's point of view, all such restrictions in fact curb their potential for credit and deposit creation. However, the hindrance is short- rather than long-term. By cooperative credit and deposit creation, the banking industry, supported by quasi-automated fractional refinancing of the central banks, creates for itself what it needs in order to extend the limits and fulfill the requirements, by building up equity, providing sufficient liquidity, acquiring enough collateral and so forth. The 'masters of the universe' will not create what it needs in six days and rest on the seventh. But they might be able to do it in seven months or a couple of years.

As a result, the ability of the banking sector to extend credit and create bankmoney seems to be limitless in the long term. Not quite. As will be seen in chapter 5 on the dysfunctions of the bankmoney regime, real economic output will always be a gravitational limit that cannot arbitrarily be outsmarted. Banks and financial markets can overshoot that mark and in fact they recurrently do. It regularly proves to be unsustainable, resulting in violent self-corrections of the markets, and in general crises causing damage to the entire economy and population.

4.9 Creation of Bankmoney: The Entire Picture

So far, we have discussed how a bank creates bankmoney by making loans and granting overdrafts. It has not yet been discussed that banks also create bankmoney when they purchase financial and real assets for their own account, such as securities, equity and real estate, also including office equipment, IT infrastructure, software, company cars, licences and so on, all items which are entered into the books as tangible or intangible assets.[24] Securities may gain or lose value, and the equipment and other durables are subject to scheduled write-down.

---

[24] Also cf. Ryan-Collins et al. (2012, p. 62).

In terms of accountancy, the transactions result in an expansion of balance sheets, analogous with making a loan or overdraft. The securities and everything else are added to the asset side of a purchase-making bank. If the payment goes to an external nonbank customer, the asset adds to the balance sheet here and to the overnight liabilities there, whereby the sending bank's reserve account is debited and the recipient bank's reserve account is credited, again analogous to a loan being paid out to an external nonbank.

The latter process is indeed always the same, no matter whether it is about making loans, purchasing assets or paying for non-asset items. Equally and in terms of the final result, it does not make a difference whether the payment goes into an internal or external current account, because the bankmoney in the internal account will sooner rather than later be transferred to external accounts anyway.

This is just the same when banks settle dealings between each other on their own account, or when it is about a transfer of reserves to and from government central bank accounts. This does not have a significant impact on the necessitated reserve base, because banks as well as public households keep the reserves busy. They are barely received before they are expended again. In banks, this is because they minimize the reserve base they need and lend excess reserves they do not need to other banks; in government accounts, this is because public bodies live hand to mouth. In consequence, the reserves of banks, no matter to whom they are transferred, will swiftly come back to the transferring banks in either case, thus ensuring that only a fractional reserve base will be needed.

Banks also create bankmoney when paying for non-asset bank expenses such as purchases of expendable items from firms, paying for external services and paying for the salaries, employee benefits, bonuses, dividends, donations, or anything else. These cases have a different meaning in terms of accountancy, but they involve the creation of bankmoney nonetheless, in that respective amounts are entered into an internal current account, or transferred into an external current account at another bank. Both cases represent costs *à fonds perdu*. These are not offset by an asset entry, and result in the entry of a loss position in the earnings and loss account. Its bottom line adds to or reduces a company's capital account. As a result, this category of expenses actually bites into a bank's equity. If such costs are not to result in negative equity, they have to be offset by earning account entries in the form of interest payments received, fees and commissions, as well as by realized capital gains (higher value of securities, real estate, etc.).

As a general rule it can be said that bankmoney is created whenever a bank credits a customer's internal current account, or makes a cashless payment to an external nonbank. By contrast, when a bank makes a cashless payment to another bank or a central bank government account, this involves the same kind of interbank transfer, but does not create bankmoney.

4.10 Deletion of Bankmoney

It has been described above how moving bankmoney from a current account into some sort of savings account takes bankmoney out of circulation—temporarily, or maybe for a long time—without deleting the deactivated bankmoney. But when is bankmoney deleted?

To begin with, bankmoney is temporarily deleted when it is withdrawn in cash. This results in a balance sheet contraction, in that cash in vault (liquid asset) and bankmoney in a current account (overnight liability) is booked out in pairs. It will not last for long, however, since other customers will deposit cash to the bank. In fact, that kind of exchange is only transitory, neither initially creating nor ultimately extinguishing bankmoney.

Transactions through which bankmoney is deleted are the reverse of deposit creating transactions. If a loan or overdraft granted to a nonbank customer is paid back to a bank, the corresponding amount of bankmoney ceases to exist, because the nonbanks will pay the bank in bankmoney. If the redemption comes from an internal customer, this will result in the pairwise extinction of the credit claim and the overnight liability (i.e. the bankmoney) on the bank's balance sheet. If the redemption comes from an external customer, the transaction results in a similar pairwise deletion, in that the overnight liability is deleted at the remitting bank while the credit claim is deleted at the recipient bank. At the same time, a corresponding amount of reserves is debited to the remitting bank and credited to the recipient bank.

In the same way, bankmoney is deleted when a bank is selling financial or real assets (bonds, shares, houses) to nonbanks, because this means again that the nonbanks will pay in bankmoney. This deletes the bankmoney in the payer's bank, while in the recipient bank this results in an amount of incoming reserves and a profit entry in the profit and loss statement which adds to the bank's equity account.

Finally, bankmoney is deleted when internal or external customers pay for services a bank has provided for them. In particular this involves interest payments to a bank, and fees, commissions, dividends and similar disbursements received. Transactions of this kind result in the deletion of bankmoney in an internal or external customer account, and a corresponding earnings entry into the recipient earnings and loss account. The final profit or loss of a bank, a surplus or deficit in its equity account, depends on the balance of its earnings and expenditures, also including profits or losses from asset sales.

Regarding monetary technique, a bank could be run in negative equity. Hypothetically, a bank could even accumulate higher levels of negative equity over many years, and yet continue its banking operations as long as the bank remained liquid, that is, as long as it disposed of enough reserves and cash. In practice, however, a bank will not get away with this. The central bank and bodies of banking supervision will have to intervene on the basis of legal provisions. Rumours will spread, the bank's balance sheet trouble will make headlines, other banks will no longer want to engage in business with the affected bank, and customers will start to switch to other banks, which is like a run on that bank.

In conclusion, it can be said that bankmoney is deleted whenever a nonbank makes a cashless payment to a bank. To connect the creation and deletion of bankmoney together in a rule: all cashless payments from banks to nonbanks create and insert bankmoney into the public circuit, while cashless payments from nonbanks to banks delete bankmoney from the public circuit.

With regard to reserves, the situation is analogous. Cashless payments from a central bank to banks insert reserves into interbank circulation, while cashless payments from banks to the central bank delete reserves from the interbank circuit. Payment of reserves between banks and government accounts (with the central bank) neither deletes nor creates reserves, but keeps reserves circulating in the interbank circuit. Solid cash, by the way, is issued when it is loaned by the central bank to a bank, and retired when a bank pays back some of its liabilities to the central bank in cash.

As a matter of fact, not all the cash flows back to its source, not even in a currency reform. Some small cash hoards happen to be forgotten, and some cash may be retained as a memento. Bankmoney too can be withheld, for less sentimental reasons, for example, by way of credit claims that had to be value-adjusted, that is, written off. The corresponding amount of bankmoney continues to exist, in circulation or in some inactive deposit, representing a sort of 'eternal' Flying Dutchman deposit. Under normal circumstances, 1–2 % of outstanding loans will have to be written off. The resulting 'eternal' deposits would accumulate over time, were it not for various customer payments to banks, such as interest and fees, absorbing and thus deleting that money. Another occasion on which Flying Dutchman deposits may find deliverance from their existence is the breakdown of a bank or many banks—which, however, under the prevailing conditions of state-backed bankmoney, is now prevented for the most part by central bank aid, government bail-out and compulsory customer bail-in.

The predominant reality of an overshooting money supply should not mean forgetting about the opposite extreme. As can be seen in a recession, an ensuing credit shortage involves money shortage, forcing many actors to liquidate savings and other assets. A persistent recession or even a depression with debt deflation will reduce the money supply to a considerable extent. The consideration makes clear that bankmoney created by primary bank credit involves a constraint of indebtedness. If, for example, in a post-growth scenario, all economic actors reduced their borrowing step by step, the available quantity of money would dwindle, possibly falling below thresholds critical for reproducing GDP.

4.11 Quasi-Seigniorage of Bankmoney Creation

In view of the issues discussed, some commentators conclude that the profits or losses of banks are 'nothing but accountancy', as if this were to say 'no real thing'. Well, accountancy is real, a documentation of actual assets and liabilities, revenues and expenses. From its archaic beginnings, money has always been about accountancy. Money is indeed of an informational nature. The surpluses or deficits of companies, and public and private households result from 'mere' accountancy in much the same way—with the difference that banks can create bankmoney whereas others cannot.

By creating money, banks have a privilege over all other participants in the economy. According to an economic saying 'there ain't no such thing as a free lunch'. And yet there is one—the special profit, called seigniorage, which accrues from creating money. There are two types of seigniorage: genuine and interest-borne seigniorage.

The first goes back, as does the term seigniorage itself, to the feudal prerogative of coinage which the seigniories had reserved for themselves. Genuine seigniorage is the difference between the costs of producing a means of payment (with coins the costs of mining, melting, minting) and the purchasing power of that money. In former times, the costs of producing coins are said to have been some 40 % of the coins' face value. Genuine seigniorage from coining was thus about 60 %. Today it can be over 80 % in larger coins, while smaller ones such as one and two cent coins hardly cover the costs, which is why treasurers would like to phase them out.

The second type, interest-borne seigniorage, exists in the form of the central banks' monopoly on banknotes and reserves as issued by interest-bearing central bank credit. It is remarkable that the term is not used when commercial banks earn lending interest. In fact, the creation of bankmoney is proactive and primary. The extra profit accruing from extending primary credit thus comes down to the unique private privilege of interest-borne seigniorage. It may nevertheless be preferable, so as not to blur the difference between sovereign money and bankmoney, to retain the term seigniorage for money creation by treasuries and central banks. The banking privilege may thus be referred to as a seigniorage-like extra profit, or quasi-seigniorage.

Traditional seigniories spent new money into circulation, while modern treasurers sell the coins to the central bank. Either way, the money is free of debt in the sense that there is no interest-bearing credit involved. Banks, by contrast, create their money by making credit entries into a current account. Upon redemption of a loan, or sale of some security, the bankmoney involved is deleted. Where then does this result in seigniorage?

The banks' interest-borne quasi-seigniorage actually derives from the refinancing costs that are avoided. All actors in the economy must cover their costs in full, no matter whether they obtain the money needed for doing so as earned income, by borrowing, as a subsidy, welfare transfer or gift. A nonbank building society, for example, may take up bankmoney from their members at 4 % savings interest, and lend it on to home-building members at 7 %. The profit margin on the entire principal then is 3 %.

Banks, by contrast, operate on a fractional base of cash and reserves. Let us assume that base to amount to about 3 % of the principal, at an interest rate which shall be assumed here to be the same as the rate on savings deposits. In this case, the profit margin is 6.88 %, compared to the 3 % of the nonbank building society. This results from a lending rate of 7 % minus 0.12 % refinancing costs incurred through a 4 % borrowing rate on the 3 % of cash and reserves that have to be refinanced, while 97 % of the principal is free of funding costs. As a result, the special banking profit, the quasi-seigniorage from the creation of bankmoney is 3.88 % on top of the regular 3 % interest margin.

When a bank purchases assets from nonbanks (securities, real estate, etc.) the situation is analogous. The bank pays 100 % of the price in bankmoney and has to refinance just 3 % of it. While loans on the balance sheet exist with the risk of becoming non-performing, securities exist with the risk of losing value, but also with the chance of gaining value.

As regards the quasi-seigniorage, bankers will point to the deposit interest which is paid on all deactivated savings and time deposits, maybe also on overnight deposits. Directly attributing these costs to the asset business of a bank, however, is not appropriate. Even though deposit interest has to be paid, deposits are not loanable funds. They cannot be used for funding banking business. From time to time, single banks try to achieve a unilateral surplus of incoming reserves by luring customers away from other banks that will then have an according reserve deficit. Overall this is a zero-sum game. Having to accept deposits is an operating constraint of bankmoney creation and is also a means for maintaining customer loyalty so as to prevent customers and deposits from draining away unilaterally, which would cause a liquidity shortage.

Furthermore, one might argue that banking competition exerts pressure on the banks to pass on the benefit of low refinancing costs to their customers, through fees being less expensive than they otherwise might be. Friedman held that position. It was contested by other scholars on the grounds of imperfect competition in the banking sector.[25] Even extensive empirical studies are unlikely to find out the truth. Given the oligopolistic structure of the global banking industry, the pressure on the banks to be nice to their customers will remain within bounds. Large banking corporations are in a market position similar to pivotal corporate players in industrial supply chains. They have the clout to set prices or financing conditions rather one-sidedly. Smaller banks are in a less advantageous position. This becomes apparent, for example, when comparing the above-average salaries in large banking corporations and relatively modest salaries in small local retail banks.

In the lending business, banks have so far primarily competed with each other; in the securities business banks compete with nonbanks, whereby banks refinance fractionally, while nonbanks have to finance their business in full. In this case, nonbanks are clearly on the short end. This might be identified as a major reason for the banking industry's tendency in recent decades to set little store by their customer lending business, while having become ever more excited about turning big wheels in global investment banking, including its casino section.

Quantifying the seigniorage-like banking extra profits is difficult. The profit disclosed in a bank's balance sheet does not tell the entire story. For example, there is a trade-off between profits and salaries which can be shaped to a degree even within the framework of collective wage bargaining. A bank's earnings may add to profits or, alternatively, increase the income of all or special groups of employees. Above-average salaries and additional benefits for bank employees are carried as payroll costs. Shares or options allotted to the top management and traders are also carried as liabilities or as effective costs. This reduces the profit disclosed on the balance sheet.

---

[25] Friedman (1971, p. 846).

Investment bankers are highest paid, followed by asset and wealth managers. Colleagues in 'boring banking' branches have to content themselves with between a third and a quarter of those very high incomes. In the 1970s, investment bankers and other professionals such as lawyers, architects and engineers were on roughly equal footing. Today these groups still belong to the 10 % top earners, but the average London investment banker now earns about twice as much as their former peers.[26] Average Wall Street pay is five to six times as much as private-sector pay in general.[27] In the entire US financial sector, personal income around 1980 was at par with the real economy, in 2010 it was 40 % higher, which is even higher than in the decades before Black Friday 1929.[28] In Germany, the average income in banking and finance is 15 % higher than the average income in all sectors of the economy, compared, for example, to 10 % above average in pharmaceuticals, 7 % in specialty chemicals, cars and aircraft, through to −7 % in building, transport and tourism.[29]

As many commentators have observed, bankers in large corporations and the managers of large investment funds indulge in lavish salaries and bonuses even if the financial performance of their business turns out to have been poor or even loss-making. Trying to justify such maldevelopments on the grounds of achievement and merit is outright cynicism. Little of this has to do with market performance, much more with financial sinecure, as if the milieu of banking and finance in fact were a privileged neo-feudal aristocracy.

4.12 Growing Competition to Primary Bank Credit from Secondary Credit Offered by Financial Intermediaries

In previous sections the difference between banks and nonbank financial intermediaries has been touched upon. Banks are monetary institutions that create and delete bankmoney (deposits), whereby they do *not* on-lend or invest existing deposits. In contrast, financial intermediaries such as mutual funds, pension and state funds, building societies or insurance companies are non-monetary institutions. They operate on bankmoney, like the public in general. Nonbank financial intermediaries are subject to oversight by financial-market authorities, but they cannot create bankmoney because they

---

[26] Theurer (2014).
[27] Office of the New York State Comptroller, *The Economist*, March 15, 2014, 81.
[28] Philippon and Reshef (2009).
[29] http://www.gehaltsreporter.de/gehälter nach branchen, January 18, 2015.

have no banking license, do not actively participate in the interbank payment system and cannot refinance themselves by way of central bank credit. They operate as financial intermediaries and investors of already existing bankmoney. The loans or investments they make are secondary credit, in contrast to primary bank credit which creates bankmoney.

Just as the difference between monetary and financial intermediation must not be blurred, so the difference between banks as monetary institutions and nonbank financial institutions must not be confused either. When loans or bonds are redeemed to a nonbank creditor, the bankmoney involved is not deleted, but continues to circulate. At the same time, the banks continue to create additional bankmoney if this is in their individual business interest. Over time this results in two by-products that can prove problematic for banks. One is the problem of a savings glut, in other words an excess of monetary assets over suitable investment opportunities. The excess of capital not only stems from the newly industrialized economies, but, more importantly, from increased employment in old industrial countries and related savings for retirement, as well as from a disproportionately increased glut of financial capital and revenue in the hands of the rich.

The other by-product, related to this, is increased competition for the banks from nonbank financial intermediaries, in that banks' primary credit and deposit creation also results in an increased supply of secondary credit by way of on-lending and investing bankmoney in the possession of nonbanks. Following its emergence in the decades after the Second World War, financial intermediation, in parallel to banking, rose to 3.5 times what it had been around 1980.[30]

While the loanable funds model does not apply to primary bank credit, it certainly applies to secondary credit, including the neoclassical view that interest rates are determined by the demand for and supply of loanable funds. The bankmoney in possession of, or managed by, nonbank financial institutions is part of the entire money supply, and is offered and sought after on the capital markets where it is competing with the money offered by the banks themselves. To the banks, growing competition between nonbank-offered bankmoney and bank-offered bankmoney represents business volume lost or foregone, which means less market share than the banks would otherwise have. If the secondary supply of bankmoney represents a critical mass and exceeds demand, this will also exert some pressure on banks' primary lending rates, and interest rates will thus have to readjust downwards in both segments of the capital market.

The problem of a savings glut, or capital glut respectively, has become apparent in the aftermath of the Subprime Crisis and the European sovereign

---

[30] Turner (2012, p. 56).

debt and banking crisis. With largely undeflated financial assets and debt, in combination with reduced growth rates, the available excess capital does not find enough profitable investment opportunities. As a result, interest rates decreased depressively close to and even below zero.[31]

This is a homemade banking problem rather than the fault of central banks, even if the latter have perpetuated, and in a way aggravated, the problem by expansionary quantitative easing policies.[32] The savings or capital glut is bigger than what can be absorbed in today's circumstances of deferred debt deflation and sluggish growth.

Banks have to pay interest on deposits, in particular savings and time deposits, not by force of law or centuries-old habit, but in order to prevent these deposits from migrating in critical numbers elsewhere. Deposit interest represents a loss in the profit and loss account. In a downswing or other time of crisis, the accumulated stock of deposits then turns out to be a burden that narrows the interest margin of the banking sector. This is the case even if deposit interest is about zero, because, due to the crisis-typical lack of demand for money, lending interest tends to be still lower, resulting in a declining real interest rate. In the short term this does not by itself involve a problem for the economy, but can be a problem in many a bank balance sheet.

In order to compensate for growing competition by financial intermediaries and increased deposit interest, banks have been looking for additional business opportunities, in particular by ever more expansion of government and consumer debt on the one hand, and by massive expansion into investment banking on the other. In the latter business, banks have the described structural advantage over nonbanks, in that banks need to finance their investment activities only fractionally, whereas nonbanks have to fund everything at 100 %. Moreover, banking corporations run ever bigger nonbank investment units. All of this has happened since around 1980, when consumer price inflation was replaced with global investment banking, asset inflation and much expanded 'innovative' financial contracts, in particular money market funds, asset-backed investment vehicles as well as swaps and derivatives of any kind.

4.13 Shadow Banking

The meaning and scope of shadow banking is not entirely clear yet. Shadow banking can range from money market funds (MMFs), off-balance sheet securitization vehicles, credit default insurance, investment trusts, mutual funds,

---

[31] Cf. Sobrun and Turner (2015) and Rachel and Smith (2015).
[32] Cf. http://www.sovereignmoney.eu/monetary-puzzlement.

and so forth, to nonbank wealth management, nonbank payment services and foreign-exchange services, to nonbank credit associations, peer-to-peer lending and crowdfunding.[33] Off-balance vehicles as well as many MMFs and investment funds are sponsored by banks. The large remainder, however, is independent of banks and operates on its own.

A commonly held opinion is that shadow banks, especially MMFs and off-balance vehicles, are thought to create new money surrogates.[34] A closer look reveals that MMF shares are indeed a new type of money surrogate, while off-balance vehicles are not, but accelerate the circulation of money and MMF shares.

An MMF is normally sponsored by a bank, but is not a bank itself, rather indeed a shadow bank. MMF shares are bought by savers and institutional investors as an alternative to holding bankmoney in a bank account. MMF shares are used especially in financial transactions as deposit-like means of payment, in fact a new type of money surrogate. MMF shares are on par with the official currency (one MMF share equals one or ten currency units). The shares are managed in an MMF customer account, and central banks register MMF shares as deposit-like means of payment. MMF shares can be rebooked within an MMF as a liability swap from one customer to another. Since MMFs hold shares from other MMFs, thus maintaining an account with other MMFs, MMF shares can also be cleared among different MMFs. To the extent that rebooking of shares within an MMF and even clearing among MMFs is practiced, this means the doubling of the effect of a respective amount of money put into an MMF.

As regards the financial items created through off-balance special-purpose vehicles, such as asset-backed securities (ABSs) and collateralized debt obligations (CDOs), these do not serve as a means of payment, but as an additional method of refinancing, and thereafter as additional collateral in subsequent refinancing operations. Hitherto idle credit claims are mobilized in that they are 'packaged' and sold off as securities. These can be repackaged in a second, and then even in a third step. The effect is multiplication of the use-frequency of bankmoney or MMF shares in the financial economy. This is not creation of bankmoney or additional MMF shares, even though the accelerated velocity of their circulation has much the same effect.

MMF shares, ABSs and CDOs were designed to circumvent banking supervision, central bank reserve requirements and bank equity requirements. By doing so, MMFs have helped banks to reduce costs and multiply profits. But these 'financial innovations' have also multiplied banking risks and

---

[33] Cf. Fein (2013), Barghini (2015), and Pignal (2015).
[34] McMillan (2014, pp. 54–79).

concealed them at the same time, especially in the context of the subprime crisis when first-class rated ABSs turned out to be toxic assets. Securitization of credit claims as well as MMF shares as new money surrogates have largely contributed to financial instability.

There are presumptions that as a result of shadow banking, the regular money and banking system might have become rather irrelevant, so that measures relating to the regular system would be correspondingly irrelevant and missing the mark.[35] For the time being, however, claiming that MMF shares and securitization are replacing bankmoney and reserves is premature. More importantly, bankmoney and reserves are a prerequisite for MMF shares. It must nonetheless be taken seriously that, in the absence of monetary reform, the expansion of MMF shares and possibly other money surrogates is undermining monetary and financial market policies still further.

4.14 The Rhetoric About Endogenous and Exogenous Money

Post-Keynesianism has developed the notions of endogenous and exogenous money. The credit-and-debt money in the modern economy is considered endogenous.[36] By that is meant that money is created by economic entities themselves according to the financial needs of their business activities. To put it less mystifyingly, money is created by the banks upon market demand and the banks' preparedness to lend bankmoney or buy securities. In this sense, endogeneity of modern money, the notion going back to Wicksell, can certainly be endorsed. Exogenous money, however, is a misleading notion in that exogenous money does not exist in a modern money and banking system.

The issue may be of a somewhat academic character. It gains political relevance, however, if central bank money is considered 'exogenous', thus attributing an 'outsider' status to central bank monetary policy. Equally, the issue is relevant if market-endogenous demand for money is assumed to induce by itself an optimum money supply, or worse, if the endogeneity of money leads to rejecting quantity considerations as allegedly irrelevant, or worst, if it serves to obscure the pivotal role of the banking industry as the foremost monetary power.

---

[35] For example, McMillan (2014, p. 137).
[36] Cf. Moore (1988a, b). Rochon (1999a, b, pp. 15, 17, 155, 163, 166). Rossi (2007, p. 29) and Keen (2011, p. 358).

Post-Keynesianism tends to distance itself from neoclassical equilibrium theory. It should be seen, however, that the basic idea of endogenous money is classical Banking School doctrine and fully in tune with the Smith/Menger narrative of 'spontaneous' market-endogenous creation of money (Sect. 3.1). At the time of Smith and Menger, the idea of 'money from inside the economy' was directed against 'exogenous' control of the money by alleged 'outsiders' to the economy, in particular absolutist and mercantilist governments of the seventeenth–eighteenth centuries.

Seen in the light of history and contemporary facts, money has always been a public affair, was introduced top down, and kept under the control of the state. Today, however, aside from US Congress, no parliament or cabinet and no private firm or person is able to issue their own money into general circulation. In fact only banks and national central banks, the monetary institutions, fulfill all juridical and factual prerequisites to create official money.

In neoclassical and Keynesian mainstream economics from the 1920–1930s, the narrative of 'money from outside versus inside the economy' was specified so as to label legal tender from the national central bank or the treasury as 'exogenous', with bankmoney deemed 'endogenous'. This is reflected in the two-tier model of banking. The split between central bank money and bank-money also expresses the prevailing situation of incomplete chartalism. This means there are nation-state currencies, while the money supply consists of bankmoney, central bank notes and treasury coins in parallel, with the bank-money over time having come to dominate the entire system. The situation has not been questioned ever since.

The post-Keynesian notion of endogenous money can be misleading in as far as it comes with a flawed notion of exogenous money. It needs to be seen that both banks and central banks create credit and deposits in basically the same way. Both do it on market demand. The banks, however, apply selective supply policies of their own, also including proprietary business independently of customer demand. The central banks today, by contrast, deliver as much reserves and cash as the banks demand. At present, central banks do not intend to exert control over the quantity of money.[37] If bankmoney is seen as endogenous in the economy, so too must central bank money. If central bank money is seen as exogenous to the economy, so too must bankmoney.

Considering the status of bankmoney as endogenous and that of central bank money as exogenous is arbitrary. It represents ideological labelling which makes banks appear to be 'insiders' of the economy, whereas the central bank appears to be an alien outside agency, similar to the way in which many economists see the role of government.

---

[37] Also see Ryan-Collins et al. (2012, p. 103).

Speaking of 'exogenous' money would only make sense if a stock of money was given from some elusive economic 'outside' prior to the economic process without dynamically changing with the demand for and the supply of money. Exogenous money in this sense does not exist in a modern economy. If something that comes close to an exogenous money supply did ever exist, it was the silver and gold of traditional coin currencies, and—in concept, not in reality—national gold hoards under the old industrial gold standard. Present-day fiat money, by contrast, is always endogenous. In consequence, the distinction between exogenous and endogenous money is superfluous, prejudiced and confusing.

A distinction analogous to endogenous versus exogenous money and of largely the same meaning is that between outside money (issued by the central bank and, maybe, the treasury) and inside money (issued by the banking industry).[38] The difference between the two wordings seems to be that 'outside money' is considered the more reliable, higher ranking asset in contrast to bankmoney, because 'outside money', also called high-powered money, comes from the central bank as the ultimate source of money and is also backed by the government, whereas banks in crisis are backed by no one—except their central bank and government. One could say that both bankmoney and central bank money represent fiat money, where bank deposits are based on 'weak' bank fiat backed up by 'strong' central bank and state fiat. Correct as such a specification may be, the terminology of inside versus outside nonetheless reproduces the ideological dictum according to which the banking industry is seen as 'inside the markets', whereas the central banks are shunted off to an unreal, in fact non-existent position 'outside' the money and capital markets.

4.15 The False Identity of Money and Credit

The unreflecting identification of credit and money is another delusion of contemporary economics, no matter whether in neoclassical or Keynesian lineage. In the times of classical economics up to around the middle of the nineteenth century, including the Currency versus Banking controversy, scholars were still aware of the fact that creating money and extending credit are two different functions; as they knew at the same time that, in addition to depositing coin, credit was another way to create bank deposits. Some of them were bankers after all.

---

[38] Lagos (2006) and Roche (2012).

Around 1900, the originators of the bank credit theory of money still had a banking operational understanding of what they described. In the course of the theory's adoption, however, insight into the practices of the day was overstretched into a general credit-and-debt theory of money which was to become a normative ingredient of money theory and monetary policy. For example, in Mitchell-Innes (1913) 'credit' became a revelation of the true nature of money from time immemorial onward to forever:

> Credit and credit alone is money.... Credit is simply the correlative of debt. What A owes to B is A's debt to B and B's credit on A. ... The words 'credit' and 'debt' express a legal relationship between two parties.... Money, then, is credit and nothing but credit. ... This is the whole theory of money.[39]

Mitchell-Innes was not alone in coming to believe that money *is* credit and debt. One can also read in Soddy (1934) that 'money is a credit-debt relation'.[40] Keynes too adopted the credit theory of money, as did the early Chicago School and Fisher. At the same time, all these authors were supporters of the state theory of money and meant no harm by including bankmoney under this umbrella. Knapp was not very outspoken on the issue. He considered bankmoney rather casually, apparently not yet grasping its potential. Keynes did, but he assumed a sufficient degree of central bank control over the banks' credit and deposit creation. He could actually believe himself to have contributed to such control with the monetary policy proposals from his *Tract on Monetary Reform* in 1923, based on setting reserve positions and central bank rates.

The state theory of money was thus wedded to the bank credit theory of money. The monetary system was considered a central bank-led sovereign currency regime that also includes private bankmoney as far as deemed admissible or useful. In fact, however, the system has mutated into a regime of private bankmoney backed by central bank and government, and paradigmatically built on pure Banking doctrine. Against the background of Currency versus Banking teaching, the marriage was a serious historical mésalliance.

To orthodox scholars today, the split-circuit system based on bankmoney and fractional central bank reserves seems to be an unshakeable matter of fact. To many post-Keynesians, partial chartalism and bankmoney even seem to have become unshakeable matters of faith too. 'Modern money' theorists have unearthed Mitchell-Innes as a forefather of their project of 'integration

---

[39] Mitchell-Innes (1913, pp. 392 | 30, 394 | 31). Similar statements in Mitchell-Innes (2014).
[40] Soddy (1934, p. 25).

of creditary and chartalist (state money) approaches'.[41] He now serves as the central witness for the mantra 'money is credit, money is debt', as if this were a timeless truth by nature and necessity. This goes way beyond a mere description of the operational practice of issuing banknotes and bankmoney by way of making bank loans, purchases and other payments to nonbanks.

'Money is credit' or 'money is debt' makes for a witty remark in an armchair conversation; if taken literally, it is simply nonsense. Why should the fact that credit and debt historically existed long before money be 'proof' of money actually being credit and debt? Rather, it may be seen as evidence that money (the means of payment) came as a social innovation that helps to deal with real economic transactions and financial credit-and-debt transactions in a much more efficient way than was previously possible.

The separate existence of money and credit was obvious for 2500 years of coin currencies, when the money was not lent into circulation against interest, but spent into circulation by the rulers of the realm, free of interest and redemption. Even today, the national treasuries sell rather than loan the coins to the national central bank. The creation of coins and the genuine seigniorage thereof were in no way tied to a credit-and-debt relationship. To the contrary, the money served to settle a debt or fulfill a credit contract.

Money, the means of payment, is indeed different from currency as the monetary unit of account, and different from capital that can be built up by investing or lending and borrowing money. Strictly speaking, the latter represents credit-and-debt relations. Payment upon sale, however, does not involve credit and debt but settles the transaction, in the same way as providing money settles a financial credit liability, and as paying back the principal plus interest settles a financial debt. Similarly, state subsidies and transfer payments may be tied to special purposes or entitlements, but do not involve monetary or financial credit and debt. Donating money is just a gift anyway. Even though this can involve social obligations and dependencies, it does not involve a monetary or financial credit-and-debt relationship.

Walsh and Zarlenga conclude of the credit-and-debt doctrine of money that:

> money need not be something owed and due, it's what we use to pay something owed and due.... Money and debt are two different things, that is why we have different words for them. We pay our debt *with* money.[42]

---

[41] Wray (ed.) (2004, pp. 11, 255, 259, 269).

[42] Walsh and Zarlenga (2012, p. 2). Also cf. Zarlenga's critique of Innes' 'Credit Theory of Money' written in 2002b. Distinctness of money and credit/debt also covers the circuitists' understanding of money as a means of payment for the final settlement of a debt; which is remarkable, because circuitism clearly also

Knapp and Lerner put it similarly. Knapp: 'Money is no debt.... it frees us of debt, in particular of our tax debt to the state'.[43] Lerner: 'Money is what we use to pay for things'.[44]

Graziani, as a main representative of circuitism, has also concluded that money is neither a commodity nor credit, but

> something different from a regular commodity and something more than a mere promise of payment ... money has to be accepted as a means of final settlement of the transaction, otherwise it would be credit and not money.[45]

The being different and the necessary distinction between money and credit has not always been maintained in circuitism, but has become a key feature in quantum theory.[46] Its monetary reform program is based on the separation of (a) money creation, (b) payments management and (c) capital building, that is, lending and investing money, a separation which is thought to be implemented in terms of bank accountancy.[47]

In summary, one can say that providing money by way of credit creates a mutual obligation to pay, a claim and a liability (a debt), whereas the transfer of money discharges an obligation to pay. This is no hairsplitting. It is about the basic monetary stipulation of whether one asserts a false *identity of credit and money*, as Banking teachings do, or whether one maintains their being different and exacts a clear *separation of money and credit*, or say, monetary and financial powers, as Currency teachings do. Connected to this is the equally fundamental question of whether money comes necessarily with a corresponding debt, or whether the circulating stock of money can be debt-free.

Even with credit-issued money, the credit and the money are not one and the same, but continue to represent two different functions, in fact two separate realities. Consider what bankmoney is in the balance sheet of a bank and what it is in the account of a customer. In a bank's balance sheet, a demand deposit is a liability of the bank to the customer, a debt, in combination with the promise to settle that debt anytime on demand by paying it out in cash or

---

stands for the theory of credit-based endogenous money. Basically the same position is also shared in the writings of Goodhart.

[43] Knapp (1905, p. 42); author's own translation.
[44] Lerner (1947, p. 313). Both Knapp and Lerner, by the way, are considered by MMTers as their chartalist forefathers together with Mitchell-Innes. The quotes above, however, conflict with MMT's absolute identification of money = credit = debt.
[45] Graziani (1990, pp. 11–12, 2003 pp. 61–62).—Also cf. Bjerg (2014, pp. 105, 121).
[46] Cencini and Rossi (2015, pp. 30–37) and Rossi (2005, p. 144).
[47] Cencini and Rossi (2015, pp. 226–240) and Rossi (2001, pp. 169–184, 2007, pp. 126–132).

transferring the deposit by transferring reserve. With regard to the customer, bankmoney is a claim on cash or bankmoney transfer to which a respective bank is subject.

In the bank account of a customer, by contrast, bankmoney is but money, a liquid means of payment. Most people obtain it by receiving a salary or sales proceeds, that is, without incurring debt, and spend it no differently from paying with notes and coins or e-cash. Paying with bankmoney is not the transfer of a credit-and-debt document, as is the case, for example, with a commercial bill of exchange. It is simply a transfer of money, regardless of its being a cash-receivable against the banks, and regardless of the credit claim of the bank and the corresponding debt of the customer that were at the origin of the creation of that bankmoney. Accepting a commercial bill of exchange is an individual and singular affair, while bankmoney circulates as an official regular means of cashless payment.

Strictly speaking, there is no such thing as 'debt money' or 'credit money'. What really exists are credit-and-debt relationships on the one hand, and money—just money—on the other hand, once a deposit has been entered into bank account and starts circulating. It keeps circulating irrespective of the creditor-bank and debtor-customer that were at the origin of a respective amount of bankmoney. Only as the debtor pays back an according amount of money (principal plus interest) to the creditor-bank is that amount of bank-money deleted.

Pragmatically, one may speak of 'credit money' when meaning 'credit-issued money', or 'debt money' as short for 'debt-borne money'. No problem exists as long as it is understood that money is but money, a tool for the settlement of transactions, different from the socioeconomic relationships of credit and debt, claims and liabilities, which are settled by paying money. Credit and debt are properties of capital formation.

A brief look at the semantics of the word 'credit' may finally be useful. The word has a double meaning. On the one hand it just denotes any entry into some sort of account. Students receive credits for a successful test. The two sides of double-entry bookkeeping are credit and debit, where credit means a positive addition, such as an incoming payment, and debit has a negative sign and means an outgoing payment. Beyond this, however, granting credit means making a loan, or buying bonds or shares, or similar. Any positive entry into a bank account is thus credited to that account, but is not necessarily the payment of a 'credit' (a loan); more often it is earned income (e.g. sales proceeds, salary) or a transfer (e.g. pension, donation).

It follows from the above that the contemporary practice of issuing banknotes and bankmoney by way of commercial bank credit is neither self-evident nor a functional necessity. It has been a practice of the last 200–300 years, but it was only after the Second World War that credit-borne bankmoney established itself as the customary general practice. On grounds of its economic dysfunctions and its questionable legitimacy, the bankmoney regime cannot last forever.

References

Barghini, Tiziana. 2015. Shadow Banking—the Future of Banking? *Global Finance*, April 2015. https://www.gfmag.com/magazine/april-2015/shadow-banking-are-nonbanks-future-banking-cover-story?page=1.

Bindseil, Ulrich. 2004. The Operational Target of Monetary Policy and the Rise and Fall of Reserve Position Doctrine. *ECB Working Paper Series*, No. 372, 2004.

Bjerg, Ole. 2014b. *Making Money. The Philosophy of Crisis Capitalism*, London.

Cencini, Alvaro, and Sergio Rossi. 2015. *Economic and Financial Crises. A New Macroeconomic Analysis*. London: Palgrave Macmillan.

Constâncio, Vítor. 2011. *Challenges to monetary policy in 2012*. Speech at the 26th International Conference on Interest Rates. Frankfurt: European Central Bank.

Fein, Melanie L. 2013. The Shadow Banking Charade. *Fein Law Offices Working Paper*, 15 February 2013. Available at: http://papers.ssrn.com/sol3/papers.cfm?abstract_id=2218812

Friedman, Milton. 1971. The Revenue from Inflation. *Journal of Political Economy* 79: 846–856.

Galbraith, John Kenneth. 1995. *Money. Whence It Came, Where It Went*. New York: Houghton Mifflin (1st edn. 1975).

Gocht, Rolf. 1975. *Kritische Betrachtungen zur nationalen und internationalen Geldordnung*. Berlin: Duncker & Humblot.

Goodhart, Charles A.E. 1984. *Monetary Policy in Theory and Practice*. London: Macmillan.

Graziani, Augusto.1990. The Theory of the Monetary Circuit. *Économies et Sociétés* 7: 7–36.

———. 2003. *The Monetary Theory of Production*. Cambridge: Cambridge University Press.

Häring, Norbert.2013. The Veil of Deception Over Money: How Central Bankers and Textbooks Distort the Nature of Banking and Central Banking. *Real-World Economics Review* 63: 2–18.

Jackson, Andrew, and Ben Dyson. 2012a. *Modernising Money. Why Our Monetary System is Broken and How It Can Be Fixed*. London: Positive Money.

Keen, Steve. 2014. Endogenous Money and Effective Demand. *Review of Keynesian Economics* 2(3): 271–291. Autumn 2014.

———. 2011. *Debunking Economics*. London: Zed Books.

Keynes, John Maynard.1923. *A Tract on Monetary Reform*. London: Macmillan.

———. 1930. *A Treatise on Money*. London: Macmillan. Dt. 1931. *Vom Gelde*. Berlin: Duncker & Humblot.

Knapp, Georg Friedrich. 1905. *Staatliche Theorie des Geldes*. Leipzig: Duncker & Humblot.—Engl. 1924. *The State Theory of Money*. London: Macmillan & Co. Republ. 1973. New York: Augustus Kelley.

Krüger, Malte, and Franz Seitz. 2014. *The Importance of Cash and Cashless Payments in Germany*. Proceedings of the International Cash Conference 2014: The Usage, Costs and Benefits of Cash, Deutsche Bundesbank, Frankfurt.

———. 1914. The Credit Theory of Money. *The Banking Law Journal* 31:151–168. Reprinted in: L.R.Wray (ed) 2004, 50–78.

Kumhof, ichael, and Zoltan Jacab. 2015. Banks Are Not Intermediaries of Loanable Funds—And Why This Matters. *Bank of England Working Paper*, No. 529, May 2015.

Lagos, Ricardo. 2006. Inside and Outside Money. *Research Department Staff Report*, No. 374. Federal Reserve Bank of Minneapolis, May 2006.

Lavoie, Marc. 2014. A Comment on 'Endogenous Money and Effective Demand' by Steve Keen. *Review of Keynesian Economics* 2(3): 321–332. Autumn 2014.

Lerner, Abba P. 1947. Money as a Creature of the State. *American Economic Review* 37(2):312–317.

McLeay, Michael, Amar Radia, and Ryland Thomas.2014. Money Creation in the Modern Economy. *Bank of England Quarterly Bulletin* Q1: 14–27.

McMillan, Jonathan. 2014. *The End of Banking. Money, Credit, and the Digital Revolution*. Zurich: Zero/One Economics.

Mitchell-Innes, Alfred. 1913. What is money? *The Banking Law Journal* 30(5):377–408. Reprinted in: L.R.Wray (ed) 2004, 14–49.

Moore, Basil J. 1988a. *Horizontalists and Verticalists: The Macroeconomics of Credit Money*. Cambridge: Cambridge University Press.

———. 1988b. The Endogenous Money Supply. *Journal of Post Keynesian Economics* 10(3):372–385.

Nichols, Dorothy M. 1961–1982, and Anne Marie L. Gonczy. 1992–1994. *Modern Money Mechanics. A Workbook on Bank Reserves and Deposit Expansion*. Chicago: Federal Reserve Bank of Chicago.

Palley, Thomas I. 2013. Horizontalists, Verticalists, and Structuralists: The Theory of Endogenous Money Reassessed. *Review of Keynesian Economics* 1(4):406–424.

Philippon, Thomas, and Ariell Reshef. 2009. Wages and Human Capital in the US Financial Industry 1909–2006. *NBER Working Paper*, No. 14644.

Philipps, Chester Arthur.1920. *Bank Credit*. New York: The Macmillan Company.

Pignal, Stanley. 2015. Slings and arrows. Financial technology will make banks more vulnerable and less profitable. *The Economist Special Report on International Banking*, May 9 2015.

Rachel, Lukasz, and Thomas Smith. 2015. Drivers of long-term global interest rates—Can weaker growth explain the fall? *Bank Underground*, July 27. http://bankunderground.co.uk/2015/07/27/drivers-of-long-term-global-interest-rates-can-weaker-growth-explain-the-fall

Roche, Cullen. 2012. Understanding Inside Money and Outside Money. *Pragmatic Capitalism*. http://www.pragcap.com/understanding-inside-money-and-outside-money

Rochon, Louis-Philippe.1999a. *Credit, Money and Production. An Alternative Post-Keynesian Approach*. Cheltenham: Edward Elgar.

———. 1999b. The Creation and Circulation of Endogenous Money. *Journal of Economic Issues* 33(1): 1–21.

Rossi, Sergio.2001. *Money and Inflation A New Macroeconomic Analysis*. Cheltenham: Edward Elgar.

———. 2003. *Money and Banking in a Monetary Theory of Production*. In *Modern Theories of Money*, eds. Louis-Philippe Rochon, and Sergio Rossi, 339–359. Cheltenham: Edward Elgar.

———. 2005. Central Banking in a Monetary Theory of Production. In *The Monetary Theory of Production*, eds. Giuseppe Fontana, and Riccardo Realfonzo, 139–151. Heidelberg: Springer.

———. 2007. *Money and Payments in Theory and Practice*. London: Routledge.

Ryan-Collins, Josh, Tony Greenham, Richard Werner, and Andrew Jackson.2012. *Where Does Money Come From? A Guide to the UK Monetary and Banking System*, 2 edn. London: New Economics Foundation.

Schemmann, Michael. 2011b. *The Euro ist Still the Strongest Currency Around. Analyses and Solutions for the Money and Sovereign Debt Crisis of the 2010s*. IICPA Publications.

Seiffert, Horst. 2012. *Geldschöpfung. Die verborgene Macht der Banken*. Nauen: Verlag H. Seiffert.

Sobrun, Jhuvesh, and Philip Turner. 2015. *Bond Markets and Monetary Policy Dilemmas for the Emerging Markets. BIS Working Papers*, No.508. Basel: Bank for International Settlements.

Soddy, Frederick.1934. *The Role of Money. What it should be, contrasted with what it has become*. London: George Routledge and Sons Ltd..

Theurer, Marcus. 2014. Wie die Investmentbanker reich wurden. *Frankfurter Allgemeine*126, June 2, 22.

Turner, Adair. 2012. Monetary and Financial Stability. Speech at South African Reserve Bank, 2 November 2012. Available at: http://www.fsa.gov.uk/static/pubs/speeches/1102-at.pdf

Walsh, Steven, and Stephen Zarlenga. 2012. *Evaluation of Modern Monetary Theory. American Monetary Institute Research Paper*. http://www.monetary.org/mmtevaluation.

Werner, Richard A. 2014a. Can Banks Individually Create Money Out Of Nothing? The Theories and the Empirical Evidence. *International Review of Financial Analysis* 36:1–19.

————. 2014b. How Do Banks Create Money, and Why Can Other Firms Not Do the Same? An Explanation for the Coexistence of Lending and Deposit-Taking. *International Review of Financial Analysis* 36:71–77.

————. 2015. A Lost Century in Economics—Three Theories of Banking and the Conclusive Evidence. *International Review of Financial Analysis*. Preliminarily published at: http://www.sciencedirect.com/science/article/pii/ S1057521915001477

Wray, L. Randall, ed.2004. *Credit and State Theories of Money. The Contributions of A. Mitchell-Innes*. Cheltenham: Edward Elgar Publishing.

5

Dysfunctions of the Bankmoney Regime

5.1 The Monetary System: The Misjudged Root Cause of Financial Crises

This chapter deals with the dysfunctions inherent in the split-circuit fractional reserve system, such as proneness to inflation or asset inflation and crises of banking and finance due to the GDP-disproportionate growth of the money supply and the levels of financial assets and debt, non-safety of bankmoney, questionable banking privileges, and disproportionate financial income at the expense of earned income. The existing bankmoney regime is a complicated constellation which recurrently proves to be a faulty design in its functional and political aspects.

An often-quoted IMF study has identified 425 systemic financial crises from 1970 to 2007 in migratory hot spots around the world, intensifying in number and severity. Of these, 145 were sector-wide banking crises, 208 currency crises and 72 sovereign debt crises.[1] It does not seem to be self-evident, however, that such problems are rooted in the bankmoney regime. Only a few scholars attribute financial instability and crises to fractional reserve banking. In contrast to preceding stages in the development of modern economies, the fundamental role of the monetary system in banking and finance is nowadays largely neglected. In view of the increased weight of banking and finance, this is paradoxical.

Saying that fractional reserve banking is the root cause of financial crises does not mean it is the main driving force. Drivers are the different actor groups in the economy and financial markets, including the banks themselves

---

[1] Laeven and Valencia (2008) and Reinhart and Rogoff (2009).

as well as nonbank institutional investors. They may in turn be driven by various constraints, including a generalized self-perpetuating expectation of ever-growing income and wealth. But the money system underlies it all in that the funding of financial and real economic transactions depends on whether and how and under what conditions money can be made available. In this sense, the monetary system of banks and central banks exerts, or fails to exert, a controlling function, a selective and restrictive function. It determines the primary creation, issuance and allocation of money and thereby enables or inhibits benign developments as well as harmful ones.

Neo-Austrian scholars are among the few to have developed a criticism of the bankmoney regime which overlaps in a number of aspects with the criticism from a new Currency point of view as expounded in this book. Neo-Austrians, however, blame the dysfunctions of fractional reserve banking on central bank policies and government interference, and thus campaign for 'free banking' beyond central banks and the state, even perhaps on the basis of a renewed gold standard.[2] By contrast, the way out shown in this book is full chartalism, that is, sovereign money only, but under conditions of separation of monetary and fiscal responsibilities, and financial market functions beyond.

Another case in point is post-Keynesianism. In comparison to orthodox economists, post-Keynesians have worked out a more or less up-to-date description of credit creation, and yet they have no problem with bankmoney. Some see themselves as critics of financial market capitalism, but do not recognize the state-backed rule of private bankmoney as the root cause of the phenomena they criticize.[3]

Across the academic world today a simple and fundamental question is no longer being raised: where does all the additional money come from that is needed for funding ever more credit and debt in relatively short periods of time? The simple answer is: the money comes from the banks, and in the first instance the banks do not have the money but create it at their own discretion.

5.2   Incomplete Analysis of Financial Crises

In the process of coming to terms with the transatlantic financial crisis, it took quite a few years to grasp the structural problems. The easily visible causes were examined first, such as greed in combination with bonuses luring traders

---

[2] Hayek (1976) and Huerta de Soto (2009), Mises Institute, Austin, Texas: mises.org/about-mises.

[3] For example, Pettifor (2014), Dow et al. (2015), and van Dixhoorn (2013).

into irresponsible risk taking. One of the reform measures proposed in this respect is capping top salaries and bonuses.

Subsequent thoughts were on risk-spoofing by questionable practices of securitization, pseudo-hedge gambling in derivatives, and risk management and accounting in general. A number of culprits were identified, among them off-balance conduits, accommodation ratings and banking via offshore centers.

Proposed reform measures include converting over-the-counter trade into registered exchange trade, closing down offshore financial centers, the interdiction of special types of securities, for example, 'structured products' such as asset-backed securities in the form of good–bad loan sandwiches, or ruling out naked (uncovered) short selling, or the issue of credit default swaps in excess of actually existing credit. Moreover, tougher statutory provisions for rating agencies, and more transparent accounting in general, particularly ruling out risky off-balance items in bank accountancy, have also been advocated.[4]

Another line of risk analysis focused on the loss-absorbing capacity of equity buffers. In the nineteenth century, bank equity as a percentage of book assets was as high as 40–50 % in America and at about 30 % in Europe (which did not prevent bankruptcies and crises). In recent decades, equity had come down to 3–12 %, depending on the calculation method.

Bulking up equity and liquidity requirements is the preferred approach of central bankers, supervisors, and also bankers themselves, as they have been facing additional restrictions anyway. They are familiar with rules on liquidity and solvency, and even though it did not work in the past—so the thinking goes—a higher dose of the medicine might help in the future. The Basel rules on bank equity and liquidity, generations I and II, were thus updated by generation III, including provisions for minimum liquidity lasting 30 days and a leverage ratio, in other words a ceiling on credit creation in terms of a maximum ratio of outstanding loans and items in a bank's trading book in relation to the core equity base.

Analyses became still more structural by pointing out the role of deregulation of international banking and capital movements. This was implemented in the name of free trade which is assumed to be beneficial to all parties involved—which is certainly true for the beneficiaries of structural change, less so for those who are losing out. In this particular case, and rather independently of industrial globalization, financial-market deregulation paved the

---

[4] For an extended analysis of the crisis see Turner (2015, Parts I–III), Wolf (2014), Blinder (2013), Peukert (2012), Liikanen Report (2012), Financial Crisis Inquiry Committee (2011), and Reinhart and Rogoff (2009).

way for all too footloose portfolio management and gambling in the global financial casino, to a considerable extent detached from the real economy. As a consequence, there were calls for re-regulation, including financial transaction taxes (supposed to have a dampening effect), and, with regard to high-frequency trading, minimum time limits for holding financial positions.

In the global context, and in relation to national dimensions, the sheer size of the top banking corporations and financial markets gained attention, discussed under the heading of 'too big to fail' or 'too interconnected to fail' respectively. Lists of systemically relevant banks have officially been compiled. These lists still conceal the fact that it is the banking sector as such which is of systemic relevance in a monetarized and financialized economy. This is certainly not a new insight, but it was ignored for more than half a century. Collapsing banks now helped to recall this, including the blackmailing capacity of the banking industry to exact government support and bail-outs in order to prevent the meltdown of finance and payment transactions, which would result in a breakdown of the economy.

The reform measures derived from this type of analysis include the dismantling of large banking corporations. Before considering a government bail-out, struggling banks will now first have to resort to a bail-in. This comes down to holding bank customers liable prior to calling on a contribution from taxpayers. In fact, this represents an impudent violation of property rights, and is outright expropriation, even more explicit than in the case of negative interest on customer deposits, given the fact that customer deposits are very different from external capital in that they *cannot* be used by a bank as loanable funds and are entrusted to a bank for safekeeping rather than for the proprietary business of said bank. Banks and bankers themselves are still not being called to account.

In addition, banks are obliged to prepare a 'living will', that is a resolution plan in the event of insolvency, aimed at leaving third parties as unaffected as possible. The latter measures overlap with the concept of firewalls between different business lines in a bank. This involves approaches to separate banking, in other words keeping apart from each other (a) basic money services such as currency exchange, account management and cashless payment, (b) the lending business and (c) investment banking. Today, as in the 1930s, the importance of (a) is normally misjudged, and the separation of (b) from (c) is largely ineffective as long as (b) is not prevented from providing leverage to (c). A related approach is the Volcker rule, which calls for the interdiction or limitation of proprietary trading, or the separation of a bank's proprietary trading from its customer business.[5]

---

[5] Cf. Independent Commission on Banking (2011) (Vickers Report) and Liikanen Report (2012).

All the contributory crisis factors mentioned here have their points. Measures may be appropriate to a degree within their special scope of application. It is predictable, however, that after another period of wound licking and some restructuring, the effect of such reforms will not be lasting. The reason is that things will basically not change as long as the banking industry continues to be the defining monetary power, itself creating the money supply on which it operates. All the causes identified in those analyses have a common basis, a cause of causes so to speak, the *monetary* cause of the *financial* and *political* causes of the banking and sovereign debt crisis, which is overshooting creation of bankmoney, financial assets and debt in the bank-led fractional reserve system.

5.3   The Monetary Quantity Equation

To analyze the relation between money and the economy, monetary quantity theory is a means of choice. It is one of the oldest and most proven elements of economics. It links the money supply with the price level of items. In its most widely quoted formulation it states that 'too much money chasing too few goods' results in inflation. This evokes the Spanish colonial silver inflation of the sixteenth century, upon which quantity inflation theory was formulated. From a contemporary point of view that statement is somewhat simplistic; it is still broadly true, but does not represent the entire truth.

Since the eighteenth century, economists have been aware of the fact that additions to the money supply, if spent on the activation of idle workforce and the development of productive capacities, can be expected to result in growing production and higher levels of income. Inflation would only arise if such productive potentials do not exist or cannot promptly be realized, so that wilful additions to the money supply represent 'empty money', as this is termed in quantum economics, that is, money not representing a real value counterpart, converging at this point with the Austrian and Neo-Austrian view.

The link between paid prices, in other words the turnover value of economic output, and the quantity of money in circulation is covered by the famous equation of exchange in its transaction form as introduced by Fisher:

$$M \times V = T \times P$$

where M is the quantity of money, V the velocity of circulation (the use-frequency of money), T the transactions carried out, and P the prices of these transactions.[6]

---

[6] Fisher (1911, p. 195).

The equation had a history before it was cast into its now most widespread formulation about a hundred years ago.[7] More variants have been added since. The equation has often been criticized, but survives for its robustness. One might see it as just another example of over-aggregate model building. It has nonetheless an undeniable truth to it: If M is increased, and V kept the same, this results in an increase in transactions (the economic product), or an increase in prices, or both. As a sensitivity relationship, the equation can also be read in the reverse: more transactions or higher prices will induce an extended endogenous money supply.

The critical part of the equation is V, the use-frequency of money units. V is a black box including all processes of the circulation and non-circulation of money, in actual fact the entire economic process as far as it includes the use of money. To assume V as constant is not plausible. Supposing V to follow some stable trend seems to be closer to reality. In an increasingly cashless money system with real time electronic payments, one has reason to assume a long-term trend towards increasing overall velocity of the circulation of bank-money. This will apply all the more to the financial circulation of money. For example, half a century ago, investors held stocks in their portfolio on average for five years, today they do so for one minute.[8]

Seen from a contemporary perspective, the equation lacks two important specifications. One is the distinction between active and inactive money, and the other is the distinction between GDP-contributing transactions and non-GDP transactions.

As explained in Sect. 4.6, part of what is considered to represent money supply today is deactivated deposit savings. The liquid part of the public money supply consists of the cash and demand deposits, whereby also a certain percentage of the cash and even of demand deposits is simply held ('hoarded') rather than actively used, particularly in times of very low interest. An additional component of active money is MMF shares used as a means of payment in financial transactions. In the above equation, M ought to refer to the active part of the money supply only; otherwise, results are misleading.

The expression 'equation of exchange' rests on the traditional understanding of money as a 'medium of exchange', and of the economy as a huge barter system where goods are 'exchanged', not expressly including the more fundamental role of money as a means of finance. The equation lacks that dimension, that is the financial economy as being distinct, though certainly not separate, from the real economy. When including this distinction, it may be

---

[7] Humphrey (1984). For an in-depth analysis and critical discussion see Rossi (2001, pp. 63–88).
[8] Chesney (2014, p. 50).

preferable to speak in a more encompassing sense about the monetary quantity equation. The equation then needs disaggregation into a real economic and financial hemisphere, as the active part of the money supply is partly used for real economic transactions, partly for GDP-related financial transactions (funding real economic activity), and partly circulates in the non-GDP asset economy.[9] Finding out more about this, in order to be able to specify empirically related sub-flows in the circulation of money, is a major research desideratum.

Scholars have been wondering about the supposed riddle of a decelerating velocity (V) of money circulation. If calculated as the ratio of nominal GDP to M1 (cash and demand deposits), V seems to have been slowing considerably in the run-up to the crisis, in the UK, for example, from 6.14 in 1980 to 1.93 in 2008, and in Germany from 7.71 to 2.43. Figures are similar for most old industrial nations, except for the USA where that coefficient has increased from 7.32 to 9.02.[10]

Velocity of money circulation calculated in this way, however, is an aggregate cipher that covers rather than uncovers the real multitude of use-frequencies of money in different segments of the real and financial economy. The overall reduction in V is an arithmetic artefact. General deceleration is counterintuitive, especially in view of computerization, online banking and high-frequency trading. The supposed riddle dissolves when including the many transactions in the financial economy that regularly absorb large amounts of money. The disaggregated uses of money include the following.

1a. Immediate use as a means of real economic transactions, in buying goods and services and paying for personnel
1b. Financial use for funding GDP-contributing expenditure, such as creating credit for real capital expenditure, initial placement of sovereign and corporate bonds, but also taxes as well as donations and other private transfers
2. Financial use for funding non-GDP asset transactions, such as trading in foreign exchange and derivatives, or the secondary trading of stocks, bonds and other securities.

---

[9] Such disaggregation has been suggested by Werner (2005, p. 185) and Huber (1998, p. 224) in the form of subdividing equations of circulation into a financial and a real economic hemisphere. Also cf. Ryan-Collins et al. (2012, p. 109). Hudson (2006, 2012, pp. 55, 297, 333) basically pursues the same idea when he suggests introducing a separate FIRE sector (Finance, Insurance, Real Estate) into macroeconomic models and Post-Keynesian public–private sector balances.

[10] Based on data from Bank of England, Quarterly amounts outstanding of M4, of M1 (UK estimate of EMU aggregate). Office for National Statistics, http://www.ons.gov.uk/ons/datasets-and-tables/index.html; Quarterly National Accounts, Time Series.—Bundesbank, Monatsberichte, Tables I.2, II.2, VIII.1, X.1.—https://research.stlouisfed.org/fred2/series/M1, series/M2, series/GDP, series/GDPCA.

There are delimitation problems. One may think about

- Whether (1b) is part of (1a); which, however, is not that simple, given that new debt is partly used for servicing old debt, in corporate as much as in public uses.
- As far as sales of real estate, stocks, bonds and so on result in earnings or losses, the latter, complying with today's accountancy practices, are GDP-effective, but not the amounts of money transacted in each case. One may think about keeping real and financial profits and losses apart; it might improve economic transparency.
- When industrial companies recapitalize, the revenue from the respective initial offering can be expected to result for the most part in real economic expenditure; when banks and nonbank financial intermediaries do so, this will for the most part result in non-GDP transactions.
- Building of homes adds to GDP; real estate acquisitions for drawing rent and capital gains do not.
- Holders of foreign exchange may have a legitimate interest in forex trading for wanting to avoid devaluation of their holdings; but value-defensive trading seamlessly switches to aggressive and quite often leveraged forex speculation. By analogy, this applies to wealth management in general.
- Derivatives represent pure betting business to the extent to which they surmount the quantity of existing underlyings.

Non-GDP transactions are not generally 'bad', as GDP-transactions are not automatically 'good'. In a modern economy, people need savings over their lifetime, as firms need a capital base and business reserves. The more savings and capital there are, the greater the need for wealth management, including a degree of portfolio trading. Wealth is fundamentally desirable, also in the form of financial assets—were it not for two awkward problems. One is that in a meritocratic society, wealth ought to be based on achievement rather than financial sinecure privileges. The other problem is that there are limits to the total stock of financial assets in relation to GDP, that is, limits of financial carrying capacity (Sects. 5.7 and 5.8).

The monetary quantity equation does not give proof of anything. It is just a plausible systemic sensitivity link, explaining that an overshooting money supply, that is more money than is absorbed by economic capacities, is to be seen in inflation or asset inflation; or in the reverse, that inflation and asset inflation, whatever other factors may cause them, induce additions to the money supply unless there is accelerated money circulation (use frequency) or alternative means of payment.

Seen overall, additions to the money supply can contribute to real economic growth, to inflation, to the growth of inactive monetary assets, the growth of financial assets and asset price inflation in the narrow sense of rising stock quotes or real estate prices. The contribution of these factors also depends on the prevailing use-frequency of money in the specific hemisphere and sector of circulation.

5.4   Overshooting Money Supply

To detect monetary overshoot, the conventional monetary quantity equation can be misleading as long as it does not include the differences between active and inactive money, and between GDP-related and non-GDP-contributing financial uses of active money. In this respect, present monetary statistics are not helpful. They are based on systematics different from one currency area to the other, and they mix active and inactive positions in the monetary aggregates M2/3/4.

Inactive monetary assets neither contribute to inflation, nor to asset inflation and bubbles. Only active money and money surrogates do. Consequently, deposit savings are relevant for monetary overshoot only indirectly in that they induce additional credit and debt.

As regards the active part of the stock of money, let us first consider liquid bankmoney and cash, which is referred to as narrow money M1. It can be assumed that in order to generate the annual economic output (nominal GDP) an active stock of money M1 of about 1/12 of that GDP is needed. The fraction 1/12 is meant to give an idea of the magnitude involved, a rough proxy on the grounds that most payments in the economy, rather than being quarterly, annually or non-regular one-off expenditures, follow a monthly or sub-monthly pattern, as is the case with salaries and pensions, most tax payments, allowances, rents, fees, interest and redemption payments, and current household and company expenditure in general. Also the findings on the use of cash, as mentioned in Sect. 4.2, support the assumption that a money supply at the magnitude of about 1/12 of GDP sustains the entire GDP-related turnover: only 10–20 % of the stock of cash is actively used in domestic transactions.

- In the UK in 2008, when the American subprime crisis fully hit, GDP was £1550 billion. Rather than accounting for the assumed amount of 1/12 of GDP, which would have been £127 billion, M1 was £1029 billion, 8.10 times that amount.[11]

---

[11] Bank of England, Quarterly amounts outstanding of M4, of M1 (UK estimate of EMU aggregate) http://www.bankofengland.co.uk/boeapps/iadb—Office for National Statistics, http://www.ons.gov.uk/ons/datasets-and-tables/index.html; Quarterly National Accounts, Time Series Data.

- In the euro area at the same time, nominal GDP was €9259 billion. 1/12 of this would have been €772 billion. In actual fact, M1 in 2008 was €3974 billion, thus 5.15 times higher than what was to be assumed. In 1997 that ratio had still been 3.55.[12]
- In Germany, GDP was €2496 billion, M1 was €1028 billion. M1 was thus 4.97 times the expected amount. In 1980, that ratio had been only 1.56.[13]
- In the USA, nominal GDP was $14,369 billion. The assumed 1/12 of this would have been $1193 billion, while M1 was actually $1616 billion, 1.36 times higher than was to be assumed. That difference was much less pronounced than in Europe. The reason behind this is the earlier and more extensive use of money market fund shares (MMF shares) in the USA, as discussed below.[14]

The part that contributes to inflation corresponds to the difference between nominal and real GDP. The other part of active money that goes into inflated volumes and prices of financial assets is directly indicated by the figures given above, because nominal GDP includes inflation, and what exceeds nominal GDP then is to the account of the asset economy and asset inflation.

The above findings become similarly visible in the Marshallian 'k', named after nineteenth-century economist Alfred Marshall. The value 'k' referred to the ratio of the money base M0 to economic output. Since nowadays bank-money (rather than merely cash and central bank reserves) is the relevant reference, and nominal GDP as a measure of output is readily available, M1 to GDP may be preferable.

- In the euro area within the short period from 1995 to 2008, M1 to GDP went from 0.25 to over 0.5, actually a very strong GDP-disproportionate increase.[15]
- In post-war Germany, M1 to GDP was oscillating at 0.16, but from 1980 to 2008, which is the time span of the Great Immoderation (Sect. 5.13), M1 to GDP grew threefold to 0.45.[16]

---

[12] European Central Bank, Monthly Bulletin, Tables 2.3, 2.4, 5.2.1.

[13] Bundesbank, Monatsberichte, Tables II.1, XI.1.

[14] https://www.federalreserve.gov/Releases/H6/hist/h6hist1.txt—FRED Economic Data St. Louis Federal Reserve, https://research.stlouisfed.org/fred2/… series/M1, series/GDP.

[15] Data from http://epp.eurostat.ec.europa.eu/portal/page/portal/national_accounts/data/database

[16] Data from www.bundesbank.de/statistik/statistik_wirtschaftsdaten_tabellen.php#wirtschaftsentwicklung—www.bundesbank.de/statistik/zeitreihen—Bundesbank, *Monthly Bulletins*, tables II.2.

- In the UK from 1986 to 2008, M1 to GDP increased in even stronger disproportion from 0.16 to 0.52.[17]
- Such an increase in M1 did not occur in the USA. From 1980 to 2008, M1 to GDP actually went sideways from 0.14 to 0.13.[18] Instead, there was something more spectacular: an unprecedented takeoff in MMF shares.

Between 1980 and 2008 US dollar-denominated MMF shares grew from about $90 billion to $3800 billion, a 42-fold increase, compared with a less than five-fold increase in GDP. A comparable takeoff in Europe started only towards the year 2000 and had reached a value of $1300 billion in 2008, an increase equally exceeding GDP growth many times over.[19] In the USA, the $3800 billion in MMF shares were 2.4 times M1 (the stock of demand deposits and cash). In the euro area, the $1300 billion represented 'only' a third of M1.[20]

Using MMF shares as a new money surrogate actually means a doubling of the bankmoney invested in MMFs because an MMF that issues the shares (debtor) obtains an amount of bankmoney to be invested in short-term money market papers, while the buyers of the MMF shares (creditors) can nevertheless use the shares they bought in lieu of bankmoney.

5.5   Channels of Bankmoney Issuance

There are three major channels through which the expansion of bank balance sheets contributes to an overshooting money supply: real estate and mortgages, speculative leverage, and government debt. 72–80 % of bank credit is allotted to these purposes, only the rest accounts for loans for other purposes to firms and households.[21]

In many countries, the biggest share of bank credit goes into building loans and mortgages. Part of this is reflected in private household debt, but also in

---

[17] http://www.ons.gov.uk/ons/rel/naa2/second-estimate-of-gdp/q3-2015/tsd-gdp-q3-2015.html—http://www.ons.gov.uk/ons/datasets-and-tables/index.html—Bank of England, Quarterly amounts outstanding of M4, of M1 (UK estimate of EMU aggregate) http://www.bankofengland.co.uk/boeapps/iadb.

[18] FRED Economic Data St. Louis Federal Reserve, https://research.stlouisfed.org/fred2/series/, add / GDP for Nominal Gross Domestic Product, add /graph/?id=GDPCA, GDPC96 for Real Gross Domestic Product.—Bureau of Economic Analysis, https://www.bea.gov/national/index.htm#gdp

[19] Baba et al. (2009, p. 68) and Hilton (2004, p. 180).

[20] Mai (2015). www.federalreserve.gov/Releases/H6/hist/h6hist1.txt. ECB, Monthly Bulletin, Table 2.3.1.

[21] Liikanen Report (2012), Financial Crisis Inquiry Committee (2011), and Turner (2015, p. 61).

public debt (as in the case of government-sponsored entities such as Fannie Mae and Freddie Mac in the USA). Private mortgages can easily amount to a multiple of a household's annual income. Real estate is of ambivalent financial character. It has use value and involves real economic expenditure as far as construction works or maintenance is involved, which contributes to GDP. At the same time, real estate is subject to the dealings of a specialized financial industry and, like securities, to secondary trade after initial production, as a real asset investment, analogous to putting money into gold, oil, timber and such like. Sales proceeds result in a profit or loss which affects GDP. The fees and commissions involved also add to GDP. The price of a respective property, however, is a financial non-GDP item, and normally of a substantial amount. The lion's share of sales proceeds is recycled into financial investment rather than spent on real economic expenditure.

Speculative leverage means to take up debt for use in financial investment expected to yield enough for paying off the debt and yet making money from it. The newly created bankmoney is put into real estate, stocks, derivatives, foreign exchange or private equity, also including hostile leveraged buyouts which are almost completely credit-funded.

Financial market trading absorbs large amounts of liquid money. The volume of foreign exchange trading, for instance, is several hundred times the volume of real economic trade in goods and services.[22] The notional value of derivatives is ten times the world's GDP. In only 2 % of futures contracts, however, will the underlying finally be delivered, meaning that 98 % of futures trading is pure betting business.[23] Prices and volumes of financial assets are generally very high, in fact multiples of GDP. This is to say, again, that much of the money supply is used in the financial markets.

The third main channel of creating money overshoot is public finance, that is debt in the form of sovereign bonds, treasury bills and book credit to public households. Consortia of large banking corporations serve as bond underwriters. They keep a significant part of the sovereign debt on their own books and sell the rest on the open market. In the eurozone, for example, and prior to the sovereign debt crisis, half of public debt was held by domestic and foreign banks, a third by funds and insurance companies, and only the rest by private individuals and central banks, the figures somewhat varying from country to country.[24] Book credit to public households is financed freehand by all types of banks. As a result, more than half of public debt is funded by newly created bankmoney, with only the rest by secondary on-lending of already existing bankmoney.

---

[22] Bjerg (2014, p. 25).
[23] Chesney (2014, pp. 33, 50). Also cf. Financial Crisis Inquiry Committee (2011).
[24] Arslanalp and Tsuda (2012, p. 12). ECB, *Monthly Bulletins*, Table 6.2.1.

5.6   Inflation

Inflation may not necessarily be 'always and everywhere a monetary phenomenon', as Friedman alleged.[25] But quite often it is, and as far as there are other factors causing inflation, this too will induce additions to the money supply by way of additional credit and debt taken up by public, corporate and private actors.

For example, in the USA from 1980 to 2008, nominal GDP (at current prices, that is, including inflation) grew by 386 %, real GDP (deflated) only by 129 %.[26] The respective figures for the UK were 392 % and 121 %.[27] The figures for Germany in the shorter period from 1992 to 2008 were 51 % nominal GDP, and 23 % real GDP.[28]

According to these figures, only half to one third of the growth in nominal GDP was real, whereas between half and two thirds of it consisted of inflation. This is to say that the bigger half of active money that was spent on GDP-contributing transactions added to consumer price inflation, while only the lesser half added to real output and increases in real income. This fact can be taken for granted, the more so as official statistics may underreport rather than overstate inflation.[29]

The difficulty is now to determine the share of active money that was absorbed by non-GDP asset transactions rather than having contributed to GDP. Considering the figures on monetary overshoot given above, and taking a conservative stance, one might conclude that in recent decades half up to two thirds of the entire active money supply went into the asset economy. This then allows one to assume, roughly speaking, that about 20 % or much less of the active money supply went into real GDP, and another 20 % or less in inflation, while about 60 % or more fed into the asset economy.

It is clear enough that there has been a steady decline in the purchasing power of money, in many cases also including devaluation of the respective currency. One may wonder whether it is appropriate to speak of 'low inflation', which is considered to be irrelevant or even desirable, in a situation in

---

[25] Friedman (1991, p. 16, 1992, p. 198).

[26] FRED Economic Data, St. Louis Federal Reserve, https://research.stlouisfed.org/fred2/series/GDP, series/GDPCA.

[27] Office of National Statistics, www.ons.gov.uk/ons/rel/elmr/explaining-economic-statistics/long-term-profile-of-gdp-in-the-uk/sty-long-term-profile-of-gdp.html

[28] www.bundesbank.de/Navigation/DE/Statistiken/Zeitreihen_Datenbanken/ESZB_Zeitreihen/eszb_zeitreihen_node.html; http://epp.eurostat.ec.europa.eu/portal/page/portal/national_accounts/data/database; Bundesbank, *Monthly Bulletins*, Tables II.2.

[29] Cf. Häring and Douglas (2012, p. 32).

which the larger half of growth just represents growing prices (inflation) and only the smaller half is real. A dollar or yen is presently only a fifth or sixth of its worth in the 1950s.

In old industrial countries, inflation was a big issue in the 1960–1970s when inflation rates in many countries, quasi in parallel with nominal interest rates, were in the double digits. A similar situation has existed in many newly industrializing countries over the last 30 years until the present slowdown set in. Inflation rates in countries such as China, Indonesia, Brasil, South Africa or Russia ranged between 6 and 12 %, occasionally even being at 15 %, thus at levels comparable to those seen before in old industrial countries. In the latter countries, inflation came down to 5–3 % in the course of the 1980s. Politicians and central bankers like to take credit for having brought down inflation rates. Given the poor effectiveness of monetary policy in the present bankmoney regime, it is more likely that low inflation rates have resulted from a number of era-specific financial and real economic factors.

Among the latter are generally lower growth rates and a certain saturation of mass consumer markets as well as re-internationalization of trade and production (globalization). This made industrial capacities available across the globe and brought about strong price competition in mass products from newly industrializing countries, as well as international competition among industrial locations. A by-product of increased global competition was the weakened national collective bargaining position of the trade unions. This put an end to the notorious price–wage spiral of the 1950–1970s, but also put many employees and self-employed people in various types of precarious employment. What then brought inflation rates down to still lower levels of 2–0 % was the most recent financial and economic crisis in combination with the so-called savings glut. This represents stocks of active and inactive money exceeding the demand for money; or, say, it represents demand for favorable investment lacking corresponding opportunities.

5.7   Asset Inflation, Bubbles and Crises

Compared with inflation, the much bigger concern in advanced economies since the 1980s is asset inflation. The term asset inflation refers here to both increasing asset prices and disproportionately growing volumes of financial assets such as securities and derivatives. As explained above, towards the end of the period of strongly expanding investment banking and asset markets from around 1980 to 2008, half to two thirds of the entire active money supply served the asset economy, and not much has changed since.

Some economists do not like the subject of asset inflation and even deny its existence, particularly if they are firm believers in efficient markets.[30] Asset owners do not like the subject either; for them it is like spoiling the party. When quotes go up, one feels like a winner and would prefer not to hear about wealth delusion, bubbles and crises. If during the dotcom bubble, which lasted until March 2000, one remarked that the New Economy was likely to look old soon, reactions ranged from a pitiful smile to excommunication.

Various studies on hundreds of crises that occurred in the last century have conclusively identified the GDP-disproportionate expansion of lending/borrowing and leverage as the harbingers of asset inflation, financial market bubbles and ensuing banking and debt crises.[31] What these studies fail to consider, however, is the difference between primary and secondary credit, as if asset inflation and bubbles were funded just through on-lending and investing of already existing money. Howsoever large the share of secondary credit may have become over time, all of the money involved is bankmoney originating from primary bank credit, now also including MMF shares as a money surrogate based on bankmoney.

Generally, bubbles and crises are the result of domestic and foreign collaboration. Bankmoney is created by banks in a particular nation, but quite often in an international context, be it upon foreign demand, or for investing abroad. National financial hotspots tend to be amplified by inflows of foreign portfolio capital.[32] Finally, the effects are all the stronger to the extent that banks and nonbank financial intermediaries not only act as enablers of a financial bonanza, but also as actively involved speculative traders themselves.

Measuring overall asset price inflation has certainly not been done as consistently as recording the growth of monetary aggregates, but is basically not more cumbersome than measuring consumer price inflation, or GDP, both as possible benchmarks for growing volumes and prices in financial assets. The difference is that for the level of consumer prices the statistical offices have developed harmonized standards and routines for measuring and reporting. The legions of financial analysts, by contrast, produce a great variety of financial market indices, often difficult to compare, much less combine.

Independently, single trends in the prices of homes or stocks, or trading volumes of derivatives, are telling enough. In recent decades, the ratio of

---

[30] Eugene Fama, who is seen as the main originator of the efficient market hypothesis (Fama 1970; Fama et al. 1969), steadfastly rejects the idea of asset inflation.

[31] Aliber and Kindleberger (2015, pp. 78–103), Jordà et al. (2010, 2014), Gourinchas and Obstfeld (2012), Borio (2012), Duncan (2012), Schularick and Taylor (2009), Kick et al. (2015), Reinhart and Rogoff (2009), Kindleberger and Laffargue (1982), and Minsky (1982a, 1982b, 1986).

[32] Brunnermeier and Schnabel (2015).

financial assets to GDP grew across the board. For example, the value of US financial assets as a percentage of GDP was oscillating sideways in the post-war decades at around 450 % of GDP until 1979–1982, at which point they started taking off to reach over 1100 % in 2007 when the subprime bubble burst.[33] US financial assets under wealth management represented 50 % of GDP in 1946, reaching 240 % in 2014.[34] From 1980–2014, the aggregated average valuation of bonds, stocks and residential property in fifteen rich countries rose fourfold, while inflationary nominal GDP doubled or tripled.[35]

Real estate and housing prices in industrial countries ballooned until 2007. According to Shiller, *real* home prices in the USA rose by only 7 % in a hundred years from 1890 to 1997, but from then on until only 2006 by an incredible 85 %.[36] In all industrial countries from the late 1970s to the present day, nominal housing prices rose on average by fourteen times, ranging from three times in Germany to 21 times in Australia (except in Japan, where the housing bubble burst in the early 1990s, and the USA, Ireland and Spain where it burst in 2007).[37] On long-term average, the price–earnings ratio of US shares is at sixteen. At the height of the dotcom bubble from 1982 to 2000, according to Shiller 'the largest stock market boom ever', US shares traded at 47 times the earnings.[38]

A crisis is the bad time when impending damage actually occurs. What paves the way for it, in what is seen as the previous good times, is barely restrained bankmoney creation feeding inactive monetary assets as well as non-GDP financial investment, superimposing itself onto real investment and expenditure. The result is money overshoot, financial over-investment and over-indebtedness. It may be impossible to know exactly when a bubble will burst. But recognizing the formation of a bubble is entirely possible, on the basis of experience as well as analytical statistics which help to monitor growing disproportions and imbalances. The US subprime bubble was pos-sibly the most clearly spotted bubble ever, including continued media cover-

---

[33] Federal Reserve Statistical Release Z.1, 2102, Flow of Funds Accounts of the US. Flows and Outstandings. Board of Governors of the Federal Reserve System, Washington, DC. Compiled in J. Rutledge: http://rutledgecapital.com/2009/05/24/total-assets-of-the-us-economy-188-trillion-134xgdp. Thomson Datastream, Federal Reserve cit. *The Economist*, March 22, 2008. Trader's Narrative, November 7th, 2009. Other delimitations lead to somewhat lower levels, but same proportions, for example in Bhatia (2011, p. 8).

[34] Andrew Haldane, Bank of England, in a speech on large institutional investors, rep. in *FAZ*, April 8, 2014, 25.

[35] Deutsche Bank Markets Research (2014, pp. 8–33); OECD data www.data.oecd.org/gdp/gross-domestic-product-gdp.htm.

[36] Shiller (2015, p. 20).

[37] Jordà et al. (2014). *FAZ*, October 18, 2014, 32.

[38] Shiller (2015, pp. 3, 6).

age in the years prior to its collapse. The narrative that 'no one saw it coming' is simply not true. It may be a little closer to the truth that those directly involved—subprime lenders with government backing, as well as banking and finance beyond—did not want to leave the bonanza, while the Federal Reserve and the US government were partly not willing and partly not able to do something about it.[39]

Economics has never systematically addressed the question of financial carrying capacity, that is, the capacity to service financial claims without impairing real productivity and earned income, the question of how big the price volumes and rent claims of financial assets can grow in relation to GDP without becoming economically dysfunctional and a threat to current incomes and existing wealth. Two, three, four times GDP? Certainly not ten times, as in the USA at the onset of the crisis. As regards financial assets, economics seems to suggest you can never have too much of that good thing. That would be a mistake, because the claims of income-yielding assets (stocks, in a general sense) have to be satisfied from current income (flows), or by adding additional claims and debt. At a certain point, stocks risk becoming too big to be smoothly serviced by current flows; flows will not keep pace with the build-up of financial stocks.

Many scholars in the Keynesian world of thought now particularly refer to Minsky's financial instability theory. This is a cyclical model starting with a situation of relative stability. Stability eventually induces more risk-taking by ever more actors, resulting in accelerating expansion and growing instability, until reaching a point of implosion and contraction, leading back to the relative stability from where the game will start anew. The pattern can be seen as a variant of the model of rising expectations, in this case the expectation of rising returns on financial market investment. In Shiller there is a similar approach to a feedback theory of bubbles, based on self-propelling expectations, and resulting in the irrational exuberance of Ponzi processes.[40]

Minsky distinguishes three stages of risk-taking in the course of a financial cycle.[41] In the first stage, called hedge financing, investment is funded through current receipts from owned assets at relatively low debt levels. Debt is redeemed upon maturity, or revolved on a prudent basis of calculations. In the second stage of speculative financing, ever more debt is taken up, while maturing debt is rolled over rather than redeemed, supposedly justified by

---

[39] Cf. Mian and Sufi (2014).

[40] Shiller (2015, pp. 70–97).

[41] On the theory of financial cycles, as distinct and also independent from business cycles to a considerable extent, also cf. Debt and the financial cycle: domestic and global, in Bank for International Settlements, 84th Annual Report, Basel 2013/2014, pp. 65–83. Also see Rey (2013).

higher future receipts from current investment. The third stage, Ponzi financing, is the overheated endgame situation in a financial cycle. Actors resort to ever more leverage in acquiring financial assets, while maturing debt is serviced with still more debt—the typical untenable situation bound to result in the breakdown of the respective bonanza and ensuing bankruptcies.[42]

The Minsky model attributes recurrent financial instability to a cyclical pattern of financial investment behavior. The banks come in not as speculators themselves, but as financers only, which is inappropriate. Minsky is not explicit about whether he supposes banks to carry out their financing function as financial intermediaries or as money creators. He too does not reflect on the role of *primary* credit creation, bankmoney and debt accumulation, which is of course also the basis of *secondary* on-lending and investing of bankmoney.[43] His view of fractional reserve banking remains unclear—as is typical of Keynesianism as well as of post-monetarist neoclassical economics.

Minsky refers to the up and down of interest rates in the course of a cycle. But he does not reflect on the distortion of interest rates in a bonanza through instant cheap bankmoney leverage. Interest rates may go up, but far less than would be natural with restrained money creation, and would be necessary for choking self-propelling feedback loops in financial markets.

On one occasion, though, in connection with the final repeal of the Glass-Steagall Act on separate banking in the 1990s, Minsky expressly thought about restricting the power of banks to create credit by separating the services of account management and payments from their lending and investment business.[44] It would seem, however, that Minsky did not give further consideration to that idea which was heading in the right direction. Instead, he then promoted the idea of the state as the 'employer of last resort'. This is but another variant of the Keynesian concept of compensatory debt-funded government expenditure which is expected to result in growth and jobs—which may or may not be the case, but is bound over time to result in public over-indebtedness.

In whichever way one investigates banking and financial crises, one will find—if the money and banking system is given due consideration rather than being blanked out—that almost all *financial* causes of crises also have a common *monetary* cause, that is, an overshooting creation of primary bank credit and bankmoney. Bankmoney is the initial primary source of funding GDP-disproportionate financial assets. Together with secondary on-lending

---

[42] Minsky (1986, p. 206).
[43] Minsky (1982b, 1986, pp. 218, 223, 294).
[44] Kregel (2012).

it leads to over-investment and over-indebtedness which in turn will unavoidably precipitate crises. According to IMF data, economies affected by a banking and financial crisis will be underperforming for many years to come. On average, seven years after the beginning of a crisis they remain 10 % below their long-term path of economic growth.[45]

5.8 Over-indebtedness

Since bankmoney is credit-borne, it comes with a corresponding debt, and so does secondary credit. In parallel to inflation and asset inflation, indebtedness was increasing in recent decades in disproportion to GDP in all actor groups, except real economic companies. In the USA, for example, financial businesses were the least indebted private-sector group until the 1980s. Since then, however, they started to outpace non-financial firms and households and had become the biggest debtor of all when the subprime crisis set in, at over 100 % GDP. Households were reported as the second biggest private debtor group.[46]

Public debt tends to be given most attention. After the Second World War, the high levels of public debt were brought down to lower levels until the 1970s, not in absolute terms, but relative to GDP, thanks to high inflation and growth rates.[47] The debt ratios were much lower then, but began their rise to present-day exceptionally high levels in the 1970–1980s, with the most recent boost owed to crisis-borne deficits and bailing out the banking and financial industry.

As a percentage of GDP, public debt in 2014 was at 235 % in Japan, 95 % in Europe (including a great variance), 90 % in the USA and 55 % in China.[48] In relation to taxes, the public debt level is at about two to over three times the entire tax revenue, in the USA even 408 %, Greece 475 % and Japan 900 %.[49]

Besides government debt, underrating private debt would be a mistake. Private debt levels are of equal importance and combine with the public debt to the level of total national debt, including the state, the financial sector, firms and households. Total national debt to GDP is now highest at 690 %

---

[45] IWF 2009: World Economic Outlook. Available at http://www.imf.org/external/pubs/ft/weo/2009/01/pdf
[46] Data sources: Bureau of Economic Analysis, Federal Reserve Board; Turner (2015, pp. 64–87).
[47] Cf. Abbas et al. (2014).
[48] IMF data, Government finance, General government gross debt as percent of GDP. http://www.imf.org/external/pubs/ft/weo/2014/01/weodata/weoselgr.aspx
[49] Dorfman (2014).

in the Netherlands and Ireland, lowest at 265 % in the USA and Germany. On average, the total national debt to GDP in 2014 was 350 % in advanced economies and 180 % in emerging economies.[50]

We are supposed to have been in a 'debt supercycle' since the Second World War.[51] Whether this is now coming to an end we do not know, but we know that growing economically out of the malaise has become unlikely under today's more mature stages of industrialization. At the same time, the room for government maneuver has been shrinking, for example, regarding the options of fiscal stimulus, still more sovereign debt on top of the high levels in place, or interest rate trickery even in negative terrain.

As debt continues to grow, an increasing share of the public debtors' money is devoted to interest payments to the banking and financial industry. Estimating the ratio of total public debt service (all levels of government) to total tax revenue in OECD countries at between 5 and 25 % might not be entirely wrong.[52] The principal is habitually rolled over rather than paid back—which is, so to speak, the debt elephant in the room. Everybody knows about it, but is acting as though it was not present, while some are suggesting the presence of the debt elephant is irrelevant or even most welcome.

In a crisis, debt service is offset to a degree by lower interest levels. It remains a constrictive burden nonetheless since employment, income, tax revenue and inflation also tend to be lower in a crisis. Occasional attempts at financial retrenchment have so far been short-lived. In clientelistic democracies, regular debt deflation is bound to be given up sooner rather than later.

Over-investment and over-indebtedness can be defined in various ways. In any case, over-investment involves oversized volumes of financial assets, or oversized real capacities respectively; oversized, in that beyond a critical point they will deliver stagnant or declining returns on investment.

As regards over-indebtedness, and from the creditor's point of view, the decisive aspect is a debtor's ability to pay. From the debtor's point of view, over-indebtedness arises as soon as debt service is paid for at the expense of other expenditure necessary for maintaining the status quo, or by having to sell assets to the same end. Over-indebted actors thus suffer losses, shrinkage, declining standards and possibly insolvency. Proneness to crisis increases as financial assets and total debt become disproportionately detached from GDP, that is, detached from current income.

---

[50] Sources: McKinsey, Eurostat, cit. *FAZ*, 6 Feb. 2014, 15. Morgan Stanley, McKinsey, cit. *The Economist*, May 16, 2015, 20.

[51] Cf. BCA Research (2014), http://blog.bcaresearch.com/primer-on-the-debt-supercycle

[52] Bazot (2014).

As obvious as this is with regard to firms and households, many experts today, especially in the Keynesian world of thought, are reluctant to apply the explanation to public households, claiming that government finance is different. In 'modern money' theory, sovereign debt is even considered irrelevant, on the grounds that a state with its own currency and national central bank will always stay liquid and need not default on debt denominated in its own currency.[53] Hypothetically it may look that way; in the real world it looks like economic surrealism. Creditors will shy away from holding debt in a currency called into question. Such a country will lose external credit and trade, and also domestic credit to a degree. It will suffer currency devaluation and domestic inflation, thereby suffering domestic decline as well. As Roche has concluded: 'Although a sovereign currency issuer cannot be forced into a legal default, this does not mean their liabilities are always considered creditworthy.'[54]

There is no mechanical threshold at which over-indebtedness sets in, either for private or public actors. Initially, taking up debt procures options that would not be available otherwise. On the other hand, ever more debt-to-cashflow will increasingly restrict a debtor's free choices and their scope of action. According to an IMF study,

> a 10 percentage point increase in the initial debt-to-GDP ratio is associated with a slowdown in annual real per capita GDP growth of around 0.2 percentage points ... with higher levels of initial debt having a proportionately larger negative effect on subsequent growth.[55]

One US dollar of additional sovereign debt in the 1960s added 80 cents to American GDP, in the 1990s the effect was down to 30 cents, and to only 10 cents in the 2000s.[56] Seen like this, almost all old industrial states are now over-indebted. At the same time, they cannot significantly reduce expenditure and debt without harming the economy and the wealth of their nations in the short term. If public expenditure is about half GDP, a 1 % reduction in public expenditure will result in a 0.5 % decline in GDP.[57] Over time, increased private expenditure of firms and households may step in. But this will only

---

[53] For a summary and discussion of the MMT positions in question cf. Huber (2014b).

[54] Cullen Roche 2014: Can a sovereign currency issuer default? http://www.pragcap.com/can-a-sovereign-currency-issuer-default.

[55] Kumar and Woo (2010).

[56] Stelter (2015).

[57] Also see the analyses in IMF (2012, p. 42).

occur in the long term, and no clientele–democratic government is likely to survive the hard re-adaptation period in between.

The volume of sovereign bonds and bills is nothing but just another bubble, in fact the biggest bubble of all.[58] As is the case with every bubble, there is no pleasant way out. At already high levels of public debt, debt accumulation owed to deficit spending is a highly problematic element of contemporary economies.

Nowadays, most governments have interdicted themselves to resort to printing money. Banks are now doing this for governments, recklessly and basically without limit. They do it as long as they collectively believe in a government's ability and willingness to pay. If they reassess the situation one day, public finances and the entire economy are bound to collapse—as this was impending when the banks and bond markets triggered the euro debt crisis upon realizing that bailing them out was creating another surge in public debt, with the weakest debtor governments threatening to default.

Of late there have been attempts to learn more about critical thresholds of public debt. The 60 % debt-to-GDP threshold set for the euro member states was but an arbitrary convention, a snapshot of the state of affairs at the time. Recently, Reinhart/Rogoff identified a 90 % threshold for advanced economies and 60 % for emerging economies.[59]

The general pattern is fairly clear. Going into debt—no matter whether it is about firms, households or government—gives a boost if one starts from low debt levels and expends the money on mobilizing unused capacities and other untapped potential. Upon reaching critical levels, however, there is the threshold of financial carrying capacity when debt ceases to be beneficial so as to become a burden which reduces productive expenditure. In financial terms, the game is over at the latest when potential debtors have no margin left for additional debt. In real economic terms, the threshold is where additional debt no longer results in corresponding additions of economic output, so that debt increasingly exceeds and departs from output. This will result in inflation or asset inflation or a combination of both. If strong, both are harmful in their way. Asset inflation, in particular, takes an unearned toll on that output and furthers the formation of Ponzi spirals when debt services debt.

The bankmoney regime pushes over-investment and over-indebtedness more intrusively than previous monetary regimes. But the threshold

---

[58] Also see Deutsche Bank Markets Research (2014, pp. 6–33).
[59] Reinhart and Rogoff (2010, 2009, pp. 21, 224). Also cf. IMF (2012, p. 102), where a 100 % threshold is investigated.

problem of financial carrying capacity, the existence of critical limits to credit and debt, is not limited to the bank-led fractional reserve system. Violating tolerable systemic limits will always result in crises. Dealing with debt according to the motto 'In the long run we are all dead' is cynical, as teaching the irrelevance of sovereign debt is foolish. Living on debt beyond one's means will always be fool's gold.

5.9   Financial Market Failure

In real commodity markets, a supply curve and demand curve working in opposite directions is an evident assumption. By contrast, as emphasized by Shiller, rising asset prices and expectations of increasing returns and capital gains will induce rather than deter additional demand for expensive assets.[60] That is why, in many cases, volumes and prices of financial assets tend to grow or stagnate together. There is a positive feedback loop overriding the negative one, which is also at work, in that market participants certainly worry about too high levels of asset prices, but feel forced to carry on unless 'the music stops'. This is another example of a social trap, or prisoner's dilemma, where the rationally chosen option suggests behaving unreasonably, and the crowd intelligence of markets turns into crowd foolishness.

Adding fuel to the fire, modern money has no natural anchor of 'scarcity', no tie to a real value base such as productivity, or the potential of output at structural capacity. The bankmoney regime amplifies positive financial feedback loops so that in actual fact there is an in-built mechanism of continued market failure. There are short-term restrictions to the creation of bankmoney, but none over time (Sect. 4.8). In consequence, rather than reaching a self-limiting point of equilibrium, money and capital markets tend to overshoot. As Chesney concluded, 'financial markets are insatiable by nature'.[61] Under conditions of basically unrestrained bankmoney creation, expansionary lending and financial investment are set to cross critical lines. Since banks have immediate advantages in creating money, they will not stop doing so until the next crisis imposes involuntary and often brutal corrections.

Although banks are largely free to create as much money as suits them, they cannot give value to the money, for monetary value derives from productivity, from actual output. The farther the banking and financial industries try to escape that gravity, the harder the ensuing crash. But if one has the privilege

---

[60] Shiller (2015, esp. Chaps. 5 and 11).
[61] Chesney (2014, p. 25).

of creating additional money, being the first user and the first to benefit from the immediate advantage, and expecting the disadvantages to fall upon all at a later point in time, the conclusion, often against one's better judgment, is straightforward. Allowing banks to create the money on which they operate engenders a massive collision of interest—which, no wonder, is regularly resolved in the self-interest of the banking industry.

Neo-Austrians address the matter under the aspect of the Cantillon effect. In 1730, Richard Cantillon was the first to write about the extra profit of the producers and first users of money. Their additional expenditure was assumed to result in a concentrically spreading increase in the level of prices, eventually of production, and putting at a disadvantage the marginalized and those at the ends of the market chains.[62] Later on, other economists, among them D. Hume and J.St. Mill, also realized that the creation and first use of money followed by subsequent uses constitutes a sequence from privileged to disadvantaged use. Leaving the privilege of creation and first use of money to private rather than public bodies creates a situation of 'systemic inequity'.[63]

By exercising the monopoly of bankmoney, the money supply is determined by the banking sector. Maybe it is so that in a cyclical trough the credit business is a buyer's market in that banks chase customers rather than the reverse. In a cyclical upturn and boom, by contrast, the credit business is a supplier's market and customers clearly chase the banks and secondary financial intermediaries. Either way, the market demand for money is met by the banks selectively, and central bank cash and reserves are supplied reactively as a fraction of the proactive supply of bankmoney. Money and primary credit is thus a supplier's market (seller's market) rather than a demand market (buyer's market). In general, borrowers are on the short side.[64]

This also means that primary credit markets do not clear at an equilibrium price or interest rate. On the primary credit markets, the banks are deliberately setting the factual limits, or not setting such limits. In other words, prices, in this case interest rates, may reliably reflect the situation of demand and supply, in particular the market power of the supply and demand sides, but prices are neither right or wrong. Prices are what they are, actual prices, most often reflecting some sort of 'disequilibrium' or 'asymmetry' in terms of equilibrium economics.

---

[62] Richard Cantillon, 'Essai sur la Nature du Commerce en Général', 1730, first official publication in 1755; several re-editions, one by H. Higgs, http://oll.libertyfund.org/titles/285.

[63] Köhler (2015, pp. 11, 22–31, 37).

[64] Werner (2005, pp. 193, 195). Häring and Douglas (2012, p. 48).

5.10 Monetary Policy Failure

If markets do not get it right, are central banks not supposed to fulfill the task? Not officially, even if many people think so and things ought to be so. Central banks do not consider asset inflation and levels of indebtedness. Their official mission is the stability of consumer prices. How high or low an inflation rate will be considered to reflect 'stable prices' is arbitrary. In most currency areas the central bank's mission also includes supporting economic growth, employment and a government's economy policy as far as this is not at odds with consumer price stability.

Central banks have two pathways available for fulfilling their mission. One is monetary quantity policy, the other interest rate policy. According to the above finding, quantity policy should be the primary approach, but has in fact been suspended under present bankmoney conditions, while interest rate policy, the weaker lever anyway, is largely ineffective.

On account of the strong consumer price inflation in the 1960–70s, and influenced by Friedman-style monetarism of the time, the central banks of industrial nations tried to pursue monetary quantity policy until the mid-1980s. The idea was to restrain the overshooting growth of bankmoney and expand the money supply in relation to the economic growth potential, or, respectively, the economic capacity or factor utilization. The respective quantity target was thought to be attainable by imposing reserve positions. According to the predominant multiplier model, minimum reserves were supposed to determine the maximum multiple of bankmoney that the banks are able to create (Sect. 4.5).

Capacity-oriented monetary policy was basically the right idea. However, it was based on a false premise and thus turned out to be a complete failure. In consequence, central banks had to resort to short-term interest rate policy, which is a weak substitute for quantity policy. The false premise is easy to identify. In the present money system, the proactive and defining initiative is with the banking sector. Central banks just react to and refinance the banks. Banks do not multiply central bank money, but central banks refinance after the fact a fraction of the bankmoney that was created beforehand (Sects. 4.2–4.4).

Central banks today are limited to being mere refinancers of the banks, without controlling the volume of bank credit and thus the quantity of money. In a banking crisis, central banks simply continue to be refinancers of the banks, albeit on a much larger scale, keeping banks in trouble afloat. The minimum reserve requirements imposed by the central bank do not make a difference, except, perhaps, for the (relatively modest) amount of interest-borne seigniorage which the central bank is able to deliver to the treasury.

The reserve position fallacy was not officially admitted, but monetary quantity policy was in fact abandoned. From around 1990, central banks have stopped pretending to control the money supply. They have, however, thrown the baby out with the bathwater by downgrading the importance of the quantity of money, not officially, but again as a matter of fact. Central banks have completely shifted to short-term base rate policy, whereby the target is no longer the money supply but the inflation rate. The link between the money supply and inflation/asset-inflation has been 'removed', or made implicit, respectively.

Central bank interest rate policy—for good or ill—is just a contributory factor. The only interest rates a central bank can definitely pin down are its own. It cannot set interest rates in loan and asset markets. Interest rates are determined by the dominant players in those markets themselves. Insofar as the availability of money has an impact on this, it is linked to primary bank credit and secondary on-lending of bankmoney through financial intermediaries, not to central bank interest rates.

The core central bank interest rates are referred to as the base rate, sometimes also as the lead rate. Lead rates, however, do not take the lead in setting interest rates. Likewise, base rates, named after the money base, or base money M0 which includes cash and reserves, are not the 'basis' for the deposit and lending rates of bankmoney, as they are in no way fundamental to defining the entire structure and level of interest rates. Base rates are merely the lending rates of the central banks.

The conventional wisdom underlying monetary policy has it that there are transmission mechanisms that would transmit central bank impulses to the banks, and via the banks to the financial and real economic markets. How is that supposed to work? As regards quantity policy, the transmission is broken and has been reversed. The banking sector transmits its impulses onto the central bank.

With regard to interest rates, the situation is not really different. A base rate guideline such as the Taylor rule clearly suggests that central bank base rates follow the inflation rate rather than leading its way. The rule suggests that in response to a 1 % increase in inflation above the desired target rate, a central bank should increase its base rate by about 1.5 %; upon a 1 % decrease in inflation below target, the base rate should be cut by about 0.5 %. How this is supposed to correct a respective deviation from the inflation target is not obvious. Rather, it is a description of what central banks are doing anyway.

The interest rates a central bank can influence best are money market rates, particularly the overnight rates for interbank lending of reserves, such as the Fed Funds Rate or the EONIA in the euro area. It is often supposed that changes in central bank rates influence these interbank money market rates, but there is no mechanical link between the two. The more effective way for a central bank to influence interbank rates is to buy securities from banks (mostly treasury bonds) if the central bank wants to provide banks with additional reserves, which induces lower interbank rates; and to sell securities back to banks if the central bank wants to absorb excess reserves from the banks, which induces higher interbank rates. There is no doubt in this respect that central banks can effectively influence the interbank rate. It should be noted that this is an example of quantity policy rather than interest rate policy, an example of effectively influencing interest rates by controlling the quantities of money involved.

Explanations of a supposed transmission mechanism linking interbank rates to bank and capital market rates are rather far-fetched. Normally these explanations try to link short-term to long-term rates in a general way. The truly relevant subject here, however, is the difference between interest on a fractional amount of reserves, and deposit and lending interest on bankmoney.

There are four reasons why a transmission effect from central bank rates to the banking industry and the markets is implausible. Firstly, central bank interest rates have no short-term effect on banks' credit and deposit creation because the related bank demand for additional cash and reserves is price-inelastic. The facts that have been created proactively have thereafter to be fulfilled, regardless of the expense, although just fractionally. In the longer term, there may be some feedback, but it is unclear to what extent.

The reason for the uncertain effectiveness of base rates, secondly, lies in the fact that base rates affect reserves and cash amounting to only 2.5–3 % of bankmoney. In the USA the rate is somewhat higher, which is certainly more noticeable, but is not a true lever of control either. Base rates are comparatively low, and banks are paid deposit interest on the reserves at about half the base rate, which makes the actual base rate even lower. How should a refinancing rate on just 2.5 % or somewhat more of the bankmoney have a decisive transmission effect on the entire 100 % of bankmoney?

Thirdly, higher/lower base rates and interbank rates contribute transitorily to lower/higher profit margins of the banks. Whatever the central bank and interbank interest rate will be, however, it will not deter banks from creating additional bankmoney, because the lending interest and expected capital gains on the 100 % of bankmoney are normally much higher than central bank rates, interbank rates and deposit rates.

Fourthly, and as mentioned already, the central bank rates do not determine the spectrum of interest rates and the general level of interest. The latter is determined on the markets for financial and real economic capital. This is why open market buying of vulnerable sovereign bonds on a large scale (which, it should be noted, is quantity policy rather than interest rate policy) has proved to be the most effective measure of central bank policy with regard to supporting the market value of those bonds, thus stabilizing bank balance sheets as well as the interest rates at which sovereign bonds can successfully be offered by the treasuries.

Banks pretend that an increase in central bank rates forces them to raise their own lending interest. In fractional reserve banking, however, there is no immediate link between the interest rates of a central bank and those of the banks. If a central bank raises or cuts its rates, this does not exert immediate pressure on the banks to do likewise, and certainly not 1:1. The crucial point with fractional reserve banking is that banks can *avoid* refinancing costs on about 90 % (USA) to 97 % (EU) of bankmoney. But a rise in central bank rates is of course an excuse for the banks to raise their lending interest. Remarkably, they are not equally prompt to raise deposit interest; or to cut lending interest upon a cut in central bank interest.

It seems to contradict the thesis of minor importance of central bank rates that central bank rates serve as a reference for many banks in setting their own lending and deposit rates. Whatever is at work here—a need for the reduction of complexity, or habitual practices—it is about behavioral conventions. It looks like a market mechanism, but in actual fact this is not about price changes according to supply and demand, but about some contractual, administered link between banking interest and central bank interest.

In line with this assumption, many banks in the euro area, on an individual and voluntary basis, have adopted the practice of raising and cutting their overdraft rate in line with the interbank rate (EURIBOR) of three months previously. Similarly, interest payments on mortgages are often contractually linked to the central bank's policy rate. Behavioral rules like this may help the banks to avoid annoying queries, and they contribute to believing in a mechanical 1:1 link between the rates on reserves and the rates on bankmoney—a price link that only exists by way of contractual price administration, not through markets.

What central banks really and effectively can do is create central bank money for refinancing banks on the banks' demand. Rather than characterizing central banks as the *lender of last resort* to banks, it might be more honest to call them the *anytime refinancer* of the banks, regularly in good times, and all the more so in times of crisis when central banks now routinely implement quantitative easing, that is flooding the banks with reserves, or even acting as a *dealer of last resort* in threatened financial assets, thereby possibly ending up as a kind of bad bank of the banking sector.[65]

---

[65] Cf. Mehrling (2011, p. 132).

If a bubble bursts and central banks step in to save threatened assets, this delays rather than solves the problem, resulting in more of the same, that is, additional credit and debt, in particular more central bank book liabilities and additional public debt, rather than reducing them to levels more compatible with GDP and actual economic productivity. Expectations of stabilizing threatened assets or debt, and kickstarting economic recovery will however be met insufficiently, simply because there are still too high levels of toxic assets and undeflated debt.

For sure, billions of asset value had to be written off in the subprime crisis 2007–2009 and the ensuing sovereign debt crisis of a number of euro countries. Nevertheless, bank bail-outs by governments and continued bank-aid by central banks (quantitative easing, emergency credit, non-settled inter-central bank liabilities) have saved most of the overshoot, that is a glut of liquid money, hypertrophic financial assets and, most importantly for the real economy, public and private debtors being strongly hampered by their unabated debt burden. The instructive case in point is the Japanese economy ever since Japan's real estate bubble burst in the beginning of the 1990s, driving public indebtedness above 235 % of GDP, after breakneck credit and money expansion during the 1970–1980s.[66]

The ostensible purpose of quantitative easing in combination with extremely low and even negative central bank rates is to be an indirect economic stimulus which may also help raise inflation to the notorious 2 % target. However, in reality the measures fail to meet these objectives, while they are clearly supporting financial assets and debt, also including over-indebted governments and their sovereign bonds that would otherwise be subject to strong losses in market value. The ensuing soaring interest rates would make it impossible for affected governments to refinance. This in turn might trigger the financial meltdown that has been averted so far. Over the years, however, the counter-intentional flipside of such desperado policies of zero and negative interest are becoming evident, especially in the form of shrinking margins even in 'boring banking', and too low revenues for example in insurance, including real losses for middle- and lower-class savers. Central banks are thus in train to checkmate themselves.

5.11 Bankmoney is Unsafe

Most people know from hearsay that deposits in a bank are not really safe. Anyone who had forgotten was reminded by the closure and impending bail-in of Cyprus banks in 2013. Normally, customers do not worry because they

---

[66] Iwata (2008, p. 323).

experience no difficulty transferring bankmoney or cashing bankmoney out. If, however, a bank is in trouble, its deposits are at stake too.

As a reaction to Black Friday and the Great Depression in the 1930s, and admitting to the non-safety of bankmoney, various schemes of deposit insurance and government guarantees have been introduced. In the USA, the Federal Deposit Insurance Corporation, a state body, guarantees deposits up to $250,000, while in Europe governments promise to stand bail for €100,000, or £75,000 and £150,000 for joint accounts under the Financial Services Compensation Scheme in the UK.

Such schemes help to reassure customers. But deposit insurance funds account for something between 0.1 % and 1.7 % of eligible deposits, little more than a fig leaf. When it comes down to it in a bank run, those insurance funds are insufficient to bail out the deposits in a large bank or a larger number of banks. At the critical moment, banks never have enough reserves and insurance. Instead, private insurers, for example emitters of credit default swaps, will go bankrupt too.

Government guarantees have never been tested, luckily, in a general banking meltdown. During the recent crisis, most people have preferred to believe rather than test their government's reassuring promises. The test was averted by saving the entire banking industry at public expense and much increased government debt.

The money of customers in a bank will never be safe as long as the money is a balance sheet position of bank debt, rather than being a customer asset in its own right off the banks' balance sheet, like having coins in the pocket, notes in the wallet, or financial assets in a separate securities account that may be managed by a bank, but is not itself a bank asset or bank liability.

Unsafe bankmoney is apparently not seen as the most important monetary problem. It is nonetheless a highly telling one. The mere existence of deposit insurance and government guarantees proves bankmoney to be unstable and unsafe by its very nature. How can a monetary system be stable and reliable if even the existence of the money is unreliable?

The state guarantee on money reflects the state-backed regime of bankmoney, in contrast to full chartalism (Sect. 3.4). That regime has to a large extent ceded monetary sovereignty to the banks as a private privilege, including the privatization of profits and seigniorage-like extra margin gains, whereas the regime socializes losses, and makes governments unilaterally dependent on banks and financial markets. The latter, rather than exerting monetary and financial 'discipline', are more reckless and undisciplined than most governments would have dared to be.

Finally, the non-safety of money also reflects the non-segregation of customer money (Sect. 4.4) and the fact that bankmoney is not the safe and positive property of the customers which it is supposed to be by any economic, legal and moral standard.

5.12 The Distributional Bias of Bankmoney

Inequality in old industrial welfare states rose significantly during the decades before the financial crisis of 2008. The trend has been inherent in the present regime of bankmoney since around 1980. Expanding financial income at the expense of real earned income can actually be seen as the main result, if not purpose, of bankmoney-based finance.

According to the facts, the income distribution between labor and capital, which tended to be in favor of earned income during the pre- and post-war real growth periods until the 1970s, has shifted towards an increasing share of capital revenue since the 1980s. 'Shareholder value' was the last rallying cry of supply side economics. More specifically, it proved to be geared towards investment banking and global casino capitalism more than towards investment in real production and consumption.

In Sect. 4.11 on the quasi-seigniorage of bankmoney, the sequence from the privileged creation and first use of money to subsequent disadvantaged uses has been addressed (Cantillon effect). That effect has become significantly stronger with globalized financialization and the GDP-disproportionate take-off of investment banking and finance. This has brought about above-average salaries throughout the banking and financial industries, also including lunatic salaries and bonuses in investment banking, financial businesses and other strands of global corporate top management. Financial capital revenues have in general been on the rise, the middle classes have been struggling to maintain their standard of living, while earned income and household purchasing power in lower social strata have been declining.[67] The distributional structure of financial and earned income from the late 1970s to 2008, and the continued crisis since then, shows the same extreme pattern as in the decades leading up to Black Friday 1929 and the Great Depression of the 1930s.[68]

The mechanism underlying these developments is not difficult to make out. All expenditure in a period of time has to be funded either by current

---

[67] For example, see Atkinson (2015), Piketty (2013), Atkinson et al. (2011), and Kaplan and Rauh (2009).

[68] Atkinson (2015, pp.17, 180) and Bakija et al. (2010).

income or by additional credit and debt taken up during that time, or, individually, by liquidation of assets. Financial and earned incomes add up to 100 %. If financial assets grow disproportionately to GDP, an increasing share of income from whatever source will have to be allotted to financial income, to the detriment of earned income. A build-up of monetary and financial assets disproportionate to GDP thus creates a distributional bias in favor of financial income, resulting in a reduced share of earned income. Lower interest rates dampen the effect without setting it off. The more financial assets grow GDP-disproportionately, the bigger the share that goes into unproductive non-GDP transactions which nonetheless demand to be serviced by the flow of actual income and additional debt.

5.13 From c. 1980 to 2008: The Great Immoderation

The complacent half of experts and politicians considered the period from the 1980s to the onset of the crisis 2008 as the time of 'Great Moderation'. This referred to the perception of the long-term decline in growth rates in the USA (and old industrial societies in general), including reduced amplitudes in the business cycle, prompting premature ideas of such cycles fading away, and low inflation and low interest rates in comparison with the preceding period.

Not included in such considerations were the effects of globalization (intensified structural change and international low-cost competition) and growing levels of indebtedness and external imbalances, the famous double deficit (which was promptly declared by some augurs to be irrelevant), as well as asset inflation replacing inflation, which was seen as the most pleasant of recent experiences, while repeatedly turning a blind eye to the recurrent experience of financial crises in the USA and elsewhere across the globe.[69] The dotcom bubble of the late 1990s was anything but an expression of great moderation.

Whitewashing the years from around 1980 to 2008 as a period of Great Moderation is another fallacy. It might be more appropriate to view that period as one of Great Immoderation, characterized by compensating for a number of real deficits by way of monetary and financial overshoot. A number of empirical core indicators of this have been discussed in previous sections of this book:

- The supersession of chartal money (coins and notes) by bankmoney and subsequently by MMF shares

---

[69] For a critical discussion of the Great Moderation see Quiggin (2010, pp. 5–34).

- Overshooting money supply in relation to the growth of GDP
- The GDP-disproportionate growth of investment banking and the financial industry, and the growing ratio of financial assets to GDP
- The growing ratio of public and private debt to GDP
- An increasingly unequal distribution of income and wealth, including the bias towards financial income at the expense of earned income
- An end to low unemployment from the second half of the 1970s and a rising level of structural unemployment with each downturn in the business cycle ever since, as well as
- The famous double deficit of the USA, that is, a public sector and foreign sector deficit at the same time.

These trends all appear to follow either a transsecular S-curve or a multi-decade cyclical trend, passing from their post-Depression and post-World War II emergence to a fulminant takeoff around 1980 until the onset of the crisis in 2008, and now somewhat descending from that zenith. Looked at soberly, the period from around 1980 to 2008 was a time of big bubble formations, including various housing bubbles, stock market bubbles, derivatives bubbles and the sovereign debt bubble in almost all old industrial countries.

The bankmoney regime is designed for private privilege and self-enrichment, less often by financing productive investment, more often nowadays by the formation of financial assets whose sheer volume has become counterproductive.

5.14 The Question of Lawfulness of Bankmoney

In recent years, lawyers and campaigners critical of banking have questioned the legal status of bankmoney. According to one argument, bankmoney is not real money, which is to say, not legal tender, but a bank-issued substitute of arbitrary validity. A related second argument describes bankmoney as a void promise, at least in the sense of not conferring positive property on the respective holder.

Some have concluded from the latter aspect that bankmoney, rather than being 'something' could therefore be said to be 'nothing'. Borrowers from a bank should not hesitate to go on 'debt strike', refusing to pay back that 'nothing'. A less radical conclusion states that, if bankmoney does not confer seizable property, then no value-equivalent property has to be returned except the bankmoney itself. This does not justify 'debt strike', but is a verdict against foreclosure or other compulsory executions.

So far, such lines of argumentation have not become widely shared legal opinion. In view of fractional reserve banking as a common practice, and given the existence of numerous regulations on banking, contracts, accounting, payment services and so forth, and the remarkable fact that government bodies today demand to be paid in bankmoney rather than legal tender, it would seem impossible to prove bankmoney unlawful.

Nonetheless, the legal foundations of bankmoney are shaky and those lawyers and campaigners have a point. Even if there are many regulations presupposing the existence of bankmoney, there is no law which expressly constitutes bankmoney and entitles banks to create money for regular public circulation.

By tradition, there is a law in every country which ascribes coinage to the state. Nowadays there is also another such law in every country which ascribes the right to issue banknotes to the central bank. Coins and banknotes are declared to be legal tender. There is no law, however, on the legal status of bankmoney. It simply exists without being legal tender. Similarly, the legal status of central bank reserves is uneven. In some countries, such as Switzerland, central bank reserves are legal tender, in other currency areas, such as the eurozone, they are not.

It is quite remarkable that there is no legal foundation for bankmoney, and almost none for central bank reserves. These monies constitute the modern money system after all, whereby bankmoney has the lead and determines the entire money supply. The situation is owed to the ambivalence of partial chartalism, that is, the state-backed rule of private bankmoney. Sooner or later the ambivalence will need to be overcome—either by stripping the banking sector of its illegitimate monetary powers, or by entirely stripping the state of its monetary sovereignty to the benefit of unimpaired banking rule.

As regards the supposed 'nothingness' of bankmoney, one should not wilfully add to the existing ambiguities. Bankmoney, like all modern fiat money, may be 'nothing' in terms of material, but as an informational unit bankmoney clearly gives fully valid purchasing power to the banks and all successive bearers of bankmoney. Or, as Soddy put in an aphorism: 'Money is the nothing you get for something before you can get anything.'[70] Similarly, bad loans and other irrecoverable claims on the 'nothing' of bankmoney cannot be interpreted as meaning 'nothing' to an affected bank, in the sense of not representing an actual loss. If asset positions have to be written off, this of course *is* a loss in the profit and loss account and the balance sheet. If a bank incurs too many losses at once it will be bankrupt.

---

[70] Soddy (1934, p. 24).

While it is clear that bankmoney gives purchasing power, and that default-ing on bank credit can ruin a bank, two other legal questions remain ambigu-ous, namely, the property right of bankmoney, and the question of what is paid out to whom when a bank makes a payment. Consider any demand or savings deposit. On the surface, the deposit is the property of the depositor, in other words the customer. But what do customers actually possess? They possess but a promise of their bank to pay out cash or transfer the deposit on demand of the customer. The cash, however, unless paid out, is owned by the bank, as much as the reserves involved (whereby central banks retain a reser-vation of title on central bank money).

With regard to the duties and rights of lenders and borrowers, civil law stipu-lates that the lender must divest a respective item or position (amount of money) from their property, and transfer it into the possession of the lender. The bor-rower has to pay interest on the loan and redeem the principal. In terms of accountancy this clearly involves a swap of lender assets, that is a liquid money position (going to the borrower) being swapped for a claim on money (from the borrower). But this is not exactly what really happens in reserve banking.

The banks actually do pay out a corresponding amount of money, smaller amounts in cash, larger amounts in reserves to the recipient bank. This now is the salient point: in contrast to cash, the reserves in a bank's central bank account are not transferred to the customer, but to the customer's bank, while the customer gets but a promissory credit entry, that is bankmoney instead of central bank money.

A bank thus actually divests reserves from its property, not however to the respective customer, but to the recipient bank. Creating claims against and liabilities to customers in bankmoney, but not having to pay out the full amount of money involved *to the customers*, does not appear to be what civil law actually stipulates: a 1:1 divestment of an item by the lender and its full transfer to the borrower. Seen from this angle, bankmoney accounting is in a way 'fictitious' indeed.[71]

Banking lawyers will argue that customers may not receive reserves, that is, central bank money (legal tender), but they receive a valid equivalent amount of bankmoney. Bankmoney, however, according to the 'outside–inside' the-sis (Sect. 4.14), does not have the same status and properties as 'high-powered' central bank money, especially with regard to safety and validity when a bank or the entire sector is in trouble. This is not far-fetched given the frequency of banks being in trouble and the proneness of the bankmoney regime to asset and debt bubbles and financial crises.

---

[71] Cf. Schemmann (2011b, pp. 16–25, 2015).

5.15 The Disregarded Constitutional Dimension of the Monetary Order

In discussing the dysfunctions of reserve banking, reconnecting to chartalism as expounded in Chap. 3 will finally round off the picture.

In terms of Currency versus Banking, the contemporary regime of bankmoney is a near-complete Banking regime. Its ingredients of Currency teaching have been ever further driven back. The reality of chartalism has been one of partial or incomplete chartalism for over a hundred years now, in fact a state-backed and central bank-backed rule of bankmoney. Of the three sovereign monetary prerogatives—the currency, the official means of payment (money) and the seigniorage from the creation of money—only the principle of nation-state currencies is still in place, even though private, globally transferrable currencies and new money surrogates may yet grow to become another challenge in the future. The second and third monetary prerogative, that is money creation and the benefits thereof (seigniorage), have almost completely been left to the banking industry.

This represents a worrying disregard of the traditions and spirit of state law, or constitutional law as in the USA, where Article 1, Section 8 of the US Constitution from 1787 assigns 'the power to … coin money' to Congress. Later on, starting in 1861, for financing the American Civil War, the government issued US Treasury notes in parallel with private banknotes. From 1913, however, Treasury notes were largely phased out for private Federal Reserve notes, while banknotes from individual private banks were no longer admitted. The Federal Reserve itself is a kind of private–public hybrid. The question of whether the constitutional 'power to coin money' includes printing paper notes became ambivalent again, and applying that power to creating credits on account has never been a topic under debate. It definitely should have been.

The regime of bankmoney deprives the state of its sovereign monetary prerogatives and renders government finance dependent on banks and bond markets, and subject to extortionate arm-twisting on their side, to a much higher degree than would otherwise be the case. At the same time, the bankmoney regime is the major source of the dysfunctions discussed in the preceding paragraphs, in that the root cause of those dysfunctions is out-of-control bankmoney creation, restrained neither by the markets nor the central banks.

The constitutional aspect of the money order is of utmost importance. Sovereign money makes for the monetary and financial sovereignty of a nation-state. The monetary prerogatives are of no lesser importance for the territorial and functional integrity of a state than other sovereign prerogatives such as legislation, public administration, jurisdiction, taxation and the use of force. Modern states need a comprehensive monetary prerogative too, that is, full chartalism.

Among earlier economists, it was particularly Irving Fisher who had an understanding of the existence of money as a sovereign prerogative of constitutional importance.[72] Ceding monetary prerogatives to the banking industry is like entrusting private lobbyists with lawmaking; like having a parallel private administration managing the same thing that the government tries to manage, but not being accountable in imposing its private preferences; like allowing a state's legal system to be superseded by another, such as Sharia law; or like replacing the police and military with private militias and mercenary forces—all of which is actually happening to various degrees in various countries. If left unchecked, this is bound to put end to the liberal rule of law based on civil rights and separation of powers.

In ancient society, money was the weapons-defended prerogative of kings and warlords. In the middle ages, coinage was the feudal prerogative of high-ranking secular and ecclesial principalities. With modernization, money became sovereign money, the legally, sometimes even constitutionally codified prerogative of nation-states.

A modern democratic state ought to be keen on its monetary prerogatives of the currency, money and seigniorage, in the same way as it ought to defend its other sovereign prerogatives. The kind of money that will prevail—sovereign or private, debt-free or interest-bearing—depends on prevailing power relations. Those who have the power to impose their concept of money will do so. But a monetary regime also needs to be economically functional and acceptable to a broader range of clientele. It will not endure if it only serves the self-interest of the money issuers and financial oligarchs, but is dysfunctional with regard to the safety of money, the value of money, and the stability of the financial system, affecting the real economy and everybody's living standard, except that of the super-rich. Legitimacy in modern society, in the words of Jefferson, is based on 'equal rights for all; special privileges to none', including achievement rather than sinecure.[73] For banks to exert monetary functions is an illegitimate private privilege, not a legitimate right, the more so as the bankmoney regime works in dysfunctional and unjust ways.

---

[72] Fisher (1935, p. 241).
[73] De Fremery (1960–1976).

The bankmoney regime as it stands today is not far from being a 'free banking' regime of a global oligopoly of huge banking corporations which would operate on the basis of denationalized money, or on the basis of one or two privileged national reserve currencies under their defining influence. Even then the banking corporations and financial markets need the law and institutional arrangements of nation-states supporting them. Ultimately, the banking industry, beyond having captured the monetary prerogatives, would also have to capture the institutional and legal structures of existing states. This certainly makes intriguing stuff for dystopian fiction. But could it be real? Presumably not. It is telling that real bankers do not really want to be that 'free', on their own and fully exposed to the risks and losses of what they are doing. Private money without state backing is unlikely to survive its own crises. The banking industry feels quite comfortable with the present situation of state-guaranteed private bankmoney.

References

Abbas, S.M. Ali, Laura Blattner, Mark De Broeck, Asmaa El-Ganainy, and Malin Hu. 2014. Sovereign Debt Composition in Advanced Economies: A Historical Perspective. *IMF Working Paper*, WP/14/162, September 2014. Washington, DC: IMF, Fiscal Affairs Department.

Anderson, Andy, Ronnie Morrison. 2014. *Moving On*. Helensburgh: Scottish Monetary Reform. www.scottishmonetaryreform.org.uk.

Aliber, Robert Z., and Charles P. Kindleberger. 2015 [1978]. *Manias, Panics, and Crashes. A History of Financial Crises*, 7th edn. New York: Basic Books.

Arslanalp, Serkan, and Takahiro Tsuda. 2012. Tracking Global Demand for Advanced Economy Sovereign Debt. *IMF Working Paper*, WP/12/284.

Atkinson, Anthony B. 2015. *Inequality. What Can Be Done?* Cambridge, MA: Harvard University Press.

Atkinson, Anthony B., Thomas Piketty, and Emmanual Saez. 2011. Top Incomes in the Long Run of History. *Journal of Economic Literature* 49(1): 3–71.

Baba, Naohiko, Robert N. McCauley, and Srichander Ramaswamy. 2009. US Dollar Money Market Funds and Non-US Banks. *BIS Quarterly Review* March 2009: 65–81.

Bakija, Jon, Adam Cole, and Bradley T. Heim. 2010. Jobs and Income Growth of Top Earners and the Causes of Changing Income Inequality: Evidence from U.S. Tax Return Data. *Department of Economics Working Paper* 2010–24. Williamstown: Williams College.

Barrdear, John, Michael Kumhof. 2016. The macroeconomics of central bank issued digital currencies, Bank of England. *Staff Research Paper*, No. 605, July 2016.

Bazot, Guillaume. 2014. Financial Consumption and the Cost of Finance: Measuring Financial Efficiency in Europe (1950–2007). *Research Papers*. Paris School of Economics.

Bhatia, Ashok Vir. 2011. Consolidated Regulation and Supervision in the United States. *IMF Working Paper*, No. 23, 2011.

Bjerg, Ole. 2014c. *Making Money. The Philosophy of Crisis Capitalism*. London: Verso Books.

———. 1982b. The Financial Instability Hypothesis. In *Financial Crises. Theory, History, and Policy*, ed. C.P. Kindleberger, and J.-P. Laffargue, 13–39. Cambridge: Cambridge University Press.

Blinder, Alan S. 2013. *After the Music Stopped: The Financial Crisis, the Response, and the Work Ahead*. New York: Penguin.

Borio, Claudio. 2012. The Financial Cycle and Macroeconomics: What Have We Learnt? *BIS Working Papers,* No. 395, December 2012. Basel: Bank for International Settlements.

Broadbent, Ben. 2016. *Central Banks and Digital Currencies*. Speech at the London School of Economics documented by the Bank of England. http://www.bankofengland.co.uk/publications/Pages/speeches/default.aspx.

Brunnermeier, Markus K., and Isabel Schnabel. 2015. Bubbles and Central Banks. Historical Perspectives. *Working Paper*. Princeton and Mainz University, 21 January 2015. http://scholar.princeton.edu/sites/default/files/markus/files/bubbles_centralbanks_historical_0.pdf

Chesney, Marc.2014. *Vom Großen Krieg zur permanenten Krise*. Zürich: Versus Verlag.

De Fremery, Robert. 1960–1976. *Rights Versus Privileges*. San Anselmo, CA: Provocative Press.

Deutsche Bank Markets Research. 2014. *Long-Term Asset Return Study*. London: Deutsche Bank Markets Research.

Dorfman, Jefrey. 2014. Forget Debt as a Percentage of GDP, It's Really Much Worse. *Forbes*, December 7. http://www.forbes.com/sites/jeffreydorfman/2014/07/12/forget-debt-as-a-percent-of-gdp-its-really-much-worse.

Dow, Sheila, Guðrún Johnsen, and Alberto Montagnoli. 2015. A Critique of Full Reserve Banking. *Sheffield Economic Research Paper Series*, No. 2015008, March 2015.

Duncan, Richard.2012. *The New Depression: The Breakdown of the Paper Money Economy*. Hoboken, NJ: Wiley.

Fama, Eugene.1970. Efficient Capital Markets. A Review of Theory and Empirical Work. *Journal of Finance* 25: 383–417.

Fama, Eugene, Lawrence Fisher, Michael C. Jensen, and Richard Roll.1969. The Adjustment of Stock Prices to New Information. *International Economic Review* 10(1): 1–21.

Financial Crisis Inquiry Committee. 2011. *Report of the National Commission on the Causes of the Financial and Economic Crisis in the United States*. Washington, DC: US Government Printing Office.

Fisher, Irving.1911. *The Purchasing Power of Money; Its Determination And Relation To Credit, Interest and Crises.* New York: The Macmillan Company.

Fontana, Giuseppe. 2000. Post Keynesians and Circuitists on Money and Uncertainty. *Journal of Post Keynesian Economics* 23(1): 27–48.

———. 1935. *100%-money.* New Haven: Yale University. Reprinted in William J. Barber et al., eds. 1996. *The Works of Irving Fisher.* London: Pickering & Chatto.

Friedman, Milton.1991. *Monetarist Economics.* Oxford, UK: Basil Blackwell.

———.1992. *Money Mischief.* New York: Harcourt Brace Jovanovich.

Gourinchas, Pierre-Olivier, and Maurice Obstfeld. 2012. Stories of the Twentieth Century for the Twenty-First. *American Economic Journal: Macroeconomics* 4 (January):226–265.

Häring, Norbert, and Niall Douglas. 2012. *Economists and the Powerful. Convenient Theories, Distorted Facts, Ample Rewards.* London: Anthem Press.

Hayek, Friedrich A. von. 1976. *Denationalisation of Money.* London: Institute of Economic Affairs.

Hilton, Adrian. 2004. Sterling Money Market Funds, Bank of England. *Quarterly Bulletin* Summer 2004: 176–182.

Huber, Joseph. 1998. *Vollgeld.* Berlin: Duncker & Humblot.

———. 2014a [2010]. *Monetäre Modernisierung,* 4 bearb. Marburg: Metropolis.

Hudson, Michael. 2006. Saving, Asset-Price Inflation, and Debt-Induced Deflation. In *Money, Financial Instability and Stabilization Policy,* eds. L. Randall Wray, and Matthew Forstater, 104–124. Cheltenham: Edward Elgar.

———.2012. *The Bubble and Beyond.* Dresden: Islet Verlag.

Huerta de Soto, Jesús. 2009. *Money, Bank Credit, and Economic Cycles,* 2nd edn. Auburn, AL: Ludwig von Mises Institute (1st edn. 2006).

Humphrey, Thomas M. 1984. Algebraic Quantity Equations before Fisher and Pigou. *Economic Review of the Federal Reserve Bank of Richmond* 70(5): 13–22.

IMF. 2012. *World Economic Outlook October 2012, Coping with High Debt and Sluggish Growth.* Washington, DC: International Monetary Fund.

Independent Commission on Banking. 2011. *Interim Report. Consultation on Reform Options (Vickers Report).* London, April 2011. http://bankingcommission.independent.gov.uk/bankingcommission

Iwata, Kazumasa. 2008. The Role of Money and Monetary Policy in Japan. In *The Role of Money: Money and Monetary Policy in the Twenty-First Century,* eds. Andreas Beyer, and Lucrezia Reichlin, 321–330. Frankfurt: European Central Bank.

Jackson, Andrew, and Ben Dyson. 2012b. *Modernising Money. Why Our Monetary System is Broken and How It Can be Fixed.* London: Positive Money.

Jordà, Òscar, Moritz Schularick, and Alan M. Taylor. 2010. Financial Crises, Credit Booms, and External Imbalances. 140 Years of Lessons. *NBER Working Papers,* No. 16567, December 2010.

———. 2014. The Great Mortgaging: Housing Finance, Crises, and Business Cycles. *NBER Working Papers,* No. 20501, Sep 2014.

Kaplan, Steven N., and Joshua Rauh. 2009. Wall Street and Main Street: What Contributes to the Rise in the Highest Incomes? *The Review of Financial Studies* 23(3): 1004–1050.

Kick, Thomas, Thilo Pausch, and Benedikt Ruprecht. 2015. The Winner's Curse. Evidence on the Danger of Aggressive Credit Growth in Banking. *Bundesbank Discussion Paper*, No 32/2015.

Kindleberger, Charles P., and J.-P. Laffargue, eds. 1982. *Financial Crises. Theory, History, and Policy*. Cambridge: Cambridge University Press.

Köhler, Michael. 2015. *Hume's Dilemma. Das Geld und die Verfassung*. Berlin: Duncker & Humblot.

Kregel, Jan. 2012. Minsky and the Narrow Banking Proposal. *Public Policy Brief*, No. 125. Levy Institute of Bard College, 4–8.

Kumar, Manmohan S., and Jaejoon Woo. 2010. Public Debt and Growth. *IMF Working Papers* WP/10/174, Washington, DC.

Laeven, Luc, and Fabian Valencia. 2008. Systemic Banking Crises. A New Database. *IMF Working Paper* WP 08/224.

Liikanen Report. 2012. *High-Level Expert Group on Reforming the Structure of the EU Banking Sector*, Chaired by Erkki Liikanen. Final Report. Brussels: EU-Commission.

Mai, Heike. 2015. Money market funds, an economic perspective. *DB Research, EU Monitor Global Financial Markets*, February 26, 2015.

Mehrling, Perry. 2011. *The New Lombard Street. How the Fed Became the Dealer of Last Resort*. Princeton: Princeton University Press.

Mellor, Mary. 2016. *Debt or Democracy. Public Money for Sustainability and Social Justice*. London: Pluto Press.

Mian, Atif, and Amir Sufi. 2014. *House of Debt*. Chicago, IL: University of Chicago Press.

Minsky, Hyman P. 1982a. *Can 'It' Happen Again? Essays on Instability and Finance*. Armonk, NY: M.E. Sharpe.

——— 1982b. The Financial Instability Hypothesis. In Financial Crises. Theory, History, and Policy, eds. C.P. Kindleberger, and J.-P. Laffargue, 13–39. Cambridge: Cambridge University Press.

———. 1986. *Stabilizing an Unstable Economy*. New Haven: Yale University Press.

Pettifor, Ann. 2014. Out of thin air—Why banks must be allowed to create money. 25 June 2014. http://www.primeeconomics.org/?p=2922

Peukert, Helge. 2012. *Die große Finanzmarkt- und Staatsschuldenkrise*, 4 überarb Auflage. Marburg: Metropolis.

Piketty, Thomas. 2013. *Le capital au XXI siècle*. Paris: Éditions du Seuil. Engl. 2014. *Capital in the Twenty-First Century*, Cambridge, MA: The President and Fellows of Harvard College.

Quiggin, John. 2010. *Zombie Economics. How Dead Ideas Still Walk Among Us*. Princeton, NJ: Princeton University Press.

Reinhart, Carmen M., and Kenneth S. Rogoff. 2009. *This Time is Different. Eight Centuries of Financial Folly*. Princeton: Princeton University Press.

———. 2010. Growth in a Time of Debt. *NBER Working Paper* 15639, Cambridge, MA, January 2010.

Rey, Hélène. 2013. Dilemma not Trilemma. The Global Financial Cycle and Monetary Policy Independence. *Proceedings of the Jackson Hole Economic Policy Symposium*. Federal Reserve Bank of Kansas City, August 2013, 286–333.

Rossi, Sergio.2001. *Money and Inflation A New Macroeconomic Analysis*. Cheltenham: Edward Elgar.

Ryan-Collins, Josh, Tony Greenham, Richard Werner, and Andrew Jackson.2012. *Where Does Money Come From? A Guide to the UK Monetary and Banking System*, 2 edn. London: New Economics Foundation.

Schemmann, Michael. 2011b. *The Euro ist Still the Strongest Currency Around. Analyses and Solutions for the Money and Sovereign Debt Crisis of the 2010s*. IICPA Publications.

———. 2015. *Putting a Stop to Fictitious Bank Accounting*. IICPA Publications. http://www.iicpa.com

Schularick, Moritz, and Alan M. Taylor.2009. Credit Booms Gone Bust: Monetary Policy, Leverage Cycles, and Financial Crises 1780–2008. *American Economic Review* 102(2): 1029–1061.

Shiller, Robert J. 2015. *Irrational Exuberance*. Revised and expanded 3rd edn. Princeton, NJ: Princeton University Press.

Soddy, Frederick. 1934. *The Role of Money. What it should be, contrasted with what it has become*. London: George Routledge and Sons Ltd..

Stelter, Daniel. 2015. Börsencrash. Jetzt starten die Helikopter. *Manager Magazin*, August 24.

Turner, Adair. 2015. *Between Debt and the Devil. Money, Credit and Fixing Global Finance*. Princeton: Princeton University Press.

van Dixhoorn, Charlotte.2013. *Full Reserve Banking. An Analysis of Four Monetary Reform Plans*. Utrecht: Sustainable Finance Lab.

Walter, Johann. 2011. Geldordnung—eine ordnungspolitische Alternative. *Wirtschaftsdienst. Zeitschrift für Wirtschaftspolitik* 91 Jg, 8/2011: 543–549.

Werner, Richard A. 2005. *New Paradigm in Macroeconomics*. New York: Palgrave Macmillan.

Werner, Richard A. 2012. How to Turn Banks into Financial Intermediaries and Restore Money Creation and Allocation Powers to the State. *CBFSD Policy Discussion Paper*, No. 3–12, University of Southampton.

Wolf, Martin.2014. *The Shifts and the Shocks. What We've Learned from the Financial Crisis and Have Still to Learn*. London: Allen Lane.

Yamaguchi, Kaoru. 2014. *Money and Macroeconomic Dynamics. An Accounting System Dynamics Approach*. Awaji Island: Muratopia Institute/Japan Futures Research Center. www.muratopia.org/Yamaguchi/MacroBook.html.

Zarlenga, Stephen A. 2014. *The Need for Monetary Reform*. Presenting the American Monetary Act. Valatie: American Monetary Institute. http://www.monetary.org/wp-content/uploads/2011/12/32-page-brochure-sept20111.pdf.

6

Bankmoney to Sovereign Money

In view of its dysfunctions, the unstable hybrid constellation of state-backed private bankmoney requires resolution, and the solution is full chartalism. This chapter deals with the basic features of the changes involved in a transition from the present regime of bankmoney to a plain sovereign money system, including the continuities and changes for central banks, banks, government and bank customers, as well as the related advantages and supposed disadvantages.

As already mentioned in the introduction to this book, sovereign money is not another Chicago Plan or some other approach to full reserve banking, or narrow banking. This will be discussed in Sect. 6.14. A sovereign money system represents a single-circuit system, easier to understand, to manage flexibly and to keep control of than any kind of complicated split-circuit reserve system.

Furthermore, it should be pointed out that a transition from bankmoney to sovereign money is not a cure-all. Bankmoney is the root cause of current problems in banking and finance, but, as discussed in Sect. 5.2, there is a number of other contributory factors too. A transition to a single-circuit sovereign money system does not make redundant certain other measures aimed at stabilizing banking and financial markets, for example, transparent and complete reporting on risk exposure, increased adequacy of bank equity, or ringfencing various business lines of banking. Most of these measures, however, cannot become effective without putting an end to bank-led money creation. Without monetary reform those measures will ultimately

© The Author(s) 2017
J. Huber, *Sovereign Money*, DOI 10.1007/978-3-319-42174-2_6

again prove not to be sustainable. Independently, sovereign money by itself immediately contributes to resolving the dysfunctions of bankmoney. Some other reform proposals would be made redundant, for example, those for separate banking, as well as much of the liquidity and solvency bureaucracy under fractional reserve.

6.1   Basic Traits of a Sovereign Money System

Sovereign money is fully valid legal tender, be it cash on hand or non-cash money, the latter on account as well as on mobile storage devices. Coins have always been sovereign money. Notes were made so 120–180 years ago. Today, the biggest and defining part of the money supply is bankmoney on account. The introduction of sovereign money on account accomplishes today with bankmoney what was accomplished with private banknotes in the nineteenth century. Bank-issued notes were phased out and replaced with central bank notes. Today, it is about replacing bankmoney on account and bank-issued e-cash with sovereign money on account and sovereign digital cash.

The notion of *sovereign money* carries with it the constitutional dimension of the monetary prerogatives, ranking among the most important sovereign rights of a state, or a community of states. To repeat, monetary sovereignty includes:

1. Determining the *currency* of the realm, the common unit of account
2. Creating and issuing the *money*, the regular official means of payment denominated in that currency, and
3. Taking the benefit from money creation, the *seigniorage*.

The entire stock of sovereign money would be created and issued by an independent and impartial state body. In most countries, this would be the national central bank. The terms money base, stock of money, quantity of money and money supply would denote largely the same thing.

With regard to terms that can be found in financial textbooks, sovereign money represents money proper in contrast to a money surrogate, or money of the first, not the second order. There are alternatives to the term *sovereign money*, such as *chartal* money (derived from chartalism), *state* money (Werner), *constitutional* money (Anderson and Morrison), *public* money (Yamaguchi, Mellor), *US* money, meaning US Treasury money, as distinct from corporate Federal Reserve money (Zarlenga), *pure* money (Striner) and *plain money*

(Huber and Robertson). *Sovereign money* seems to encapsulate best what it is all about.[1]

A sovereign money system can still be seen as a two-tier structure composed of a central bank and the banking sector. Systemically, though, this is not as important as it is in today's credit-based and bank-led reserve system. In lieu of the split circuit of reserve banking, a sovereign money system entails one single circuit. There are no 'reserves' anymore, just sovereign money circulating freely within a single circuit among banks and nonbanks alike, similar to solid cash in former times, but now in the form of central bank digital currency, in a conventional account system or maybe a blockchain system.

Accordingly, today's monetary aggregates M0 and M1 would no longer exist; there would just be one integrated money supply M, easy to handle and to control. Assets in today's aggregates M2/3/4 such as savings accounts or certificates of deposit would be customer loans to a bank or fund, documented in banking and financial statistics, though not as a monetary aggregate, or near-money, but as short-term financial capital.

Sovereign money circulates as a liquid monetary asset only. On no bank balance sheet does it appear as a liability. If the money has been obtained by incurring debt, that debt is a liability, not however the money obtained which, as a readily available means of payment, is always a liquid asset, also if it is on a bank's or central bank's balance sheet.

Transition from bankmoney to sovereign money, as conceived of in this book, can be seen as New Currency teaching upgraded to present-day conditions. The core component of any Currency teaching is control of the quantity of fiat money by separating money and credit, or to put it differently, by way of the separation of *monetary* functions (central bank), *fiscal* and budgetary functions (government) and *financial* functions beyond (banks, other financial institutions, and further financial market participants).

For some critics, replacing bankmoney with sovereign money means progressing from bad to worse. Common doctrine has it that only banks are in on

---

[1] Werner (2012), Anderson and Morrison (2014), Yamaguchi (2014), Mellor (2016), Zarlenga (2014), Striner (2015), Huber and Robertson (2000).

The term *sovereign mo ney* is different from the term *sovereign currency* as used by modern money theory (MMT). The usage of 'sovereign currency' in MMT is part of a questionable construction in which banks' credit and deposit creation in the fractional reserve system is seen as a benign part of what is misleadingly portrayed as a 'sovereign currency system', as if what still needs to be achieved already exists. Cf. sovereignmoney.eu>money theory>modern money and sovereign currency.

A group of French social anthropologists also used the term *monnaie souveraine*, but in a different sense. The group started from the systemic hierarchy of money and finance being prior to real economic transactions, but then overstretched the position. In the vein of Marxist ideas on economic alienation, money itself is seen in the role of an independent sovereign entity rather than being a means of payment originated *from* a sovereign body. Cf. Aglietta Orléan (1998).

money while governments are suspected of not even knowing how to spend it sensibly. Bank-issued money is supposed to be functional, government-issued money to be inflationary. The analyses given in this book as well as historical facts indicate the contrary and result in a more differentiated picture.

Comparing times when either the government or the banking industry had decisive control of the money supply, the historical record for governments shows a mixed performance, whereas the result of the banking industry's 'control' of the money supply regularly results in inflation, asset inflation and boom and bust cycles, leading to recurrent panic and crises.[2]

At the same time, one should be aware that the monetary performance of governments is mixed indeed, partly responsible, but also partly abusive, and that throughout history many a government has tended to spend beyond its means and thus become over-indebted, be this for pomp and splendour, war or welfare. For sovereign money to be sound and stable it is therefore essential to entrust it to an impartial monetary authority, on the basis of a well-defined legal mandate, but independent in the operational details of its monetary policies and not subject to directives from the parliament and government cabinet of the day.

Another sweeping criticism of replacing bankmoney with sovereign money portrays it as terribly radical, even revolutionary. In terms of money and banking theory, the paradigm shift involved in fact challenges certain elements of hitherto prevailing wisdom. Practically, however, the transition to sovereign money is but an obvious next step in the evolution of money and finance in the context of state- and market-organized modern societies. The program requires only a few changes in legal and practical terms. Besides banks and central banks, money users would not even notice unless informed about it.

6.2   Central Banks as the Fourth Branch of the State

Modern fiat money has no natural anchor of scarcity and indeed should not be scarce. However, some mechanism needs to ensure that the quantity of money is tied to a real value base, that is, economic output and related finance. Financial markets, though, as discussed in Sect. 5.9, recurrently fail rather than continually succeed in achieving such necessary anchorage of

---

[2] Benes and Kumhof (2012, p. 26) have compiled a number of studies on the issue, among these the groundbreaking works of Del Mar (1895), Shaw (1896), and Zarlenga (2002). One would also include Aliber and Kindleberger (2015, Chap. 4), and other writings by Kindleberger.

money in its value base. Thus, a specific institution needs to be entrusted with the task of providing and flexibly readjusting the entire stock of money. The obvious candidate for fulfilling this function is the central bank of a nation-state.

In the USA, it does not seem to be as obvious as elsewhere that it is the Federal Reserve that should be entrusted with the task of being the monetary authority. Historically, America has had mixed experiences with central banks, as Europe had mixed experiences with governments in control of the money. Nations often had to suffer from their governments' financial mismanagement, in particular when resorting to the printing press. Americans, by comparison, have a different view of government-issued money. Colonial bills in the eighteenth century, promoted by Franklin as a substitute for a lack of coins, greatly helped the newer states to prosper until the bills were banned by the British Parliament. Continental dollars then helped to finance the War of Independence. During the Civil War the Greenback dollars as well as Confederate demand notes acted similarly.[3] Although these monies, except the colonial bills, proved to be rather weak due to the circumstances of war, they have retained a patriotic nimbus.

American monetary reformers in the 1930s (as well as those of today) thus preferred the idea of conferring money creation to a currency commission under the auspices of the Treasury. In the USA, it appears, there are remarkably few reservations about mingling monetary and fiscal functions.

In Europe and Japan, it is less controversial that the task of being the monetary authority falls to the national central banks. Similar to the bank-owned Federal Reserve, some of the European central banks still have to shed private co-ownership. Central banks should definitely cease to be incorporated companies. Balancing rules may require them to account for equity, but there is no problem carrying out this as a body under public law. In the Eurosystem, it is the European Central Bank that would take on the role of the monetary authority, certainly not without a more precisely stated legal mission and a thorough overhaul of its statutes, and provided the euro survives its persistent problems.

Whatever institutional arrangement will be chosen, the sovereign money-issuing body would then be a fourth branch of government, the monetary power, complementing the legislative, executive and judicial powers. Quite a number of national banks today are already in a position that comes close to such a status—without being able to live up to their task because in the bank-led fractional reserve system they have lost control.

---

[3] Zarlenga (2002, Chaps. 14–20), Striner (2015, pp. 27–46), Hixson (1993, Chaps. 7, 8, 18–20), and Galbraith (1995, Chaps. 5–8).

Central banks began their development as commercial *banks of the state*, directly financing government expenditure. Today, overt monetary government financing by central banks is interdicted by law, while it is allowed for banks at any time and for any amount. Except for managing central bank accounts for state agencies, central banks today are exclusively *bank of the banks*, but *bank of the state* no more; and rather than being the banks' *lender of last resort*, central banks have become the *anytime fractional refinancer of the banks*, on a regular, quasi semi-automated basis, under conditions of business as usual and more so in times of crisis.

As central banks have gradually changed from the private commercial banks they once were, 200–300 years ago, into monetary authorities responsible for the currency and money of their country, it is no longer adequate to see a central bank as a 'bank' in the traditional and commercial sense, less so in a sovereign money system. Central banks are in fact 'banks' increasingly less, and have become ever more what they are bound to be under full chartalism: the monetary authority of a currency area, the provider and guardian of a nation's currency and money supply denominated in that currency. In this capacity, central banks will be the sole source of official money, be this in the form of money on account and digital cash, or notes and coins for as long as solid cash is in use. The central bank would be the only agency to expend money in its own currency without taking it in or up before.

As the fourth power in a state, central banks must be independent and impartial, in a way that is analogous to the independence and impartiality of the courts. Central bank independence is a notorious bone of contention. To most mainstream economists, independence of central banks means that these must not be subject to directives or other interference from the government. At the same time, the cosy relationship between the banking industry and 'their' central bank is blinded out. In actual fact, today, as the banking industry has largely captured the prerogatives of money creation and seigniorage, it has also captured the respective functions of the central banks, putting the latter in a role of more or less willing agents serving the private interests of banking and finance.

It is exactly this cosy relationship between banks and the central bank that annoys other people throughout the political spectrum. If these people are decidedly left- or right-leaning or otherwise statist, they want the central bank to be bank of the state in the first instance, susceptible to the spending preferences of the parliament and the cabinet, perhaps also including direct central bank credit to the government (monetary financing).

In a well-run sovereign money system none of these attitudes should have its way. Central banks, to fulfil their legal mandate, must be independent from other state agencies as well as from the banking and financial industry, and be impartial and neutral towards any kind of particular interest. Especially they must not be biased towards the interests of banks and financial markets, or the desirabilities of public households. It might no longer make particular sense to refer to central banks as *bank of the banks* or *bank of the state*.

The parliament and cabinet of the day would have no right to demand money from the central bank and would have no say in a central bank's decisions. Parliaments make laws but do not administer justice. By analogy, the task of a national parliament is to provide a legal framework for the monetary order and the central bank, the financial markets and taxation, while the treasury, in cooperation with the parliament, should focus on the government budget, but must not be allowed to create money itself. However, there might be exception rules for the central bank to collaborate with the parliament and cabinet in a declared national state of emergency.

Whether the present strict taboo of monetary financing would be maintained or loosened in a sovereign money system can be left open here (Sect. 6.4). This element is not necessarily part of a sovereign money reform. In any event, government would fully benefit from the entire seigniorage accruing from additions to the money supply (Sect. 6.13). Some of the seigniorage can still be interest-borne from central bank loans to banks. If, however, the banks are allowed to borrow from the central bank to a limited extent, why should the government be prohibited from borrowing from the central bank to a limited extent? The important thing here is neither bank nor government borrowing, but for the independent central bank to make sure that the money it can supply in various ways keeps within the boundaries set by its publicly defended monetary policy on the basis of its detailed mandate.

The head and members of a central bank's governing council can be appointed in a way similar to how constitutional judges or other highest judges are appointed. In contrast to judges, who are often appointed for the whole of their active life, the office incumbency of central bank top personnel should be limited to a number of years, after which follow-up terms might be possible.

Comparable to the judiciary, again, a central bank acts in compliance with the law and the specific legal mandate assigned to it. A central bank, like any government body, must be under administrative jurisdiction and be subject to auditing and supervision by respective national offices.

The legally specified criteria and limitations a central bank has to observe would have to include the following aspects:

- The growth potential of the economy at structural capacity
- The domestic levels of consumer prices and interest rates, and the external exchange value of the currency

- The levels of asset prices and the ratio of financial assets to nominal and real GDP, complemented by
- The ratios of public and private indebtedness.

Different currency areas have developed different preferences for monetary policy. Certain elements will remain controversial to a degree, for example, whether or not monetary policy should support economic, labor-market and welfare policy, and whether it is actually capable of doing so. The extent to which asset inflation and indebtedness should be considered is hence an additional controversy.

In general, central banks ought to be able to pursue their policies in a discretionary rather than a mechanically rule-bound way. The reason is that additions to the money supply will have to keep within the boundaries of productive potential and related finance. Economic growth evolves in cycles that are caused by more than just monetary factors. Economic variables such as GDP-growth and employment, in particular inflation, asset inflation, interest rates and the currency exchange rate, are moving targets. Continually anticipating the need for money, and readjusting the quantity of money to these moving targets, requires the ability to act and react flexibly.

Neo-Austrians as well as crypto-currency enthusiasts please themselves in accusing sovereign money of 'centralism' and establishing a money monopoly. The terms 'central bank' and 'monopoly' alone seem to trigger some conditioned reflex here. As regards the money monopoly of full chartalism, which would indeed be established, it is of the same nature as the state monopolies of legislation, public administration, taxation, jurisdiction and the use of force. Modern nations would not exist and could not function without these monopolies, and the problems and dysfunctions of the bankmoney regime are in fact the best proof of this. A nation-state, or community of nation-states, must not share its sovereign prerogatives with private agencies; nor in particular its monetary prerogatives with commercial money makers.

Independently, bankmoney is everything but a model of decentralization. Banks have the sectoral monopoly of bankmoney, which is monetarily determining everything else today. Comparing this to, say, the 'monopoly' of the computer industry of producing computers is an inadequate belittlement of the systemic role of money and finance which makes them completely different from any other industry. Rather than calling for *monetary* decentralization—which is misleading and counterproductive under constitutional and functional aspects—it would be more reasonable to call for more decentralization of *banking and finance*, depending on the country.

The category of central versus decentral is not adequate for the matter under consideration. More relevant here is the category of exogenous versus endogenous money. As discussed in Sect. 4.14, sovereign money is as endogenous as bankmoney. The point of contention is the criteria of endogeneity. The demand for money alone is not yet the conclusive criterion, either with regard to banks' bankmoney or central banks' sovereign money. The banking industry today applies selective supply preferences and proprietary business priorities, while the central bank in a sovereign money system would have to apply the criteria of GDP-proportionate and capacity-oriented monetary quantity policy.

6.3 Separation of Money Creation from Banking, and of Monetary from Fiscal Functions

Critics often demand central banks to be more 'democratic' or 'democratically accountable'. What, by comparison, is a 'democratic' lawsuit and court decision? Applying ideas of representative and participatory democracy to monetary policy is beside the point. The mode of democracy relevant to monetary policy is the separation of powers, or the division of functions, in the spirit of Montesquieu within a setting of liberal rule of law—which of course includes having to justify and defend publicly decisions to be taken, in compliance with the law.

Liberal rule of law based on democratic separation of powers is in fact the political foundation of the concept of sovereign money. It is designed to ensure stable money and sound finances by separating monetary and fiscal powers, as well as by keeping the monetary functions apart from the financial functions of banking and financial markets. Separation of money and credit will ensure that a nation's money is no longer hostage to the particular interests of the banking and financial industry. The separation of state powers between the central bank and the parliament/administration will prevent sovereign money from falling victim to the fiscal and budgetary interests of the day.

Some scholars and policymakers are rather insensitive to the differences between monetary, fiscal and financial market functions and tend to blur the boundaries between them. They are possibly being misled by deficit-borne and debt-laden Keynesian demand-side policies of old and oversimplified post-Keynesian public–private sector balances of late, where the fundamental distinctions between government and central bank is made to disappear into a black box called the 'public sector'. Any monetary reform approach insensitive to the division of monetary, fiscal and financial market functions will in fact progress from bad to worse.

It should be noted, however, that keeping apart the monetary functions of the central bank and the fiscal and budgetary functions of the government does not exclude the transfer of seigniorage to the treasury. Quite the contrary, seigniorage from money creation, as well as central bank profits in general, is due to the treasuries, not to the banking industry. In comparison with today's central bank profits, seigniorage in a sovereign money system would most often entail larger amounts of money. It is seigniorage nonetheless, keeping within the boundaries of a central bank's monetary mandate.

6.4   The Prohibition of the Government from Issuing Money

In the chartal money system which we are supposed to have, but in reality do not, governments are prohibited from creating chartal money (except coins), as central banks are not allowed to finance the government directly. That taboo of monetary financing seems to be as curious as the treasuries' demand to be paid in bankmoney only. In a sovereign money system, one might be inclined to assume that the government, representing the sovereign nation, would be entitled to create its own money and that the central bank would be allowed to contribute directly to funding the public budget. Such assumptions, however, are less obvious than they might appear. Lifting the prohibition without further ado would surely run contrary to the separation of monetary and fiscal powers. It depends on who is considered to be 'the government', and how different state bodies are supposed to cooperate.

From a legal point of view, overt government funding by the central bank is ruled out today. In America, this is set by US Code (Title 12, Chap. 3, Subchap. IX) § 355, in the European Union by Art. 123 (1) of the Treaty on the Functioning of the EU (TFEU). These legal provisions allow for the purchase and sale of public debentures of any kind 'but only in the open market', as US Code § 355 (1) states. This corresponds to Art. 123 (2) TFEU, while Art. 123 (1) TFEU explicitly prohibits any central bank contribution to public budgets, such as central bank loans to public bodies or the direct purchase of initially offered government bonds.[4] Exceptions relate to interest-borne seigniorage as part of the annual central bank profit that is discharged to the treasuries, contributions to the IMF and the traditional purchase of coins from the treasuries.[5]

During the recent crisis, however, governments showed a tendency not to care about the law when systemically relevant bankers were making frightening calls over the weekend. The EU no-bailout clause (Art. 125 TFEU) was ignored without hesitation, and Art. 123 (2) has been overstretched into outright monetization of public debt and questionable bank claims. One of the next steps might be to 'readapt' central bank accounting so as to disguise negative equity. The Maastricht stability criteria of the eurozone proved not to be worth the paper they are written on. In every such case the rationale is that an 'exceptional situation requires exceptional measures'. Reasonable as this may sound it was in fact just an excuse for establishing the exception as the rule, that is, doing 'whatever it takes' to delay insolvency of overexposed banks and over-indebted governments. This traps the central banks in a dilemma, choosing between banking and financial collapse now, and stagnation from now on due to delaying the resolution of an unresolved overhang of bad loans, assets and debt.

Under the conditions of today's state-backed banking rule, the respective laws can in fact be seen as 'enabling laws', privileging the banking industry by taking the 'printing press' away from the governments and handing it over to the banking industry, with no conditionality or policy requirements attached to it. Those laws have thus contributed to rendering governments *and* central banks subservient to the banking industry and financial markets.

The situation would be different in a sovereign money system. Central banks, representing the monetary state power, would be in actual control of the stock of money. There would be several options for money issuance, in particular long-term genuine seigniorage to the government as well as short-term central bank credit to banks, both of these to a limited extent depending on a central bank's policy targets (Sects. 6.6 and 6.7). Given there are such limits, why then should the government be prohibited from obtaining central

---

[4] Art. 123 (1) TFEU: 'Overdraft facilities or any other type of credit facility with the European Central Bank or with the central banks of the Member States (hereinafter referred to as 'national central banks') in favour of Union institutions, bodies, offices or agencies, central governments, regional, local or other public authorities, other bodies governed by public law, or public undertakings of Member States shall be prohibited, as shall the purchase directly from them by the European Central Bank or national central banks of debt instruments.'

[5] Art. 123 (1) TFEU applies to all EU member states, including the UK and other non-euro states. The British Government, however, won a derogation concerning its ways-and-means facility with the Bank of England.

bank loans, subject to the same conditions that apply to the banks, and to an equally limited extent? Put differently, how could today's privileged access of banks to central bank credit be justified further on?

Since this is a highly controversial matter, it should be stressed that a sovereign money system can work with a prohibition of central bank credit to the government as well as with permitting it. The latter case, however, would presuppose strict provisions and limitations for both the central bank and the government, making sure the central bank keeps within the limits exclusively set on grounds of its monetary policy.

Moreover, it shall be repeated in this context that the transfer of newly created sovereign money to the treasury represents seigniorage, like the benefit from coinage. It thus does not fall under the prohibition of monetary government funding, should such prohibition continue to exist. If today's interest-borne seigniorage is exempted from those prohibition paragraphs as well as genuine seigniorage from coinage, then genuine and interest-borne seigniorage from the creation of sovereign money is surely exempted as well.

6.5   The Role of the Banks in a Sovereign Money System

The biggest impact of sovereign money replacing bankmoney seems to be on banking. That needs to be put into perspective. The casino section of investment banking, which has been shrinking a little in recent years, is likely to be reduced all the more. This does not apply to 'boring banking', because in advanced financialized economies there is always a high demand for funding. As Fisher observed, the banking business does well when the economy is doing well. If the banks help the economy to prosper, the economy will no doubt return the favour.

For sure, the banking sector would lose its *monetary* privilege to create the money on which it operates. Before being able to expend money, banks would have to earn and take up the money in basically the same way as other financial intermediaries. The banking industry then would no longer be a monetary power. There would be no bankmoney, just sovereign money. Banks would no longer be creators of money, but they can continue to offer account management and payment services. Moreover, they would be the financial intermediaries they are supposed to be in the present system, but are not. Banks would thus continue to be the financial power they have always been. This would still involve debiting and crediting in the booking sense of transferring existing money into and out of accounts. The money, however, would no longer be created by way of bank credit.

Moving from bankmoney to sovereign money is *not* about nationalization of banking. It is about re-completing nationalized *money creation* while retaining banks as free financial enterprises, albeit stripped of the monetary privileges they have captured today. In a sovereign money system, banks can be, and ought to be, independently acting market enterprises. Finance, income and capital ought to be as private as possible. Money, by contrast, is no private affair; rather, it is a kind of public good, or public domain.

The separation of powers between the central bank and the banks would be straightforward. The two-tier structure would stand for the separation of money creation from banking. The central bank's task then is to manage foreign reserves, provide the national money supply and keep control of its quantity in circulation to make sure there is neither too much nor too little money, thus ensuring the monetary precondition for banks and the economy to work at optimal capacity.

The banks' business would continue to be *financing* customer expenditure. To a certain extent, banks may continue to be investors, underwriters and market makers themselves. But they will no longer be able to spend, lend or invest money without having earned or taken in that money before—from their customers, from other banks, on the open market, and ultimately, if need be, from the central bank. Prior to this, banks would have a large steady flow of principal returning to them, since money in reflux would be readily available for ongoing use, rather than being deleted as is the case today. Banks would be what they are supposed to be today but are not, that is, intermediaries between savers and borrowers, between upstream and downstream, retail and wholesale investors.

Banks and central banks ought not to interfere in each other's business. As banks must not be allowed to create money, central banks ought to abstain from interfering in the banking business and financial markets, except when this is unavoidable to fulfil their monetary mandate, for example, foreign exchange trading in their own currency, or open market operations necessary for readjusting the money supply or interest rates.

Technically, the banks will have no problem dealing with the new conditions. Public and private households and small enterprises, as well as large industrial and financial corporations, all have to plan their finances and current expenditures—which is basically not an issue. The analogy with banks is the way in which they manage cash. One never hears of banks facing difficulty in providing the necessary amount of cash. Technically, it is a well-run system. Prior to the bankmoney regime, banks were perfectly able to cope with near full financing of their operations. Why should it be different with money on account? Providing for non-cash money is in fact much easier than managing cash. In some countries there are bank-like financial institutes operating on bankmoney without creating bankmoney themselves, but nonetheless engaged in money lending as well as in investment activities. Their operations function smoothly.

If banks, rather than operating on a fractional reserve base, have to finance their engagements in full, one could think that the costs of banking would be correspondingly higher, resulting to a degree in higher rates and fees charged to customers. For the most part, this would not be the case, and if it were true, the aforementioned bank-like institutes could not withstand competition from fractional reserve banks. Today, banks pay deposit interest on all classes of deposits, and they would simply continue to do so in the future. The difference is that today the interest is paid to deactivate the deposits, thus making sure the deposits will not drain away. In a sovereign money system, there is no such loss of active money in the circuit. The interest would be paid to obtain the corresponding amounts of money to fund a bank's lending and investment business. Here again, banks will do what they are supposed to do today but are not doing.

There is nowadays a tendency towards growing competition for banks from shadow banking and other nonbank financial intermediaries. Sovereign money will contribute to that tendency. Banks and nonbank financial intermediaries will be more alike. Central banks will have to decide whether to maintain exclusive access of the banks to central bank credit and whether banks will be the only institutions to manage sovereign money accounts, which includes participation in the central bank payment system. These aspects—access to central bank credit, management of money accounts and access to the central bank payment system—will decide upon the banks' distinctness from nonbank financial intermediaries.

Some proponents of contemporary green-ethical banking, as organized in the Global Alliance for Banking on Values, have objected to sovereign money. What is needed, in their opinion, are different business models for banks, not a different money system. This is a rather elusive point of view. A different money system and different business models for banks are two different things. They neither exclude nor include each other, and they go together very well.

Alternative business models of banking are of course welcome, as it is desirable, in any money system, for banks to be more aware of what kind of business their profit comes from, and for customers to be more aware of whom and for what they trust with their money. With sovereign money, the effect would be stronger because banks then actually need their customers' money. Citizens can vote not only through the ballot box, but also by purposefully allotting money—supposing they have enough money at their disposal.

6.6 Capacity-Oriented Quantity Policy

How would sovereign money be put into circulation, and according to which criteria would a central bank decide how much money to issue? The major principle would be to provide a money supply commensurate with the economy's growth potential, while observing additional targets relating to indicators such as inflation, interest rates, as well as asset inflation and related indebtedness.

Modern fiat money needs to be anchored in a non-financial real value base. To be functional, this cannot be gold or a selective basket of commodities. Much less can it be the value of land or the value of mere financial assets, since the value of such assets depends on actual income relations, meaning the long-term market value of economic output, not the reverse. The economic value of money, its purchasing power, derives from the overall productivity of the economy (Sect. 2.8).

From this it follows that the obvious candidate to serve as a real value base is economic output or, as regards additions to the stock of money, the growth potential of the economy at full capacity. Determining that potential, including the structural limits of the capacities in place, admittedly is no trivial matter. If it were, any computerized expert system would suffice.

GDP-proportionate increases in the money supply can basically be assumed to foster non-volatile stable levels of real economic prices, asset prices, interest rates, currency exchange values and volumes of financial assets and indebtedness. However, the dynamics between money supply, economic output and these other variables is quite complex. Hence, again, there is no reasonable mechanical rule applicable to monetary policy. Attempts to follow some such univariate rule should not receive consideration, for example the Friedman prescription of continually increasing the stock of money at a fixed rate, or the Taylor rule of reacting to changes in the inflation rate by changing the central bank rates. It should also be understood that stability does not normally mean unaltered permanence, but refers to non-volatile stable trends.

It is clear from the above discussion that monetary quantity policy cannot be reduced to setting money supply targets, if such targets need to be set at all. The quantity of money matters, but concentrating on quantity-of-money targets was another flawed element of monetarism. Reasonable monetary policy goals would refer to all of the variables mentioned above, certainly including projections of GDP-proportionate additions to the stock of money, but equally including price stability, non-volatile interest rates and so on. The quantity of money itself does not make for a sensible operational target. Rather, it is a flexibly readjustable means to those other ends.

Many experts doubt the central banks' ability to provide an adequate money supply. The unfavourable opinion about central banks is partially due to a mere ideology of infallibility of markets, partially based on Hayek's thesis of bureaucracies' pretence of knowledge, or due to a misconceived notion of endogenous money, or partially a result of the experience of ineffective central bank action under the present bankmoney regime. In addition, the desperado monetary policies of recent years have certainly not contributed to people having confidence in central banks. A central bank, it is assumed, simply cannot know how much money will be adequate in half a year or one year's time.

As a response to this it must be recalled that markets do not know either, but recurrently fail and overshoot. The pretence-of-knowledge verdict surely also applies to the large bureaucracies of industrial and financial corporations. A central bank, too, cannot know and actually need not know exactly how much money will be enough at any given time in the future. What it takes in a sovereign money system for central banks to pursue effective quantity policies is:

- An array of reliable long- and short-term banking data and market indicators, which they already have
- Then, in proactive issuance of money: regular *long-term* additions to the money supply based on a broad estimate of how large the future GDP-proportionate increase in the money supply can be expected to be,
- And, in continuous readjustment of the money supply: the *short-term* application of a variety of monetary policy instruments for temporarily releasing additional money or absorbing money.

In the bank-led fractional reserve system that kind of monetary quantity policy was doomed to fail because the central banks exert no control over the banks' money creation. In a sovereign money system, quantity policy will be effective because a central bank is in direct full control of the stock of money, which it can readjust at any time to any extent, literally overnight if need be. Thus, quantity policy in a sovereign money system is not backward-looking, but a step forward to an efficacious new type of monetary policy.

It is often assumed that central bank-led provision of money would result in an inflexible system with a recurrent standstill of the flow of payments when there is not enough money with the banks and other financial institutions.

An expectation like this has no real grounds, exactly because modern money is fiat money that can be created at any time to any amount and that central banks in a sovereign money system have control over the quantity of money supply. Anticipating money shortage is thus unfounded.

One should not, however, confound money shortage with credit shortage. In a sovereign money system, money and credit are no longer a dysfunctional pair of equals. Providing enough money is not the same as making sure there is enough credit. The first is the realm of monetary policy, the latter the realm of financial markets and economic policy in which the actor groups involved have cyclically fluctuating preferences. The degree to which money keeps circulating depends on the preparedness of money owners, banks and other financial institutions to lend and to finance, and the preparedness of firms and other private and public bodies to borrow and to invest and spend.

Under conditions of the identity of bankmoney and credit, monetary policy has almost unavoidably been mingled with economic policy. It remains unclear, though, to what extent monetary policy in the name of growth and employment has really achieved something useful, to what extent it may have been counterproductive with regard to inflation, asset inflation and public over-indebtedness, and to what extent it has been ineffective anyway. If there is enough money, but the actors are reluctant to make use of it during cyclical recessions and fluctuations in economic activity, the reasons for the reluctance are clearly non-monetary. Pouring in a 'monetary stimulus', that is, adding still more to what is already enough, cannot really be a reasonable policy standard then.

In a sovereign money system, in any event, there will be no difficulty in ensuring a sufficient money supply, or absorbing money if need be. Available monetary policy instruments, flexibly applied, will make sure that necessary readjustments can also be accomplished in the short and very short term.[6] Beyond the long-term emission through genuine seigniorage, the main central bank instruments for providing an adequate and flexibly readjustable money supply are already available—open market operations, in particular repos and reverse transactions, as needed, then short-term lending operations on a weekly or fortnightly basis, as well as a marginal lending facility (overdraft) with a borrowing limit. As there would be no transmission from interbank to public circulation, the immediate effect of such instruments would be much greater than today.

As discussed in Sects. 5.9 and 5.10, quantities have a stronger effect on price levels and interest rates than the reverse. The quantity of available money

---

[6] Also cf. van Lervenet al. (2015) and Dyson et al. (2015).

sets the path and pace of interest trends more effectively than the base rates in a split-circuit reserve system ever could. In consequence, a central bank with full control of the quantity of money is able to pursue monetary quantity policy rather than interest rate policy. The interest rates resulting from quantity policy will in turn be market prices in allocating the available money. If there is enough money, the level of interest cannot be too high, and if the money supply is steady and reliable, interest rates will not be volatile.

Interest rate policy, in the sense of setting central bank rates, is in no way excluded, but will in fact be of minor importance. One should stay aware that in a market economy, prices, in particular interest rates, are the last thing that should be administered. If a central bank would nevertheless find it useful to vary its lending rates in order to influence the demand for sovereign money, it could of course do so. This too would be more effective than today, because, as far as banks would have to resort to central bank credit, they would have to take up what they need in full, not only a small fraction of it.

With sovereign money, a central bank can effectively pursue moderately countercyclical quantity policies, that is, adding money to the upswing, then stopping doing so upon increasing signs of overheating, and starting adding money again at a later stage of the downswing. In contrast to the present bankmoney regime, a sovereign money supply issued by way of genuine seigniorage does not grow or shrink in one act with the lending and investment activities of banks and financial markets. As a result, the stock of money will not shrink in a downswing. Sovereign money thus opens up the perspective of effective quantity policy of the steady hand.

6.7   Channels of Issuance and First Uses of New Money

For a central bank to make additions to the money supply, two channels of money issuance would be recommendable.

One channel is to leave the bigger, *long-term* additions to the stock of money to the treasury for government expenditure. That money will be spent, not lent, into circulation and thus represents *genuine seigniorage*, comparable to the historical prerogative of coinage, free of interest and redemption and thus debt free. A certain share of that money will soon end up as savings or, say, capital reserves, in banks, investment funds or similar.

The other channel is short-term issuance of the smaller part of new money by way of primary central bank credit to banks, or bank-like financial intermediaries in general. Together with the array of open market instruments, this will ensure flexible options in monetary policy. The money that is lent to the banks will generate *interest-borne seigniorage*.

Either way, additions to the stock of money have to be determined under *monetary* criteria, while *fiscal, budgetary and non-GDP financial market* interests are none of a central bank's business.

As to the purposes for which new money should be used, these too are basically not a central bank's business. Discussions regarding the question of how the government should spend the seigniorage that they obtain tend to be vivid. It is always inspiring to imagine what one could do with money if one had it. Not surprisingly, people and politicians have plenty of priorities—investment in infrastructure, in education and research, in seed and risk capital; or reducing taxes, or paying down the public debt; or funding basic income, health expenditure; or putting the money in public and national security. Pash argues in favour of spending seigniorage on a great diversity of GDP-related investments.[7]

Such questions are actually very important, but they relate to budgetary and economic policy rather than monetary policy. As seigniorage can be used for any public purpose, the matter is best left to the government of the day. One exception, though, might be how to use the huge one-off transition seigniorage that would accrue over several years from replacing bankmoney with sovereign money (Sect. 6.13). That transition seigniorage should indeed be earmarked for the smooth redemption of public debt.

As an alternative to using seigniorage for funding the budget, S. Gesell suggested in the 1920s to transfer the seigniorage to the treasury *and* grant a corresponding tax credit to every household. One can also imagine paying newly created money out as a per-capita share to every citizen, as a national dividend, as C.H. Douglas called it. For each percentage point of GDP-growth, that dividend could amount to about 190 dollars in the US, 165 pounds in the UK, and 165 euros in the eurozone.[8] At annual growth rates in the range of 1.5–3 % the resulting several hundred dollars, pounds or euros are not exactly a fortune, but would no doubt be popular. At the same time, the magnitude of the numbers makes it clear that ideas such as funding a basic income or even replacing taxes with seigniorage are very far beyond the available means.

---

[7] Pash (2013).

[8] Calculated on the basis of M1 in the euro, and 50 % of M2 in the USA as well as 50 % of M4 in the UK, taking this as a rough proxy for what liquid M might be in a sovereign money system.

Paying common dividends from seigniorage was once a practice in Maryland from 1733 to 1751 when every taxable citizen was given government bills worth 30 shillings, the colonial scrip of the time.[9] The grievances over the oppression of colonial bills in favour of motherland bank credit are said to have been a much bigger reason for the War of Independence than the import tax on tea. As Ferguson observed, 'behind each great historical phenomenon there lies a financial secret'.[10]

With regard to central bank credit to banks, it is, again, basically no concern of the central bank what the banks intend to do with the money they borrow. Monetary policy should not interfere in the banking business. By comparison, however, banks do not hesitate to pursue their private financial market policies. They have rather precise ideas of what they consider creditworthy, and they demand to know the exact reason for customers' borrowing. Why should a central bank not do something similar?

Thus, there might be one or two exceptions in which monetary policy verges on financial market policy. One such case could be real economic conditionality of central bank credit.[11] Banks would have granted central bank credit on condition of lending or investing the money in GDP-contributing activities, such as lending to firms, or consumer and true building loans.

There are certainly questions of delimitation. As a matter of fact, all receipts serve to fund all expenditure. Nominal assignments of particular receipts to particular expenditures remain somewhat arbitrary, while actual assignments, as in public and corporate budgeting, tend to result in an inefficient waste of money. Moreover, large industrial corporations today are to a certain extent financial market actors too. Real economic conditionality of central bank credit would nevertheless be an element that contributes to preventing a preference for non-GDP finance over GDP-contributing activities.

In general, however, a central bank's business in a sovereign money system is control of the quantity, not the uses of money. It can be assumed that a money supply growing in proportion to GDP would by itself contribute to a level playing field for competing GDP-related and non-GDP uses of money.

Profit margins are not per se higher in non-GDP engagements than in GDP-contributing engagements. When this was the case in recent decades, it was based on instant cheap bankmoney leverage for self-propelling expansionary engagements in investment banking and the global casino. If the basis

---

[9] Hixson (1993, p. 56).

[10] Ferguson (2008, p. 3).

[11] Such an element of real economic conditionality, or say credit guidance, is part of 'The Chicago Plan Revisited' by Benes and Kumhof (2012) and is occasionally also expressed in the writings by Werner.

of instant cheap leverage and expansionary casino gambling no longer existed, and investors wanted to leverage the stakes regardless, the money obtainable for this would quickly become scarce and expensive. Expectable returns would decrease and the risks to be taken increase. This would significantly reduce, though not eliminate, the appetite for such investments. Financial madness, such as the prototypical Dutch tulip mania in the 1630s, would presumably occur time and again in a sovereign money future as well. The important thing is to make sure that third parties are not affected by such madness and that the money base, the payment system and the economy can carry on regardless of failing banks and bankrupt gamblers.

6.8   Is There a Necessary Sequence in the Circulation of Money?

The ways of money issuance and first uses of money raise the question of whether there is a necessary sequence in money circulation. The older classical and neoclassical models assumed 'investment first, consumption later'. Credit should first feed into capital expenditure, especially into private investment in productive capacities, not immediately into consumption, and less so into government expenditure, both of which were supposed to result in inflation; hence the distinction between capital- and consumer-goods industries, or sections I and II in Marxist economics, as well as the Austrian School five- to seven-step production model that underlies its capital theory.[12] At the beginning of industrialization, with productive capacities at a low level of development and potential consumptive demand still mostly unsatisfied, the idea of 'investment in productive capacities first, consumption second' made some sense, in market economies as much as in centrally planned economies.

Keynesian-style compensatory economic policies then attributed a bigger economic role to consumer and government expenditure, and thus helped in reshaping the class conflict between labor and capital in the form of wage earner and consumer demand-side policies as opposed to investor supply-side policies, thereby in fact complementing capital investment with mass purchasing power.

Keynes's idea of a 'monetary theory of production' was then pursued by circuitism and the quantum theory of money and production. These approaches were again somewhat closer to classical and Marxist views in that the defining circular flow of endogenous money is supposed to be banks crediting firms,

---

[12] Huerta de Soto (2009, Chap. 5, pp. 265–396).

the firms paying wage earners, who buy the firms' product, which enables the firms to repay the banks.[13] Henry Ford thought this way a hundred years ago when he wanted his workers to earn enough to buy themselves the model T they produced.

The circuitist model rejects a special focus on investment. It just refers to 'the monetary cost of output in general', that is capital expenditure with a broad meaning, including wages.[14] This is progress in a way, for any step in a vertical or horizontal chain of provision is one of consumption and production at the same time. Quite often, the distinction between investive and consumptive spending is a convention of accountancy and tax law.

The circuitist and quantum models, however, must put up with being criticized for reductionism. There is more to the circulation of money than just banks, firms and wage earners. The entirety of actor groups and flows of money cannot plausibly be reduced to these. The arena of actors also includes nonbank financial intermediaries, government bodies, and non-employed, as the flow of money also includes secondary credit, de- and reactivated money, redistribution of earned and financial income, trade not only in products and services but also in real and financial assets, GDP-contributing and non-GDP flows of money, including a certain multi-directionality of the flows of money.

The empirical evidence does not support the circuitist sequence. As mentioned in Sect. 5.5, about 70–80 % of bank credit is allotted to real estate and mortgages, government debt, and speculative leverage. Only the rest goes to firms, into consumer credit (overdraft, car, credit-card and home-equity credit) as well as, in the USA, student loans.[15] As Hudson points out, by far most primary and secondary credit

is spent on assets, not goods and services. Every day a sum larger than an entire year's GDP passes through the New York Clearing House and the Chicago Mercantile Exchange for asset purchases and sales. More than 99 percent of spending in the United States and other financialized economies is thus for real estate, mortgages and packaged bank loans, and for stocks and bonds.... The largest system is that of land, monopoly rights and financial claims that yield *rentier* returns in the form of interest, other financial fees, rents and monopoly gains.... These returns far overshadow the profits earned on investing in capital goods and employing labor to produce goods and provide actual services.[16]

---

[13] Graziani (1990, p. 12), Fontana (2000, p. 42), and Rossi (2007, p. 121)
[14] Graziani (1990, p. 14) and Rochon (1999a, p. 20).
[15] Jordà et al. (2014). Turner (2015, p. 62). *The Economist*, March 28, 2015 16.
[16] Hudson (2012, pp. 335, 298).

Lending to firms certainly continues to be part of the banking business and that of nonbank financial intermediaries. But what is thought to be the defining center of finance, that is, banks funding the relation between employers and employees ('capital and labor'), is in no way predominant and applies to small and medium-sized enterprises rather than big companies. Industrial corporations no longer depend on bank credit to a major extent. They pay for current expenditure from current earnings, and when they need more than just bridge-funding by a bank, they tap the secondary credit market by issuing corporate bonds or borrowing from funds in other ways. In addition, large corporations run banks of their own.

The empirical data no longer even clearly support the notion of primary and secondary income distribution. At the present stage of development, as public and private households take up as much primary and secondary credit as firms, it has become far less clear than it may have appeared in former times why government expenditure would be 'secondary', while the firms' allocation and distribution of available means is deemed the 'primary' function.

The narrow focus on 'banks financing firms' leaves a somewhat dated impression. Focussing questions of money and finance too narrowly on the firm and wage earners now represents an old industrial bias of economics that may have had a point from the beginning of industrialization until the 1950–1960s. One consequence of this has been building the industrial welfare state too narrowly upon the relationship between employers and wage labor. Over time, this has become another fiscal and financial market problem without lastingly resolving the respective social problems but greatly contributing to the GDP-disproportionate expansion of sovereign debt and financial assets.

Questioning the circuitist model does in no way mean to question the fundamental truth that money has value only to the degree to which there is valuable economic output; which in turn implies prior investment in productive capacities, infrastructure, education and human skills. The classical view of production chains, implying some sort of supply side policy, is certainly not wrong, but reductionist and linear, missing a variety of loops and links, and resulting in somewhat rigid policy recommendations. On the other hand, one-sided increases in mass purchasing power are no silver bullet in economic policy either. In a financial and economic crisis, the impact of household and government debt, as well as that of current account deficits induced by consumption, is more severe than the impact of non-financial firm debt.[17] What both supply-siders and demand-siders tend to overlook is the question

---

[17] Mian et al. (2015) and Denk and Cournède (2015).

of financial carrying capacity, the burden of too high levels of assets and debt in relation to GDP.[18]

It follows from the above considerations that there can be various ways of channelling new money into circulation, and many ways in the subsequent circulation of the money. There is no such thing as a natural or strictly necessary sequence regarding the issuance and circulation of money. Respective doctrines can safely be dropped. The important thing is that enough money for GDP-related supply and demand can be obtained by financial institutions, firms, private households and public bodies. In contrast, under the present conditions of bloated non-GDP finance, over-indebtedness and growing inequality, the situation is rather strained and productive investment is coming off badly in many fields.

If there is any proviso today to replace the old industrial rule of 'investment first, consumption later' then such a rule might now read 'GDP-contributing finance and real economic expenditure first, non-GDP finance last'.

6.9   Debt-Free Versus Interest-Bearing Sovereign Money

The two channels of money issuance discussed above—genuine and interest-borne seigniorage—determine whether the sovereign stock of money is debt-free or debt-laden. Genuine seigniorage from long-term additions to the quantity of money is spent, not lent, into circulation and is thus debt-free. By contrast, short-term central bank credit to banks constitutes a credit and debt relation, with the central bank as the creditor and the banks as debtors.

Certain social movements, particularly in religious and anarcho-syndicalist traditions, would like to overcome interest-bearing debt. They would probably object to issuing sovereign money by way of central bank lending. Pragmatically speaking, however, that channel needs to exist for functional reasons of monetary policy. More fundamentally, a price mechanism other than interest for allocating funds in capital markets is not available. Bureaucratic apportionment is generally no viable answer, even though it can be necessary when there is a structural lack of effective private demand. Islamic banking also does not really represent an alternative to interest in that it restructures the financial creditor–debtor relationship into a commercial partnership, and reinterprets interest as entrepreneurial or trading profit.[19] Either way, in the end, one is in surplus or deficit, having made a profit or a loss.

---

[18] Borio (2012, pp. 16–23).
[19] Iqbal (2009).

Sovereign money does not dispense with interest and interest-mediated finance. Simply, modern fiat money can easily be created and issued debt-free, in much the same way as traditional coins. Genuine seigniorage is the one free lunch that otherwise does not exist in the economy. If a thing like this exists, it should certainly benefit the public purse rather than privileging the banking industry. There is no natural imperative according to which money must be created and issued in one act with the formation of a credit and debt relationship. This is just banking doctrine. Astoundingly, it is defended nowadays by the heirs of Keynes more fiercely than by neoclassical economists. The reason can be seen in the Keynesian and post-Keynesian theory of endogenous money, which is largely appropriate, except for the notion of exogenous money, but unreflectingly biased in favour of Banking doctrine.

In general, the question of whether sovereign money should be issued free of interest and redemption, or whether it can also be brought into circulation as credit and debt money, should be dealt with in a pragmatic way, all the more so as the debt burden of a modern economy cannot be expected to shrink below a certain basic level, because, except for the casino section of the financial economy, there is a real and large need for GDP-contributing finance. This then is the good news for the banking industry.

In a certain sense, though, even debt-free money is embedded in a context of socioeconomic obligations. This involves not a banking debt or other kind of monetary obligation, but a social duty as expressed in cultural values such as work, performance, achievement and merit. Without human effort, labor, technical efficacy and the regenerative forces of nature, there is no economic product to sell and buy and no purposes for which to invest and build up capital. Money would have no function and would be worthless. Even though debt-free sovereign money is not in itself a promise to repay, it is a promise to be productive, and a promise to keep control of the money supply, excluding overextension as well as shortages, in correspondence with actual levels of economic output.

6.10 How to Account for Sovereign Money on a Central Bank Balance Sheet

The British Bank Charter Act of 1844, as it aimed to separate money and credit, and following a proposal by Ricardo, introduced within the Bank of England a special institutional arrangement giving expression to that aim, in the form of the separation of the Issue Department from the Banking

Department.[20] The arrangement still exists today, even though it was designed to implement the gold standard and did not really fulfil its function because the act did not apply to bankmoney. One might think that the arrangement will be rejuvenated by a transition to sovereign money. The approach preferred in America so far, that is entrusting a monetary commission under the roof of the treasury with the monopoly of money creation, actually comes down to ascribing to that body the function of an 'issue department' while the FED's role would be the 'banking department', that is, open-market readjustment of the money supply and the function of lender of last resort.

It needs to be seen, however, that separating money and credit means separating a central bank's monetary functions from the banking and financing business. It can be dysfunctional to separate, *within* a central bank, the decision-making on long-term additions to the money supply from short-term open market operations. This actually led to problems in the decades after 1844.[21]

Short- and long-term decisions on the money supply ought to be taken by one and the same central bank council and can well be recorded in one frame of accountancy. Today, central bank credit to banks is booked as a pair of an asset (claim) and a liability (central bank reserves or banknotes). Both banks and central banks, after all, have the same commercial origin. One could think of keeping the practice in a sovereign money system. Scarcely anyone would worry much. It would not make a difference with regard to central bank credit to banks. In relation to the transfer of genuine seigniorage to the treasury, however, this would imply some significant reinterpretation of the meaning of claim and liability. The meaning of the claim would read 'non-interest bearing credit with unspecified maturity', also referred to as 'zero-coupon perpetual bond', in fact giving eternal gratuitous credit to the treasury (even if the credit could basically be redeemed when diverting taxes to this end). The liability would look like sovereign debt, but would have to be declared not to be debt, as 'modern money' theory has it, and which does not really inspire confidence.

It would therefore be more convincing to enter new money on a central bank balance sheet not as a liability but as part of a nation's monetary *equity*, so to speak part of the national monetary *endowment* which the money issu-

---

[20] Bank of England (2015), O'Brien (2007, p. 112), P.H. Douglas et al. (1939, p. 24), and Rossi (2001, p. 170).
[21] O'Brien (2007, p. 151).

ing authority can write out to the state coffers or lend to the banks. The basic principle is to account for sovereign money on the central bank balance sheet in the same way as coins.[22] Benes/Kumhof expressed the same idea. They proposed sovereign money to be 'treated as government equity rather than government debt, which is exactly how treasury coin is currently treated under US accounting conventions'.[23]

The procedure would then be the following:

- The central bank creates money by entering the respective amount on the asset side as liquid money, booked on the other side of the balance sheet not as a liability, but as a receipt in a new type of account that adds to the equity account. This extends the balance sheet.
- When the money is transferred to the treasury as genuine seigniorage this results in a balance sheet reduction in that the money is booked out on the asset side, which is an expense that reduces the equity account. The central bank's balance sheet will thus not mirror the entire amount of existing money (which today is not the case either), but that amount in its different use forms will of course be registered statistically.
- As far as money is loaned to banks, this would find expression in a swap of assets, meaning that the money is swapped for a credit claim on the borrowing bank. If a central bank purchases securities, money is swapped for these securities. If a central bank re-sells securities, or banks redeem loans, the swap is the reverse. The money would thus not be deleted but would be available for subsequent transactions.

On a bank's balance sheet, too, the money would always be a liquid asset, never a liability to customers used as a surrogate for central bank money. A bank loan or bank purchase of an asset would result in a swap of assets, that is the money for a claim on money. Other expenses would simply result in a corresponding reduction of a bank's money. On the balance sheet of any recipient—nonbank financial institutions, government, firms and households—the money would also circulate as a liquid asset only. There would be credit and debt, but the major part of the stock of money itself would no longer be credit-borne and debt-laden.

---

[22] Gudehus (2015a, p. 434). Mayer (2013a) also contributed to working out the approach.
[23] Benes and Kumhof (2012, p. 6).

6.11 Conversion Day Transition

The preferred scenario for making the transition to sovereign money would be a conversion day scenario. Some would say a big bang. On a set date, the necessary legal provisions would become applicable, the overnight liabilities of banks to customers would be rededicated, and central bank accounting would also begin to be modified accordingly.

Conversion day does not mean that everything would completely and finally be changed in one fell swoop. Instead, it would be the beginning of a gradual transition period of about three to five years in the main, with another five to ten years of petering out. The actual time horizon is set by the maturities of outstanding debt owed to banks. From the set date, however, there would be no more bankmoney and all payments would be made in sovereign money.

The basic legal measure would be to amend the paragraph that gives a respective central bank today the monopoly on banknotes, to extend it to money on account and digital cash. If not yet undertaken, and for the sake of coherence, the residual coin monopoly of the treasury should also be assigned to the central bank as a state's monetary authority. Thus, a full money or currency monopoly in accordance with a state's unimpaired monetary prerogatives would come into existence.

At present, the pertinent passages regarding a respective central bank, depending on the country, read like this:

> ... has the exclusive right to issue banknotes. Such banknotes shall be the only means of payment to have the status of legal tender.

An amendment might read like this:

> ... has the exclusive right to issue coins, banknotes, money on account and digital cash. Such monies shall be the only means of payment to have the status of legal tender.

In the euro area, for example, this refers to Art. 128 (1) TFEU and Art. 16 of the Statute of the European System of Central Banks. In the UK it refers to the latest pertinent amendment of the 1844 Bank Charter Act. In the USA, it might involve unambiguous reformulation of Art. 1, Sec. 8, Cl. 5 of the Constitution, replacing the sovereign 'power to coin money' with something like the 'power to issue legal tender in any use form'. The 1913 Federal Reserve Act, Sec. 16 on the issue of banknotes, would accordingly need to be reformulated. The strange distinction between 'legal tender' and 'lawful money' could be repealed.

In addition, the regulations on bank and central bank accountancy would have to be modified, to reflect the following alterations. From the set date, the customer current accounts in a bank are declared money accounts, and the overnight liabilities in these accounts, in other words the existing stock of liquid bankmoney, are converted into sovereign money. The current accounts are taken off a bank's balance sheet and exist as money accounts in their own right. At the same time, the overnight liabilities as of the conversion day will remain on a bank's balance sheet, but will be converted into a liability of the same amount to the central bank, as if in the first instance it had been the central bank that had loaned the money to the banks.

Customers need not change their bank, as the banks can continue to manage the individual money accounts of the customers. Money accounts could also be managed by licensend payment service providers. If managed by a bank, not even the account numbers would need to be changed. Such separate money accounts would be fiduciary accounts which are in no way at a bank's disposal. They would be run as part of the money services of a bank (management of accounts, cashless payment services, currency exchange), but outside a bank's balance sheet, like running a customer securities account on behalf of the customer.[24]

Alternatively, the customer accounts can be run by a bank or other payment service provider as a separate omnibus account with the central bank, a collective customer funds account. In this case, too, the money in such an account is a fiduciary off-balance item of a bank to which the customers retain full title.[25]

Another option seems to be central bank accounts for everybody.[26] There are, however, two problems with this. One is the huge and unnecessary sunk costs. The respective infrastructure and personnel of the banks would largely be made obsolete, while the central bank would have to build them up from scratch. Independently, a central bank would hardly be prepared to do that. Acting as the current account master of all citizens is not an obvious task of a national monetary authority. For a long time now, central banks have run accounts for banks and the government only and have refused to do so for private individuals, companies and most nonbank financial firms. Legal actions by companies for having opened a central bank account have

---

[24] Keeping individual money accounts of customers with the banks is the preferred procedure of Huber and Robertson (2000, p. 23).

[25] The omnibus variant is preferred in the draft of a 'Bank of England Act' by Positive Money. See Jackson and Dyson (2012, p. 186), and Positive Money (2011).

[26] Cf. Schemmann (2012b, pp. 51–69).

been dismissed. The idea of resorting to central bank accounts was primarily born of recent concerns about unsafe money under fractional reserve banking. Sovereign money, by contrast, is safe and secure. It cannot disappear in a banking crisis and can thus be managed by any licensed institute.

As regards the choice between individual and omnibus accounts, the answer can be left open here. Both ways are feasible and achieve the same result. Customers will be the sole and full owners of the money, in the same sense as having cash in their pocket. The proprietary means of a bank and the means of the customers will be separate. A transfer of customer money will no longer be 'mediated' by interbank transactions in reserves, but will be the direct and full transfer of an amount of sovereign money from the payer's account to the payee's account. If a customer lends money to a bank, for example by adding to a savings or time deposit, the money will be transferred from the off-balance customer account to the on-balance bank account. If a bank lends money to a customer, the money will be divested in full from the bank's account directly to the customer off-balance account.

With regard to the conversion of former bank-to-customer overnight liabilities into bank-to-central bank liabilities, an according amount will be fixed upon conversion day for each bank. It might be recommendable to use a statistical method which smooths out near-term distortions of the amount of bankmoney.

The respective amounts fixed upon conversion day represent 'old bankmoney'. More precisely, the respective amounts represent a transitory bank liability derived from the former quantity of bankmoney. These amounts will have to be paid down according to the pace and rate of outstanding payments due to banks. Most of the replacement would happen within a time span of about three to five years. The procedure should be agreed upon in redemption plans, negotiated individually or on a sector-wide basis. When the transitory bank liabilities are fully paid up, the transition from bankmoney to sovereign money is accomplished.

After the conversion day, when bank customers pay back overdrafts or loans, or when banks sell assets, the banks will no longer receive bankmoney which, in a fractional reserve system, is deleted in the process. Instead, they will obtain sovereign money which can be reused. Were the money not passed on to the central bank, the banks would make a huge windfall profit by obtaining sovereign money free of cost for the bankmoney they have created prior to conversion day on a small basis of fractional refinancing. For the sake of not overloading the transition process, it should be conceded that the transitory bank liability to the central bank is not interest-bearing.

As a counterpart to the banks' transitory liabilities to the central bank, a corresponding position of transitory claims on the banks would be added to the central bank's balance sheet. Upon receiving redemptions from the banks on this account, the transitory claims will be reduced accordingly. In exchange, and at the same time, the central bank will issue corresponding amounts of sovereign money, so that the stock of money will not shrink to an undesired extent.

The reissue of the corresponding amounts of money can be effected either as genuine seigniorage to the treasury or as short-term loans to banks. Particularly at the beginning of the transition process, this may result in leaving money with a bank, rather than the bank having to pass it on to the central bank. In this case, the transitory central bank claims and bank liabilities would be reduced all the same and replaced in the books with a new regular central bank loan to that bank.

As the present bankmoney supply represents overshoot, this raises the question of whether the exchange of old bank overnight liabilities to customers for new sovereign money should be carried out 1:1 or, say, 100:80 or some other ratio. This cannot be determined a priori. A respective central bank would certainly proceed cautiously to find out.

What about the fractional base of reserves on the banks' books? Banks will keep the cash in the vault. There is no change related to this, nor to the reserves on government accounts with the central bank; they remain what they are, that is, liquid sovereign money. The banks' fractional base of minimum and excess reserves, however, will be obsolete. Today, the reserves represent an interbank-circuit sub-amount of public-circuit bankmoney. In a single-circuit money system, the former reserves are fully redundant. As a sub-amount of bankmoney, reserves should not be part of the conversion process. If they were converted, they would unduly extend the money supply. In consequence, all reserves ought to be cancelled as an asset and a liability on both the banks' and the central bank's balance sheets. This represents a balance sheet reduction for both parties and does not involve a profit or loss for either side.

Another question is why the conversion of old bank liabilities into new sovereign money should only apply in a 'narrow' range which includes today's active cash and bankmoney, rather than applying to the 'broad' range that would also include all of the deactivated bankmoney. In the latter case, the amount of bank liabilities to be converted would be much higher, resulting in much higher amounts of both current seigniorage and one-off transition seigniorage. That much money, however, might easily be too much money.

In the split-circuit reserve system, savings and time deposits are just a passive cost factor, neither representing active money supply nor being available for effective demand until maturity. In a single-circuit sovereign money system, by contrast, savings and time positions provide active money for funding the banking business. For carrying out current transactions, the amount of cash and liquid bankmoney is sufficient today, including current liquidations of savings or time deposits that are offset by other customers making new such deposits. A comparable amount of liquid money M would thus be plenty in a sovereign money future too, the more so as the share of non-GDP finance would be smaller.

What about MMFs? There is no problem as far as MMFs exist as an instrument of financial intermediation, competing with time 'deposits' in banks. As a fund paper, MMF shares shall be freely bought from and re-sold to the issuing fund, they shall however not be transferrable within a fund or between different funds as a monetary asset on account. When MMF shares are used as a deposit-like means of payment, the shares are clearly a new type of money surrogate, and the regular general use of money surrogates on a large scale challenging the sovereign monetary prerogatives must not be tolerated. Otherwise, the control of the stock of money would again be undermined from the beginning. Non-cash sovereign money would face the same fate as banknotes in the last 120–170 years when banknotes were superimposed by bankmoney on account. Similarly, new money surrogates today might marginalize non-cash sovereign money.

It should be remembered that MMF shares developed in the 1970s in the USA due to unsuitable regulation, including a ceiling on deposit interest at around 5 % for savings and time deposits. This did not fit in with the much higher interest and inflation rates of the 1970s.[27] MMFs arose as an evasive reaction, and MMF shares turned out to be a formidable instrument of circumventing banking supervision and regulation on bank equity and minimum reserve requirements.

6.12 Little to Lose, Much to Gain: Stability, Safety, Seigniorage

As an interim result, a brief summary of the advantages of a transition from bankmoney to sovereign money follows. The overall picture opens up a perspective of little to lose and much to gain.

To begin with, the transition is not a 'revolution' that turns everything upside down, assuming incalculable risks. In terms of institutional arrangements as well as business and market routines, almost all elements of the present system would remain in place. Sovereign money retains the beneficial

---

[27] Hilton (2004, p. 180) and Baba et al. (2009, p. 68).

elements of the present monetary system, such as convenience, transactive efficiency, cost-efficiency, a necessary degree of incongruence of maturities and liquidability of financial assets, currency convertibility, and flexible monetary policies which—in contrast to the present system—exclude overextension as well as shortages in the money supply.

Nor is substituting sovereign money on account for bankmoney a currency reform. The currency and its units remain the same. One dollar continues to be one dollar. Financial property and duties remain as unchanged in the transition as the claims and liabilities of all actors (except the swap of overnight liabilities to customers for liabilities of the same amount to the central bank on the banks' balance sheet). The banking sector, certainly, would lose its illegitimate monetary privilege, which would be completely restored to the state to which it belongs.

The legal and technical measures to be decided and the changes to be implemented do not exceed the scope of so many reforms that are undertaken. Yet putting an end to bankmoney in favour of sovereign money would certainly be a step of the greatest importance.

With regard to the dysfunctions of the present bank-led split-circuit fractional reserve system, sovereign money would largely contain and partly eliminate those dysfunctions.

Sovereign money is safe money—on hand, in account, mobile sub-account, or some other form of digital cash. Sovereign money can be exchanged and circulated in these forms, domestically or abroad, but it cannot disappear. In a banking crisis it is not at stake like deposits and need not be guaranteed by the government. Invested money, by contrast, is no money but short- and long-term capital. As such, it quite naturally carries a certain risk, depending on how and for what it is invested. Whether this justifies retaining the present deposit insurance of savings and time deposits can be left open here.

As sovereign money is safe, there would be no threat of payment services breaking down in a banking crisis. Insolvent banks, regardless of their size, would no longer have to be rescued to prevent a general 'meltdown' of banking and a standstill of economic transactions.

Considering the matter from the angle of financial and economic market dynamics, probably the most important characteristic of sovereign money is full and effective control of its stock, including its flexible readjustment whenever necessary. On the basis of control over the stock of money, the central bank toolset of monetary policy instruments will also be effective in controlling inflation and asset inflation as far as these are due to monetary factors. This will curb the formation of hyper-inflated bubbles and ensuing severe crises—no matter whether they concern housing bubbles, stock bubbles, sovereign debt bubbles, commodity bubbles, derivatives bubbles, alternative-investment bubbles or anything else. As deposit creation by the banks would be brought to an end, banks would no longer be able to pour large amounts of additional bankmoney into non-GDP investment banking and financial market bonanzas. Business cycles and financial cycles would still exist but would remain on a rather moderate path.

GDP-proportionate additions to the money supply will result in a similarly proportionate increase in financial assets, curbing the bias towards disproportionately growing financial income at the expense of earned income.

Correspondingly, debtors would experience great difficulty in venturing ever deeper into debt by means of instant cheap money. The disproportionate demand for money would result in hefty price tags, that is, interest rates markedly above average. Lavish deficit spenders and Ponzi speculators would think twice.

Finally, the seigniorage—the gain from creating new money—will not be forgone to the public purse any more. Money creation will no longer add to private banking profits, but will help to balance budgets, reduce the outsized sovereign debt to more sustainable levels—which is of particular interest today—and help avoid public over-indebtedness in the future. In addition, beginning on conversion day, public coffers will benefit from a huge one-off transition seigniorage, on top of the regular seigniorage from current GDP-related additions to the stock of money.

6.13   Seigniorage to the Benefit of the Public Purse

For simplicity's sake, let us assume seigniorage would just be about genuine seigniorage of the amount of respective additions to the money supply. One percentage point of economic growth would then come with seigniorage of about the same order. A first rough idea of how much money this might be can be derived from present-day data, bearing in mind that present monetary aggregates represent overshoot. This means that actual figures on seigniorage would have to be adjusted downward, thus coming out lower than the figures in Table 6.1. According to these figures, one percentage point of economic growth in a country would amount to about 1.2–1.9 % of total public expenditure; 3 % economic growth to about 3.4–4 %. The comparatively high numbers for the UK (5.6 %) and Switzerland (8.3 %) might be due to the unusual size of the financial sector in both countries.

Table 6.1 Regular annual seigniorage as an addition to the stock of money

2014 billion \$, €, £, SFr	Money supply M	Seigniorage from Δ M of 1–2–3 %	Total public expenditure	Δ M as a % of total public expenditure
USA	8112	81–162–243	6200	1.3–2.6–3.9
Euro	5916	59–118–178	4957	1.2–2.4–3.6
UK	1380	13.8–27.6–41.4	735	1.9–3.7–5.6
Switzerland	568	5.7–11.4–17.0	206	2.8–5.5–8.3

Sources: http://www.federalreserve.gov/releases/h6/current/default.htm#t5tg1link (M2).—http://www.bankofengland.co.uk/boeapps/iadb/BankStats.asp?Travel=Nix (overnight deposits and cash); www.ukpublicspending.co.uk/total_2014UKbt_ 15bc5n. —European Central Bank, *Economic Bulletin*, Tables 5.1, 3.1, 6.1–2 (www.ecb.europa.eu/pub/pdf/ecbu).—Schweizerische Nationalbank, *Statistische Monatshefte*, Tab. B2, H1

Regular annual seigniorage to the extent of about 1–4 % of public expenditure may not sound like a lot, but in fact it is. It would contribute significantly to funding the purposes discussed in Sect. 6.7, including tax cuts. On the other hand, it becomes clear that replacing taxes with seigniorage is totally unrealistic. In a sovereign money future, too, the budget needs to be funded by taxes and satisfy the principles of sound housekeeping. But regular seigniorage will no doubt help. Budgets in countries with relatively low government expenditure and/or high growth rates will benefit more than budgets in countries with relatively high government expenditure and/or low growth rates.

Still more important than current regular seigniorage, especially under today's conditions of public over-indebtedness, is the one-off transition seigniorage. It accrues from the introduction of sovereign money on account in a way that is analogous to the transition from private banknotes to central bank notes in the nineteenth century.

As the former bankmoney liabilities are successively phased out, new sovereign money must in exchange be phased in. At the beginning of the process, a relatively high share of the new money might need to be loaned short-term to the banks. Over the months and years, an ever larger part of the new money can be issued long-term as genuine seigniorage to the treasury. It would be a great pity if that one-off opportunity to reduce the sovereign debt was not taken. To the degree that banks still hold sovereign debt, this would at the same time contribute to providing them with new money.

In this way, and measured by current figures as shown in Table 6.2, more than half of total public debt in the USA and the eurozone could be redeemed in the course of the transition period. In the UK, the respective figure would

Table 6.2 One-off transition seigniorage

2014 billion $, €, £, SFr	A. Bankmoney	B. Total public debt	A/B (%)
USA	9837	18,000	55
Euro	4976	9280	54
UK	1306	1260	104
Switzerland	501	217	231

Data Sources: USA demand deposits and other checkable deposits in M1, and small time deposits and savings deposits in M2. http://www.federalreserve.gov/releases/h6/current/default.htm#t6tg1link. For the national debt see www.usgovernments pending.com/national_debt.—Eurozone overnight deposits in M1, from 2014 for EU-18. European Central Bank, *Economic Bulletin*, Tables 6.2.3.2, 6.2.1 (www.ecb. europa.eu/pub/ pdf/ecbu).—UK overnight deposits and deposits redeemable at notice, excluding cash in circulation. http://www.bankofengland.co.uk/boeapps/iadb/BankStats.asp?Travel=Nix. For UK government debt see www.ukpublics pending.co. uk/uk_national_debt_chart.html.—Switzerland demand and transaction deposits. Schweizerische Nationalbank, Statistische Monatshefte, Tab. B2, H1

allow for full redemption. In Switzerland, the figure represents over twice the national debt. The exceptional ratios in the UK and Switzerland are presumably again due to the exceptional relative size of the financial sector in both countries.

The figures are not meant to be any kind of forecast, but, again, give an idea of the magnitude of the numbers at stake and the room for maneuver opened, while bearing in mind that the substitution of new sovereign money for old overnight liabilities of the banks would probably not be 1:1, but rather 90:100, or 80:100, or even much less.

Nevertheless, the one-off transition seigniorage offers a historically unique opportunity to pay down sovereign debt to a considerable extent—with no need for negative deposit interest or inflation, and without having to impose 'haircuts' on creditors and depressing austerity on debtor governments and the people.

The prospect of significantly less sovereign debt makes some people fret about a lack of investment opportunities. Present soaring levels of sovereign debt, though, cannot sensibly be the historical benchmark. The financial economy went through periods of high as well as low sovereign debt. The business proved to be adaptive. There is no doubt vast dormant investment potential in the real economy, including public infrastructure and medium-sized enterprises. Moreover, present ratios of financial assets and debt to GDP are hypertrophic. One will anyway have to readapt to more sustainable levels of financial assets and debt.

It should be stressed that the money for paying down public debt is not confiscated from anybody. The transition is about neither expropriation and redistribution nor taxation. In particular, the money is not taken from the banks. The money involved does not exist today; instead, it exists as the bank liability we habitually use as bankmoney, which is a money surrogate, a claim/liability on cash and central bank reserves which only exist at a small fraction of the stock of the bank liabilities. Banks will keep the cash in their vault as well as existing excess reserves in their current central bank account. Minimum reserve requirements will be obsolete and can be cancelled both as an asset and as a liability on both the banks' and the central bank's balance sheets, thus not resulting in a loss for the banks. Simply, sovereign money will replace that largely 'void' liability of bankmoney with positively existing, actual legal tender money. The seigniorage from creating new sovereign money in fact represents a free lunch.

6.14 Transition Through Raising Fractional Reserves to 100 % of Deposits?

Many commentators pass off sovereign money as a remake of the approaches to 100 % reserve banking of the 1930s, as if to say 'That's old hat', why care about yesterday's tomorrows? Nothing could be farther off the mark. Sovereign money and 100 % reserve banking are two entirely different systems. The 100 % reserve approach involves a number of shortcomings that are not easily discerned at first glance. Had it been given a chance, 100 % reserve banking would at best have achieved only partially, if at all, what sovereign money can achieve today.

It is true, however, that sovereign money and 100 % reserve share a common lineage, in particular monetary quantity considerations, Currency teaching and chartalism. They thus also share similar analyses and criticisms of fractional reserve banking and the basic goal of putting an end to banks' primary credit creation to regain control over the stock of money. Technically and operationally, however, 100 % reserve banking and single-circuit sovereign money are two different things based on different principles regarding the ways of creating and issuing money, accounting procedures, management of payment transactions and institutional arrangements.

Soddy is said to have been the first to propose a 100 % reserve on deposits in 1926. This was pursued in the 1930s by the then Chicago School (100 % banking promoted by Simons, Knight, Viner and others, including young Friedman). Fisher, who had previously supported the Gesellian stamp scrip movement, adopted a variant of the approach as 100 % money.[28] In the decades to follow, the idea was advocated, for example, by Allais, and by Tobin with his narrow banking proposal.[29]

All 100 % plans are based on raising fractional reserves, which were already 10 % at the time in the USA, to 100 % reserve coverage of all deposits. As far as this is the only measure, the approach leaves a number of problems unresolved:

Even with a full 100 % reserve it is still about a complicated split-circuit reserve system based on reserves and deposits, rather than a single-circuit system based on one integrated money supply M. Bank customers are still not in safe possession of their money on account and have only a claim on it, while the banks own the money and owe it to the customers.

The 100 % scholars argued as if reserves were all payment reserves (excess reserves), not a requirement to hold idle backing reserves on all deposits. They ignored that question, in spite of it being fundamental in a reserve system.

In a two-tier split-circuit system, new reserves and banknotes are loaned into circulation by way of central bank credit (or currency committee credit) to banks. As all of the reserves are credited to the banks, the entire stock of money is still credit and debt money.

Even with 100 % reserves on deposits, the obligatory reserve requirement is determined after the fact, for example, on the average stock of deposits during the past two months for the next month. In other words, banks can still have the proactive lead in credit and deposit creation, while the central bank accommodates the banks' demand for reserves upon or after the fact. The 100 % reformers have apparently not taken into account that a bank that creates primary credit is *not* liable for 100 % coverage of the ensuing deposits. The latter falls on the recipient banks that receive deposit liabilities from the primary credit creator or any other bank thereafter.

A bank's own money and the money liabilities to customers are still not separate. Savings and time deposits still represent deactivated bankmoney. Banks do not obtain liquid reserves from these deposits, but nonetheless have to cover them 100 %.

As a result, a 100 % reserve on all deposits would be unnecessarily expensive, because—all other things in the reserve system being the same—the banks would have to pay double: deposit interest to the customers and lend-

---

[28] Soddy (1926), Currie (1934a, b), Hart (1935), Fisher (1935), Douglas et al. (1939), Simons (1948), and Friedman (1948, 1959, 1969).
[29] Allais (1987, 1988) and Tobin (1987, p. 172).

ing interest to the central bank. This would induce an unnecessarily increased cost level for everybody, because the banks could hardly avoid charging the customers most of these additional costs. It would make the interest-borne seigniorage from the creation of reserves look like a special tax on money. It should, however, not be the intention of a sovereign money reform to generate a hidden tax on money to beef up the government budget. The intention is to provide genuine seigniorage commensurate with the increases in real output.

Recognizing the cost problem, the monetary reformers of the 1930s finally thought of leaving the reserves to the banks free of interest. This, however, was rightly seen as granting the banking sector privileged refinancing further on. As an additional measure for making the transition, the authors suggested the monetary authority could buy all sovereign bonds in the banks' portfolio.[30] This is outright monetization of public debt, a questionable practice by any measure. In comparison, outright issue of sovereign money by way of genuine seigniorage is the straightforward alternative.[31]

In response to the critical points listed here, the 100 % reserve approach could be modified by adding a number of further elements. This would boil down to emulating sovereign money within a 100 % reserve system, without, however, being identical to a genuine single-circuit sovereign money system.[32] The measures to be implemented to achieve such emulation are the following:

1. Re-declare all reserves to be payment reserves. A difference between 100 % coverage reserves (in succession of today's minimum reserves) and excess reserves would no longer exist.
2. Separate—on the books and in the payment system—bank reserves from customer reserves, that is, the reserves that represent a bank's own money from the reserves that are intended to cover customer deposits in full.
3. Enact legal and regulatory changes regarding monetary property rights and insolvency procedures to make sure that customer reserves represent a fiduciary position on a bank's balance sheet of which customers have the full title. The customer reserves must not fall under the terms of bankruptcy in the case of insolvency. It is open to legal examination whether priority customer claims on reserves that override any other claims, especially those

---

[30] P.H. Douglas et al. (1939, para 11a, b).

[31] For an appraisal of 100 % banking cf. the contributions at http://sovereignmoney.eu/100-per-cent-reserve-chicago-plan, including a critical synopsis of the core elements of 100 % money and sovereign money. A similar synopsis has been compiled by Andrew Jackson, Positive Money. This is available at http://www.positivemoney.org/2013/01/the-chicago-plan-versus-positive-money

[32] For more details of the 'emulation' problem, see my papers at http://sovereignmoney.eu/how-to-emu-late-plain-money-within-a-full-reserve-sytem, and 'Many roads lead to Rome—not all by the shortest path' at http://sovereignmoney.eu/on-kumhof-the-chicago-plan-revisited.

of the central bank, can be implemented within a reserve system. If the answer is negative, the existing property rights regarding the ownership of reserves represent a serious obstacle.

4. Ensure synchronized full transfer of reserves and deposits 1:1 in parallel, whereby

   – A transfer among customers involves customer reserves only
   – A transfer from a bank to customers involves bank reserves adding to the recipient customer reserves
   – A transfer from customers to banks involves customer reserves adding to bank reserves.

Customers can thus run savings and time deposits, or invest their money in securities, by transforming customer reserves into bank reserves. Banks can therefore finance their own lending and investment engagements largely by taking up money from their customers and on the open market, while still being able to resort to additional central bank credit if need be and if fitting the central bank quantity targets. This is to say, however, that deposit savings are no longer idle deposits. Instead, such 'deposits' represent short-term capital invested in a bank. This would also bring down the cost problem to normal levels.

The requirement of synchronizing the flow of bank and customer reserves and the transfer of deposits cannot be met in a net settlement system, that is a payment system of continued clearing of payment orders with deferred settlement or without settlement. Synchronization could best be achieved in a real time gross settlement system, in which payment orders are immediately settled in full.

Some people, who erroneously consider the differences between the two approaches to be insignificant, assume it would be easier to retain split circulation rather than to integrate the two circuits into just one. But common sense alone tells us that a split-circuit system must be more complicated and effortful than a single one. The shortcomings of the approaches to a 100 % reserve on deposits are indeed rooted in keeping the reserve system as such. It is apparent from the features discussed that emulating sovereign money within the frame of a 100 % reserve system is not a simple affair. Indeed, it is complicated and, compared with a single-circuit sovereign money system, it seems to require *more* technical and legal effort.

Raising 2.5 % or 10 % fractional reserves to 100 % could be undertaken gradually. As far as this is an advantage, it not only applies to a 100 % approach, since a simple sovereign money system also involves a transition period of about five years, and is easier to implement and to manage thereafter.

Both approaches involve some technical measures, in that the bank accountancy systems and the central bank payment system would have to be readapted with regard to the separation of a bank's own money and its customers' money.

Given these considerations, it definitely appears to be easier to quit the double-circuit reserve system altogether in favour of a single-circuit plain money system—no more reserves and deposits, no funding costs for backing idle reserves, unambiguous ownership of money, and no complicated synchronization of deposits and reserves; just one integrated money supply M, circulating among banks and nonbanks alike as a liquid monetary asset on any balance sheet.

6.15 Monetary Financing. Government Spending of Sovereign Money Adding to Bankmoney

Some economists think of 'helicopter money' as an unconventional way of kickstarting economic recovery. They suggest issuing additional reserves (sovereign money) by way of central bank funding of government expenditure rather than using today's regular channel of crediting the reserves to the banking sector. Some supporters of sovereign money welcome the idea as a first step towards monetary reform. Introducing sovereign money in parallel to bankmoney might be easier to achieve than putting an end to bankmoney.

Walter proposes that the central bank should leave newly created reserves (sovereign money) to the government. According to the author, such means ought to be limited in quantity and earmarked for specified investment in public infrastructure only.[33] Similar proposals have in recent years been put forth by American scholars and activists, given that infrastructure in the USA is a particularly urgent issue.

Wolf wrote in the *Financial Times* on 'The Case for Helicopter Money', in which he argues in favour of the creation of reserves for public spending.[34] The metaphor dates back to Friedman in 1969 who considered helicopter money to be useless, for it would simply create inflation without having real effects. Wolf, by contrast, ascribes positive investment and demand-side effects to government-spent helicopter money.

Turner shares that opinion under the term overt money finance, questioning the taboo according to which direct central bank contributions to funding government expenditure must not be allowed.[35] In particular, he refers to

---

[33] Walter (2011, 2013, p. 204).
[34] Wolf (2013, 2015, p. 209).
[35] Turner (2015, pp. 213, 218, 227–230, 237–240).

using central bank money as consumptive helicopter money compensating for effective demand, or for writing off past public debt, or for other purposes, on the understanding that this is not carried out excessively. Turner argues that helicopter money is basically no more risky than conventional quantitative easing and that printing money to fund public expenditure is the fastest way to prevent impending deflation.

The impulse was taken up by the NGO Positive Money, including a campaign entitled 'Quantitative Easing for People'.[36] The government is supposed to create sovereign money in cooperation with the central bank and use it for deficit spending, which in this case, however, does not come along with additional debt.[37] Jackson/Dyson propose that the government should issue 'perpetual zero-coupon consols' (zero-interest permacredit) directly to the Bank of England. The Bank in turn would credit the exchequer account with the corresponding amount of liquid reserves. However, the central bank alone would decide how many consols to buy.

In the meantime, American monetary reformers recollect the country's patriotic past of government-issued money, in particular the Greenback dollars that helped the Union to fund the Civil War, as the Greyback dollars did for the Confederacy. The ensuing Greenback movement in the 1870–1880s campaigned for Treasury-issued sovereign money, which, as especially the farmers thought, would keep interest rates down. Still today, even though the Treasury has not issued Greenbacks for a long time, there are US Treasury notes circulating in parallel to Federal Reserve notes.

Of late, Striner has taken up the US tradition of government-issued money again. His proposal concerns 'twin streams of money creation, one of them coming from the banking system … and the other one coming from Congress', the first being credit and debt bankmoney and the latter debt-free sovereign money 'through direct electronic deposit'. This twin system 'would constitute a merger of fiscal and monetary policy'.[38] In this case, the Treasury and the Congress themselves would create sovereign money in parallel and in addition to Federal Reserve notes and reserves.

In Wolf, Turner and Jackson/Dyson, monetary financing aims at conventional Keynesian-style compensatory demand-side policy. Regarding government expenditure, debt-funded deficit spending would be replaced with

---

[36] Jackson and Dyson (2013b, p. 16).
[37] Jackson and Dyson (2013b, p. 19).
[38] Striner (2015, pp. 84, 59–64); also cf. http://globalmonetaryforum.blogspot.de run by Keith L. Rodgers.

debt-free deficit spending without changing the budget and tax policies in place. Using money creation for purposes of fiscal policy and income policy helps to prevent additional government debt or, alternatively, higher taxation. The existing levels of debt are not reduced.

Monetary financing puts itself in the context of monetary reform. In fact it is about another variant of rather short-term countercyclical government interventionism. Monetary financing allows the banking industry and governments to continue along the path they have been following for decades, which has recurrently led to financial crises. Instrumentalizing monetary policy for fiscal and economic policy remains a controversial practice, accompanied by doubts about its effectiveness and side effects.

Monetary financing could be supported as a stimulus that would help to emerge from the current crisis. In this respect, monetary financing can be expected to be economically effective, in contrast to conventional quantitative easing, that is, central bank purchases of government debt and other sorts of badly performing credit, thus monetizing such credit and debt. This helps to maintain government debt and to keep afloat quasi-insolvent financial institutions without, however, supporting the real economy.

Monetary financing would also be more effective, and certainly more reasonable, than imposing negative interest rates on money holdings. Technocrats try to legitimize negative interest as 'a kind of fee' for banking services, while in fact it is outright expropriation violating fundamental property rights. Technically, and if fully implemented, negative interest reduces banking liabilities to customers, thereby also reducing the stock of bankmoney, that is, public purchasing power without, however, reducing nonbank debt levels. This is counterproductive in that it deters firms from taking up money for investment and, psychologically, prompts households to make additional efforts to uphold savings rather than re-activating savings for additional expenditure.

The expectable positive effects of monetary financing are, however, subject to the proviso that the economic situation in a country is characterized by a lack of real investment and capital expenditure due to a lack of mass income, tax revenue and consumer demand. Monetary financing is bound to fail, however, to the extent that the problem is postponed crisis resolution, particularly postponed debt reduction and the writing-off of irrecoverable debts.

Moreover, one should bear in mind that deficit spending has never been implemented as conceived of, that is, as a countercyclical stimulus only, with debt reduction in boom times. Instead, deficit spending has become an all-seasons habit of financing ever higher levels of government expenditure, and maintaining these levels. Why would this be any different from now on?

Another problematic aspect of monetary financing is related to the split circulation of bankmoney and central bank reserves. With monetary financing, the role of the banking sector as a monetary power might be strengthened rather than overcome. The reason is that today's money system is no longer based on cash or dominated by it, as was the case with the Greenbacks in the nineteenth century when strongboxes full of notes were shipped across the country. In today's cashless monetary and banking system, when the government spends reserves from its central bank account, firms and people get a deposit entry (bankmoney), while the banks obtain the reserves for free. The banks would thus be free riders in the arrangement. The more extensive monetary financing would be, the less the banks would still have to refinance at a cost. If traditional solid coins and notes, which banks still have to refinance to 100 %, are then abolished, any of the existing monetary policy instruments will ultimately be pointless.

Thus, extending the share of sovereign money without putting an end to bankmoney opens an ambivalent perspective. The split-circuit system of fractional reserve banking and the monetary powers of the banking sector remain untouched and the dysfunctions related to fractional reserve banking continue to exist. As soon as signs of an impending crisis occur again, the banks and the government would shift the blame onto each other. As a consequence, monetary financing, rather than being a promising halfway house on the road to monetary reform, might become stuck in a situation of uncoordinated parallel money creation, eventually losing out to bankmoney as occurred twice in the history of the USA (with colonial scrip in the eighteenth century and the Greenbacks in the nineteenth century). The Canadian experience of monetary financing from 1936 through to the early 1970s reached its end in the same way.[39]

What is more, monetary financing adding to bankmoney cannot be implemented just like this. There are legal prerequisites. The proposal encounters much the same juridical disputes as a conversion day strategy. Even in America there is no undisputed legal basis for Treasury-issued sovereign money on account, and monetary financing by the central bank requires a change of US Code Title 12, Chap. 3, Subchap. IX, § 355 in America, and Art. 123 (1) TFEU in Europe. These laws prohibit direct government funding by the central bank. Achieving an amendment of the respective laws is unlikely in the short run. Full sovereign money reform, by contrast, does not necessarily involve changing those paragraphs, however desirable certain specifications would be.

---

[39] Ryan-Collins (2015).

The key concern of sovereign money reform is putting an end to the dysfunctions of the bankmoney regime, not to provide gratuitous funds for government expenditure, even if this, to a limited extent, is a welcome side-effect of monetary reform.

6.16 Safe Sovereign Money Accounts

The calls for government-issued money in addition to bankmoney would gain in consistency if accompanied by the introduction of a new type of current account—sovereign money accounts, or money accounts for short—in addition to conventional bank giro accounts with bankmoney in them. Put differently, firms and people would in some way get access to the central bank payment system on the basis of reserves, or, alternatively, to central bank digital currency on the basis of blockchain technology. Such options are now considered by a number of central banks, but the technical aspects involved have still not been clarified in detail.

In the case of money accounts, these would serve the safekeeping and transfer of non-cash sovereign money (central bank reserves) also in public circulation among firms, nonbank financial institutions, private and public households. The split-circuit reserve system would still exist, but customers then have the choice between bankmoney and sovereign money. They could in fact maintain both types of account.

There have been proposals for introducing 'safe deposits' or 'safe accounts' before.[40] For the most part, such proposals include 100 % coverage of bank deposits by reserves. The idea put forward here is different. It is about introducing sovereign money ('high-powered' central bank money), which has so far been restricted to interbank use, into cashless public circulation too.

Money accounts can be fiduciary accounts with banks or other payment service providers. The money would be kept and managed in a separate central bank account in the form of a customer omnibus account of a bank or another payment provider. That account would have its own address in the respective real time gross settlement payment system. Money accounts could be off-balance items, separate from a bank's own reserves, analogous to customer securities accounts, so that the customers' money and the banks' or payment providers' money are kept apart. They could also be fiduciary on-balance items that are 'sterilized' against other bank assets and liabilities. Money then is the property of the customer, and is neither an asset nor a liability on a bank's or other payment provider's balance sheet. The proposal could thus also be referred to as an approach of separate accounts.[41]

---

[40] For example Mayer (2013a, b) and Gudehus (2015b).

[41] Also cf. www.sovereignmoney.eu/separate-accounts-safe-deposits

The money would be issued by the central bank. The government would obtain the money in its central bank accounts in much the same way as it does now. Further changes are not a precondition for introducing money accounts. The reserves would then get into customer money accounts through government expenditure, by transferring the money from a government central bank account into the money accounts of payees. The government could also issue e-cash on chip cards or phones, albeit on the basis of the reserves in its central bank account, rather than in a procedure based on bankmoney.

Offering money accounts to customers can for the banks be optional or made compulsory. As soon as such an offer existed, many customers would not hesitate to make use of it. The firms and people would decide which kind of account they prefer, as governments already do in that they have the choice to keep their current accounts with the central bank and commercial banks alike.

Transfers between money accounts and giro accounts would be possible, in the same way as it is possible today to transfer an amount of money from a government central bank account to any bank giro account (by way of the recipient bank crediting the respective customer account), and, in the opposite direction, to transfer an amount of money from a bank giro account to a government central bank account (by way of the remitting bank deleting the bankmoney and transferring the respective amount of reserves to the government account). The banks as monetary intermediaries receive and pay out transfers in central bank money (reserves) anyway.

With money accounts in public circulation, banks would not be free riders of the arrangement, as is the case with monetary financing without money accounts. The reason is that transactions among customer money accounts would not affect the banks, while the banks would need incoming reserves, which they obtain through transfers from money accounts to giro accounts, to fund outgoing transfers from giro accounts to money accounts. In this way, a gradual transition from bankmoney to sovereign money would be possible, depending on the market decision of money users over which type of account, or which type of money respectively, they would prefer to use.

6.17 Sovereign Digital Currency

As cash is bound to be abolished sooner or later, it would be highly desirable from a chartalist point of view to continue the traditional sovereign monopoly on solid cash by implementing sovereign digital currency as a modern equivalent. As discussed in Sect 2.6, it is presently not clear whether what is called e-cash today can have an existence independent of money on account.[42] But if such a thing as sovereign digital cash existed, it would be an alternative to bankmoney, and might even have the potential to replace it.

For one thing, there can be sovereign e-cash as a sub-amount, or mobile sub-account respectively, of a sovereign money account. Governments should in fact start emitting e-cash, based on central bank reserves (sovereign money) rather than bankmoney, which would support the use of money accounts, as money accounts would foster the use of e-cash based on sovereign money. EU Directive 2009/110/EG explicitly grants the right to issue e-cash not only to banks, but also to central banks, government bodies and other licensed agencies.

For another thing, the question arises today whether it is possible to replace solid cash with central bank issued digital cash based on blockchain technology.[43] This would be a substantial and presumably decisive step into a sovereign money future. Such digital 'currency' issued by a central bank is not intended to be an alternative to the national currency in place, rather, a cash-like legal-tender alternative to bitcoins and similar new private digital currencies. Sovereign digital cash would also be based on some special variant of blockchain technology, but created by a central bank according to its own rules.

In lieu of obscure algorithm-controlled money creation ('mining'), the only 'miner' to insert digital cash in the blockchain would be the central bank. The blockchain processing itself would need to be much faster than the present bitcoin method, allowing for many thousands up to a million transactions in a second rather than only seven as is the case now.[44] There would also need to be an interface between sovereign cash and sovereign money on account.

The blockchain technology might indeed be an additional and perhaps decisive way of modernizing money. Irritatingly, what central bankers seem to have in mind when reflecting on alternatives to traditional solid cash is the questionable aim of imposing without hindrance negative interest rather than worrying about monetary sovereignty.

---

[42] Cf. 'Digital E-Cash Accounts' by Dyson and Hodgson (2016). That proposal converges in its basic features with the proposal of sovereign money accounts as outlined here.

[43] Cf. Ali, Barrdear, Clews, and Southgate (2014a, b), Barrdear and Kumhof (2016), Broadbent (2016) as well as Dyson and Hodgson (2016).

[44] Systems with a corresponding transaction capacity already exist, for example in various electronic payment systems, or in the systems of Google, Amazon, Twitter and Facebook.

6.18 International Connectivity of Sovereign Money

In a world of global interdependencies, free cross-border flow of capital, and full convertibility of currencies, is it possible for a single country to go it alone with a transition from bankmoney to sovereign money? The answer is yes, any country can to the degree that it meets certain preconditions.

Among the preconditions are reasonably reliable state institutions, stable political conditions, the rule of law and respected division of powers, as well as functioning markets making for a fairly productive economy. By contrast, under conditions of widespread corruption, predatory elites, and financial and structural deficits on all fronts, it does of course not make a difference whether there is a run-down currency on the basis of sovereign money or bankmoney.

A well-run nation-state and economy will be an internationally respected trading partner with an acceptable currency. If any such country, whether large or small, switches from bankmoney to sovereign money, it may face political contestation, but as far as technical, operational and economic aspects are involved, basically no problem should arise. Sovereign money is not about currency reform. The cross-border conversion of domestic currency into other currencies, or the reverse, would technically be the same as before. Foreign exchange trading is currency trading, and cross-border payment procedures handle currency units as quantities of money. They do not care whether these quantities of currency units were originally created by banks, or the central bank, or the national treasury. The important thing is to be connected to a respective payment system by maintaining a current account there, or by cooperating with a bank or other payment service provider that does. The final settlement of international payments is carried out in central bank reserves anyway. International transactions thus are optimally compatible with national sovereign money systems.

As far as countries have a preference for free trade, unrestricted capital mobility, and full currency convertibility, this need not be changed due to the introduction of sovereign money. Naturally, though, the more such preferences determine the course of events, the higher the degree of exposure to foreign influences, including exposure to foreign monetary influences, and the lower the degree of national 'autonomy'. This applies in any case, independently of the particular money system.

As a result, the effectiveness and advantages of sovereign money would partly be reduced in a scenario of a single country going it alone; as the qualities of sovereign money are enhanced, the greater the number of adopter countries. For example, to the extent that monetary factors are responsible for inflation, a central bank with full control of the stock of money can pursue effective inflation policies. What it cannot influence, however, is imported inflation, which depends on monetary policies and other factors in foreign countries.

In an analogous way this also applies to asset inflation in the financial economy. Financial trends and cycles follow international patterns, detached to a degree from the particular conditions in single economies. Large amounts of portfolio capital flood into and drain away from a country, without the central bank being able to do much about it unless resorting to overt exchange rate intervention, or even restricting the movement of capital.

A country with a foreign trade surplus has a corresponding inflow of money from abroad. This adds to the foreign reserves of the national central bank that exchanges respective amounts of foreign currency into domestic currency, thus adding these amounts to the domestic money supply. This is carried out, but not actively controlled by a central bank. The respective amount of money is foreign-created and cannot responsibly be created domestically a second time. The overall effect, however, is not as important as it might appear at first glance. The reason is that countries with a trade surplus also tend to be net capital exporters. On balance of the overall external account, trade revenue inflows and foreign investment outflows largely offset each other. Remaining deficits or surpluses become only a problem if structurally entrenched over a longer period of time.

Despite such non-optimal aspects, an important part of the advantages of sovereign money remains, in particular, far-reaching control of the available stock of money, with a dampening effect on domestic inflation and asset inflation, a great deal of genuine seigniorage and interest-borne central bank profit from money creation and the management of foreign reserves, and absolute safety of sovereign money and cashless payments—which correspondingly increases economic stability irrespective of risky business lines in banking and finance.

Although any country can go it alone, there are of course countries that have more weight than others. Since the Bretton Woods conference in 1944, the USA is the only financial center country, that is, the dominant monetary and financial power in the world system.[45] The US dollar is the leading currency by any standard, putting it in a privileged position that is mirrored in a 60–80 % global share of foreign exchange and foreign currency reserves,

---

[45] Rey (2013) and Borio (2012).

cross-border payments, trade finance and international banking liabilities. The overall directions in money, banking and finance thus depend to a large extent on where the USA is heading.

Given the country's monetary privilege, the USA seems to be an unlikely candidate for monetary reform. On the other hand, sovereign money is not about currency reform. A renewed global currency system is desirable, but sovereign money by itself does neither include nor exclude related measures. At the same time, even if the dollar's privilege is 'exorbitant', it is not limitless. The country's deficit and debt problems are clearly felt to be a permanent nuisance. If the US elites could begin to see monetary reform as an important answer to the deficit and debt problem, they might see sovereign money more favorably. Since the eighteenth century, the monetary history of America has been one of alternating shifts between bank-controlled and state-controlled money. Sooner or later the tide will turn again; it may already be changing.

Independently, any country that summons up the political will can go ahead with issuing sovereign money and phasing out bankmoney, thus making the advantages of a sovereign money system observable, and inviting observers to become adopters.

References

Aglietta, Michel, André Orléan, eds. 1998. *La monnaie souveraine*. Paris: Odile Jacob.

Ali, Robleh, John Barrdear, Roger Clews, and James Southgate. 2014a. Innovations in Payment Technologies and the Emergence of Digital Currencies. *Bank of England Quarterly Bulletin* Q3: 262–275.

———. 2014b. The Economics of Digital Currencies. *Bank of England Quarterly Bulletin* Q3: 276–286.

Aliber, Robert Z., and Charles P. Kindleberger. 2015 [1978]. *Manias, Panics, and Crashes. A History of Financial Crises*, 7th edn. New York: Basic Books.

Allais, Maurice. 1987. The Credit Mechanism and its Implications. In *Arrow and the Foundations of the Theory of Economic Policy. Essays in Honor of Kenneth J. Arrow*, ed. George R. Feiwel, 491–561. New York: New York University Press.

———. 1988. *L'Impôt sur le capital et la réforme monétaire*, Nouvelle édition. Paris: Hermann Éditeurs des Sciences et des Arts. Première édition 1977.

Baba, Naohiko, Robert N. McCauley, and Srichander Ramaswamy. 2009. US Dollar Money Market Funds and Non-US Banks. *BIS Quarterly Review* March 2009: 65–81.

Bank of England. 2015. *The Bank of England Act 1998, the Charters of the Bank and Related Documents*. London: Bank of England. http://www.bankofengland.co.uk/about/Documents/legislation/1998act.pdf

Benes, Jaromir, and Michael Kumhof. 2012. The Chicago Plan Revisited. *IMF-working paper*, 12/202 August 2012. Revised draft February 2013.

Borio, Claudio. 2012. The Financial Cycle and Macroeconomics: What Have We Learnt? *BIS Working Papers*, No. 395, December 2012. Basel: Bank for International Settlements.

Currie, Lauchlin. 1934a. *The Supply and Control of Money in the United States.* Cambridge, MA: Harvard University Press.

———. 1934b. *A Proposed Revision of the Monetary System in the United States* (submitted to the Secretary of the Treasury, Henry Morgenthau). Reprinted in Currie, Lauchlin. 1968. *The Supply and Control of Money in the United States.* New York: Russell & Russell.

Del Mar, Alexander. 1895. *The History of Monetary Systems.* New York: Cambridge Encyclopedia. Reprinted by A.M. Kelley, New York, 1978.

Denk, Oliver, and Boris Cournède. 2015. Finance and income inequality in OECD countries. *OECD Economics Department Working Papers*, No. 1224. Paris: OECD Publishing.

Douglas, Paul H., Earl J. Hamilton, Irving Fisher, Willford I. King, Frank D. Graham, and Charles R. Whittlesey. 1939. *A Program for Monetary Reform.* Unpublished, but widely circulated among economists at the time. Available from the Kettle Pond Institute for Debt-Free Money. http://www.economicstability.org/history/a-program-for-monetaryreform-the-1939-document

Dyson, Ben, and Graham Hodgson. 2016. *Digital Cash. Why Central Banks Should Start Issuing Electronic Money.* London: Positive Money.

Dyson, Ben, Graham Hodgson, and Andrew Jackson. 2015. *Would a Sovereign Money System Be Flexible Enough?* London: Positive Money. http://positivemoney.org/wp-content/uploads/2015/01/Would_A_Sovereign_Money_System_Be_Flexible_Enough_WEB20140113.pdf

Ferguson, Niall. 2008. *The Ascent of Money. A Financial History of the World.* London: Allen Lane.

Fisher, Irving. 1935. *100%-money.* New Haven: Yale University. Reprinted in William J. Barber et al., eds. 1996. *The Works of Irving Fisher.* London: Pickering & Chatto.

Friedman, Milton. 1948. A Monetary and Fiscal Framework for Economic Stability. *The American Economic Review* 38:245–264. Reprinted in: Friedrich A. Lutz, and Lloyd W. Mints, eds. 1951. *Readings in Monetary Theory*, 369–393. Homewood, IL: Richard D. Irwin. Reprinted again in M. Friedman, ed. 1953. *Essays in Positive Economics*, 133–156. The University of Chicago Press.

———. 1959. *A Program for Monetary Stability.* New York: Fordham University Press.

———. 1969. The Monetary Theory and Policy of Henry Simons. In *The Optimum Quantity of Money and other Essays*, ed. M. Friedman, 81–94. New York: Aldine de Gruyter.

Galbraith, John Kenneth. 1995. *Money. Whence It Came, Where It Went*. New York: Houghton Mifflin (1st edn. 1975).

Graziani, Augusto. 1990. The Theory of the Monetary Circuit. *Économies et Sociétés* 7: 7–36.

Gudehus, Timm. 2015a. *Dynamische Märkte. Grundlagen der analytischen Ökonomie*. Berlin: Springer.

———. 2015b. *Sicherheitskonten und Geldsicherungsbanken. Gleitender Übergang zu einer neuen Geldordnung*. Available at: http://www.vollgeld.de/trennkonten-und-sicheres-geld

Hart, Albert G. 1935. The Chicago Plan of Banking Reform. *The Review of Economic Studies* 2:104–116. Reprinted in Friedrich A. Lutz, and Lloyd W. Mints, eds. 1951. *Readings in Monetary Theory*, 437–456. Homewood, IL: Richard D. Irwin.

Hilton, Adrian. 2004. Sterling Money Market Funds, Bank of England. *Quarterly Bulletin* Summer 2004: 176–182.

Hixson, William F. 1993. *Triumph of the Bankers. Money and Banking in the Eighteenth and Nineteenth Centuries*. Westport, CO: Praeger.

Huber, Joseph, and James Robertson. 2000. *Creating New Money*. London: New Economics Foundation.

Hudson, Michael. 2012. *The Bubble and Beyond*. Dresden: Islet Verlag.

Huerta de Soto, Jesús. 2009. *Money, Bank Credit, and Economic Cycles*, 2nd edn. Auburn, AL: Ludwig von Mises Institute (1st edn. 2006).

Iqbal, Jaquir. 2009. *Islamic Finance Management*. New Delhi: Global Vision Publishing House.

Jackson, Andrew, and Ben Dyson. 2013b. *Sovereign Money*, ed. Ben Dyson. London: Positive Money. http://positivemoney.org/our-proposals/sovereign-money-creation

Jordà, Òscar, Moritz Schularick, and Alan M. Taylor. 2014. The Great Mortgaging: Housing Finance, Crises, and Business Cycles. *NBER Working Papers*, No. 20501, Sep 2014.

Mayer, Thomas. 2013a. *How Can Sovereign Money be Brought Into Circulation? Accounting Options for a Central Bank*. [Monetative]. Available at: http://sovereignmoney.eu/papers-and-manuscripts; scroll down to the paper.

———. 2013b. Banish fractional reserve banking for real reform. *Financial Times*, June 24.

Mian, Atif R., Amir Sufi, Emil Verner. 2015. Household Debt and Business Cycles Worldwide. *NBER Working Paper*, No. 21581, September 2015.

O'Brien, Denis Patrick. 2007. *The Development of Monetary Economics*. Cheltenham: Edward Elgar.

Pash, Mark. 2013. Monetary Reform—'The Big One'. Encino, CA: Center for Progressive Economics. http://cpe.us.com/?article=monetary-policy

Positive Money. 2011. *Bank of England Creation of Currency Bill*. London: Positive Money.

Rey, Hélène. 2013. Dilemma not Trilemma. The Global Financial Cycle and Monetary Policy Independence. *Proceedings of the Jackson Hole Economic Policy Symposium*. Federal Reserve Bank of Kansas City, August 2013, 286–333.

Rochon, Louis-Philippe. 1999a. *Credit, Money and Production. An Alternative Post-Keynesian Approach*. Cheltenham: Edward Elgar.

Rossi, Sergio. 2001. *Money and Inflation A New Macroeconomic Analysis*. Cheltenham: Edward Elgar.

Ryan-Collins, Josh. 2015. Is Monetary Financing Inflationary? A Case Study of the Canadian Economy, 1935–75. *Working Paper,* No. 848, Levy Economics Institute of Bard College. October 2015.

Schemmann, Michael. 2012b. *Liquid Money—the Final Thing. Federal Reserve and Central Bank Accounts for Everyone*. IICPA Publications.

Shaw, William Arthur. 1896. *The History of Currency 1252–1896*. New York: Putnams. Reprinted by A.M. Kelley, 1967.

Simons, Henry C. 1948. A Positive Programme for Laissez Faire. Some Proposals for a Liberal Economic Policy, and: Rules versus Authorities in Monetary Policy. Both articles in: H.C. Simons, *Economic Policy for a Free Society*. The University of Chicago Press, 1948. First published as 'Rules versus...'. *The Journal of Political Economy* 44(1936):1–30.

Soddy, Frederick. 1926. *Wealth, Virtual Wealth and Debt*. London: G. Allen & Unwin Ltd. Reprint 1987, Noontide Pr.

Striner, Richard. 2015. *How America Can Spend Its Way Back to Greatness A Guide to Monetary Reform*. Santa Barbara, CA: Praeger.

Tobin, James. 1987. The Case for Preserving Regulatory Distinctions. *Challenge* 30(5):10–7. Available at: https://www.kansascityfed.org/publicat/sympos/ 1987/ S87tobin.pdf

Turner, Adair. 2015. *Between Debt and the Devil. Money, Credit and Fixing Global Finance*. Princeton: Princeton University Press.

van Lerven, Frank, Graham Hodgson, and Dyson Ben. 2015. *Would There Be Enough Credit in a Sovereign Money System?* London: Positive Money. http://positive-money.org/wp-content/uploads/2015/07/Credit_in_Sovereign_Money_System_ FINAL_20150609.pdf.

Wolf, Martin. 2013. The Case for Helicopter Money. *Financial Times*, 12 Feburary 2013.

Zarlenga, Stephen A. 2002. *The Lost Science of Money. The Mythology of Money—The Story of Power*. Valatie, NY: American Monetary Institute.

Index of Authors

Note: Page numbers with "n" denote notes.

© The Author(s) 2017
J. Huber, *Sovereign Money*, DOI 10.1007/978-3-319-42174-2

Whale, P.B., 46, 46n21
White, L.H., 44n17
Wicksell, K., 90
Withers, H., 40
Wolf, M., 103n4, 183n34
    183–4
Woo, J., 121n55
Wray, L.R., 38n7, 94n41

Index of Subjects

Note: Page numbers with "n" denote notes.

© The Author(s) 2017

J. Huber, *Sovereign Money*, DOI 10.1007/978-3-319-42174-2

Printed by Printforce, the Netherlands

.